METAPHYSICS . COSMOLOGY . TRADITION . SYMBOLISM

STUDIES IN COMPARATIVE RELIGION

The First English Journal on Traditional Studies — established 1963

Studies in Comparative Religion is devoted to the exposition of the teachings, spiritual methods, symbolism, and other facets of the religious traditions of the world, together with the traditional arts and sciences which have sprung from those religions. It is not sectarian and, inasmuch as it is not tied to the interests of any particular religion, it is free to lay stress on the common spirit underlying the various religious forms.

One of our primary aims is to meet the need for accurate information created by the now world-wide interest in the question of "ecumenical relations" between the great religions, by providing a forum where writers of proven authority can exchange views on various aspects of religious life, doctrinal, historical, artistic and mystical, not forgetting the element of personal experience and reminiscence.

By collecting accurate information about the great religions under their many aspects and rendering them available to interested readers we feel we are fulfilling a very pressing need of our time and also contributing in a practical manner to the cause of inter-religious understanding. If there is to be an effective measure of this understanding at any level this can only be on the basis of accurate presentation both of teachings and facts. An ill-informed benevolence is no substitute for genuine insight, based on information that is neither willfully distorted nor confined to the surface of things.

In this manner we think that we are best serving the interest of our readers in their search for truth.

(*Excerpt from the Introduction to our first publication, almost fifty years ago*)

World Wisdom

Crossing Religious Frontiers

Studies in Comparative Religion

Edited by
Harry Oldmeadow

World Wisdom

Library of Congress Cataloging-in-Publication Data

Crossing religious frontiers / edited by Harry Oldmeadow.
p. cm. -- (Studies in comparative religion)
Includes bibliographical references.
ISBN 978-1-935493-55-6 (pbk. : alk. paper) 1. Religion--Philosophy. 2. Tradition (Philosophy) I. Oldmeadow, Harry, 1947-
BL51.C715 2010
201'.5--dc22

2010027777

Printed on acid-free paper in USA.

For information address World Wisdom, Inc.
P.O. Box 2682, Bloomington, Indiana 47402-2682
www.worldwisdom.com

CONTENTS

III. Encounters

Book Reviews

Crossing Religious Frontiers

Editorial

Readers of the original series of *Studies in Comparative Religion* (1963-1987) will be familiar with the name of Marco Pallis, a regular contributor to the journal and a friend and collaborator of the other great perennialists whose work also appeared frequently—René Guénon, Ananda Coomaraswamy, Titus Burckhardt, and Frithjof Schuon among them. It is fitting, then, that in this new series we should take the title of one of Pallis' essays to identify the governing theme of this issue which also includes pieces by all of these figures. In keeping with the editorial policy of the new series, we will continue to publish landmark essays which have not previously appeared in this journal. Another token of the continuities between the old and new series is the contribution, in this issue, from William Stoddart, the Assistant Editor of the first series of *SCR*. However, the new series will also keep readers abreast of more recent writings which evince, to one degree or another, a traditional outlook. In these pages readers will not only find contributions from established authors such as Rodney Blackhirst, James Cutsinger, Peter Kingsley, Patrick Laude, Tim Scott, and Charles Upton, but pieces by younger authors here appearing in print for the first time. It is encouraging to witness the emergence of a new generation of writers who are deeply engaged with the same issues that commanded the attention of those earlier writers who took their bearings from Guénon, the towering French metaphysician whose work answered the urgent necessities of the peculiar cyclical and terrestrial conditions in which we find ourselves. Whilst Guénon laid bare the metaphysical principles which inform the world's great religious and sapiential traditions it remained to Frithjof Schuon to articulate the essence of the *religio perennis* which is the underlying theme of this issue. In many regards it might be said that the whole perennialist movement of recent times is an elaboration and application of the generative work of Guénon and Schuon.

We are living in an unprecedented situation in which the different religious traditions are everywhere impinging on each other. There has, of course, always been some exchange of ideas and influences between the great religious cultures, sometimes at quite a profound level. Nevertheless, each civilization formerly exhibited a spiritual homogeneity undisturbed, for the most part, by the problem of religious pluralism. In former times, just as man appeared as "man" and not as "yellow man" or "white man," and just as each language seemed to its practitioners to be language as such, so too each religion, for most adherents, appeared as "religion" or "the way" without further qualification. For the vast majority of believers in a traditional civilization the question of the interrelationship of the religions was one which was either of peripheral concern or one of which they remained unaware. As Martin Lings has remarked,

> Needless to say our ancestors were aware of the existence of other religions besides their own; but dazzled and penetrated as they were by the great light shining directly above them, the sight of more remote and—for them—more obliquely shining lights on the horizons could raise no positive interest nor did it create problems. Today, however those horizons are no longer remote; and amidst the great evil which results from all that has contributed to bring them near, some good has also inevitably stolen its way in.[1]

[1] Lings, *Ancient Beliefs and Modern Superstitions* (Cambridge, UK: Quinta Essentia, 1991), p. 70.

This phenomenon is addressed not only in Pallis' essay from which this issue of SCR takes its title, but, in one way or another, in all of the articles which the reader will find herein.

It hardly needs saying that the homogeneity of Christian civilization has long since been ruptured by secularist ideologies of one kind and another. In the last few centuries Europe has, in turn, been the agent for the disruption and sometimes extirpation of traditional cultures the world over. Comparative religion itself, as a field of study was, in part, the product of the cultural contacts to which an aggressive European imperialism gave rise. Since then all manner of changes have made for a "smaller" world in which it is impossible to ignore the presence of religious cultures and traditions different from our own. The interrelationships of the religions today is an issue which has taken on a new immediacy in the cyclical conditions in which we live, especially for all those concerned with fostering a harmonious world community. Furthermore, in an age of rampant secularism and scepticism the need for some kind of interreligious solidarity makes itself ever more acutely felt. At a time when "the outward and readily exaggerated incompatibility of the different religions greatly discredits, in the minds of most of our contemporaries, all religion"[2] the exposure of the underlying unity of the religions becomes an imperative task—one that can only be achieved through a properly constituted esoterism. The open confrontation of different exoterisms, the destruction of traditional civilizations, and the tyranny of profane ideologies all play a part in determining the peculiar circumstances in which the most fundamental needs of the age can only be met by a recourse to traditional esoterisms. As Schuon wrote half a century ago, "That which is lacking in the present world is a profound knowledge of the nature of things; the fundamental truths are always there, but they do not impose themselves because they cannot impose themselves on those unwilling to listen".[3] This, alas, is no less true in the religious domain than in any other. At a time of volatile intra- and inter-religious tensions it is incumbent on perennialists to affirm the "profound and eternal solidarity of all spiritual forms".[4]

Seyyed Hossein Nasr has observed that

> The essential problem that the study of religion poses is how to preserve religious truth, traditional orthodoxy, the dogmatic theological structures of one's own tradition, and yet gain knowledge of other traditions and accept them as spiritually valid ways and roads to God.[5]

The resolution of the peculiar tensions and antagonisms arising out of our new global circumstances, and the fulfilment of its inherent spiritual possibilities, is one of the most momentous tasks facing all those concerned with the spiritual welfare of humankind. The perennialist exposition of the *sophia perennis* furnishes the *only* completely consistent and coherent explication of the interrelationships of the great religious traditions—in other words, the *only* satisfactory basis on which to resolve the problems arising out of religious pluralism in the modern world, at least in the intellectual domain. The traditionalist outlook decisively resolves the problem spotlighted by Nasr by providing an understanding which affirms the

[2] Schuon, *The Transcendent Unity of Religions* (Wheaton, IL: Quest, 1993), pp. xxxiii-xxxiv.

[3] Schuon, "No Activity Without Truth", in *The Sword of Gnosis*, ed. Jacob Needleman (Baltimore, MD: Penguin, 1974), p. 28.

[4] Schuon, *The Transcendent Unity of Religions*, xxxiv.

[5] Nasr, *Sufi Essays* (Albany, NY: SUNY, 1991), p. 127.

inner unity of religions but at the same time honors their diversity. Because of its premium on the "incalculable value" of religious orthodoxy, a properly constituted perennialism does not threaten religious commitments—indeed it insists on them—but shows how the formal antinomies of different theologies can be resolved in a trans-religious metaphysical synthesis, in Coomaraswamy's words, in "an intellectual wisdom . . . independent of all environmental idiosyncrasy." *Studies in Comparative Religion* is committed to this ongoing work.

"Crossing Religious Frontiers" is a theme which can be inflected in many ways, as is evident from the range of articles gathered together here. Our material has been organized under three rubrics: "Principles", encompassing explications of those metaphysical axioms which comprise the *sophia perennis* and which must control our understanding of the proper relations between the great mythological, religious and sapiential traditions; "Perspectives" wherein those principles are brought to bear on particular interreligious issues and phenomena; and "Encounters", where we find more discursive and anecdotal accounts from and about wayfarers who have engaged directly in an experiential frontier-crossing. Of course, this organization is somewhat arbitrary and several of the articles might easily have been situated under another heading.

Let me close with another reference to Marco Pallis' essay, "Crossing Religious Frontiers". Writing of the work of Frithjof Schuon, he says this:

> It exemplifies the power to penetrate all traditional forms as well as to render them mutually intelligible for the sake of those who, not by evading but rather by faithfully observing the claims of form where they properly belong, will make of this obedience not a shuttered but an open window, one through which light and air are able to penetrate and from which the imprisoned bird can start forth on an unhindered flight.

It is my hope that the pieces assembled here will, each in its own way, serve something of the same high purpose.

Harry Oldmeadow

I
PRINCIPLES

On Crossing Religious Frontiers

Marco Pallis

Among the many phenomena of an unprecedented character to which modern civilization has given rise there is one that calls for particular attention at the present time inasmuch as it affects the religious outlook of men in a very vital, if hitherto unaccustomed, manner. Indeed it is not too much to say that every religiously inclined person whose mind is open to fresh impressions is, or soon will be, compelled to face the issue raised by this cause, and this holds good whatever may be the trend of his personal conclusions, whether these have been formed, that is to say, in the light of a traditional orthodoxy or under influences of a more aberrant kind.

In previous ages, and even until quite recently, contacts between different religions, though continually occurring as a result of geographical proximity, military invasion and other similar causes, partook, generally speaking, of an "accidental" character, while the greater number of those who were attached to the various traditional forms continued to think and believe much as if their own tradition constituted an enclosed world, one in which the ideas of those dwelling outside the form in question could safely be ignored. Inter-traditional exchanges did of course nevertheless take place from time to time, and sometimes at a very high intellectual level; such occasions must however count as relatively exceptional when regarded from the standpoint of average traditional conformity, as can still be observed, for instance, in many parts of Asia, where differing forms of traditional life, despite mingling of populations, have continued over long periods to flow along entirely separate channels in a state surprisingly uninfluenced by the ideas of their neighbors.

When it comes to defining the attitude of one religion towards another in a more specific sense, a difference is observable between those that have sprung from the great Semitic stem, including Christianity, and most others, inasmuch as the former have tended to exclude from their point of view the possibility that spirituality, for different sections of humanity, might assume different forms; whereas in the second case, for which the Indian traditions provide the type, a plurality of spiritual paths, at the level of form, is taken for granted without any fear that doing so might carry with it implications damaging to one's own tradition. It is but normal for that tradition to represent for its adherents "the highest *Dharma*," but this is a very different thing from claiming for it the status of the one and only revealed way, all the rest being written off as mere errors or, at best, as "natural religion," that is to say as part-inventions of the human mind trying to meet its own unsatisfied aspirations to the best of its limited ability. Thus where the Christian, for instance, has hitherto but grudgingly recognized (against all the weight of evidence) the presence of an authentic spirituality in other religions and, when he did so, has tended to regard it as a purely subjective phenomenon, his opposite number in the Hindu, Buddhist or Far Eastern tradition has been prepared to accept at their face value, in forms other than his own, manifestations of Grace extending even to the occurrence there of Divine Incarnations, *Avataras*: moreover this attitude goes generally with a less individualistic point of view regarding human affairs, as also with less anthropomorphic views regarding the Divinity.

This Eastern openness of mind, which anybody who has come into intimate contact with Orientals still living traditionally will be able to substantiate, deserves somewhat closer study in the present instance, if only because it does not, as some might suppose, indicate any kind of doctrinal laxity: in fact the reverse is true, inasmuch as this attitude of practical tolerance is itself an expression of traditional orthodoxy, not of its absence. Behind it lies the clear distinction which, in the more purely metaphysical traditions, is made between the formal order in all its extension and the formless Truth, unique seat of liberty and therefore of liberation: the claims of the latter alone are treated as absolute; those of the former being recognized as relative, but valid at their own level. It is in virtue of this conviction that the Eastern devotee is able to accept, according to need, the discipline of a form yet without losing sight of the transcendence of "non-form," comprising as it does the ultimate goal to which forms themselves are but so many stepping-stones. It may be added that the tolerant outlook resulting from such knowledge is at the antipodes of the attitude of the "freethinker," as we have come to call him in unconscious irony, whose vaunted disregard of religious forms springs not from an ability to get beyond them, but rather from accepting to remain bound, as it were, on their hither side.

Turning once again to the West, while it cannot be denied that in more recent times the idea of religious toleration has found general acceptance there as part of the "liberal" creed now in vogue, it must at the same time be remembered that this otherwise welcome development has to a great extent gone hand in hand with a religious in difference such as often amounts to a quasi-dogmatic skepticism, a fact which in a religious sense can scarcely be counted as unmixed gain.

This skepticism in regard to religious values, which has by now become almost instinctive with contemporary man to the point of affecting the whole background of his thought and action, negative factor though it is, has nevertheless had one important repercussion within the sphere of religious thought itself, by causing people to review certain claims to exclusive validity which had hitherto been simply taken for granted; hence the great and increasing interest taken in the doctrinal expressions of other, and especially Eastern, traditions, with the inevitable comparisons resulting from such studies. Thus the question of the spiritual value of "foreign" forms, as well as of the attitude that one should take up towards them, has become a burning one in a world where, if on the one hand everything is laid open to discussion and even doubt, on the other hand, under the quantitative conception of knowledge which now passes for "scientific," everything is grist to the mill of research, including the religious phenomena associated with every section of humanity known to have ever existed either in time or space. It is not lack of information which will hamper a would-be inquirer, but rather its bewildering excess.

An army of translators has made available in printed form the sacred writings of every tradition and their work has been supplemented by that of the ethnologists, so that a mass of factual evidence has accumulated which, however profanely it may be interpreted, cannot but have a powerful effect on all who choose to become acquainted with its contents. Nor must one overlook the parallel results of collecting the artistic products of every possible civilization, including the tribal ones: for the arts have everywhere served as a vehicle for a spiritual message according to one or other traditional pattern, and the internal consistency of the artistic language, wherever an authentically traditional life prevails, goes together with an extreme differentiation versus other forms, the power to convey universal truth being in fact proportional to formal strictness as regards the means of expression. This observation harbors no paradox, being itself an expression of the relationship uniting form as such to the formless Truth, in the sense given above, a relationship on which all true symbolism depends for its efficacy: in any case there are some truths which speak to us more freely through visual or musical forms than through the spoken or written word, if only because the immediacy of their appeal places them outside the scope of the rational mind and its subterfuges. If this flood of information presents some serious disadvantages by reason of the mental voracity it both feeds and excites, it must at least be admitted that the evidences it supplies are difficult to explain away on purely conventional lines, as in the past.

Indeed it is a most case-hardened heart that is still prepared to interpret religious phenomena of almost identical character as being somehow more than they appear in one favored case and, in all other cases, less than they appear. The cruder missionary type may still cling to this position, but here at home, in the beleaguered castle of religion with hostile forces swarming round about, the very absurdity of such a view, in the light of now common knowledge, makes such a position hardly tenable.

Thus we have to deal with a situation where a kind of indiscriminate pooling of the fruits of spiritual creativeness is taking place, admittedly at a rather superficial level, but where at the same time the very traditions which have provided the material for such an exchange are all alike threatened with disintegration under pressure of the modern humanistic teaching, for which the focus of attention, by definition, is human interest restricted to the narrowest and most external sphere, with consequent withdrawal of that same attention from whatever can by any stretch be regarded as "otherworldly."

It is from the interplay of the two factors described above that there has arisen what is, in some ways, the most unprecedented feature of the situation, namely the emergence of the idea, almost unthinkable in antiquity, of what might be termed "inter-traditional co-operation," on a quasi-corporate as well as individual basis, between representatives of different religions, a co-operation such as could only take place on reasonably equal terms of mutual respect, itself implying at least a partial recognition of a common spiritual factor underlying all the forms concerned and escaping their formal limitations—this with a view to countering a danger, world-wide in its scope, that threatens all without distinction, a danger moreover which hereditary dissensions among the religions themselves can only make worse.

"The house of spirituality," so it has been argued more than once, "has hitherto been divided against itself, and this it is which prevents religious influences from playing their proper part in solving the crisis through which mankind is passing at present, one which, if a remedy be not quickly forthcoming, may well result in the physical and intellectual suicide of mankind. Therefore this is not the time to harp on old divisions but rather to lay stress on those things which are to be found on both sides of the religious frontiers and in this way the spiritual forces of the world will be able to make themselves felt before it is too late." However one may view such an argument, it must at least be admitted that there is an appearance of rough-and-ready logic behind it. How far that logic is able to carry one is however another matter, calling for the most careful examination of the conditions, favorable or restrictive, under which even the best intentions to co-operate could be expected to yield the desired results.

For a start, it is worth calling to mind a few actual examples of attempts to establish contacts as envisaged in the foregoing paragraph, though without seeking to assess their value in positive or negative terms: in fact many such attempts have been vowed to futility from the start, for a variety of reasons, but this is beside the point, as far as the present discussion is concerned, our aim being, not to support or oppose this or that movement, but merely to investigate a state of mind which has arisen in our time, of which all these activities, whatever may be said for or against them, are but cases in point. Among movements of this kind might be mentioned the one promoted by the late Sir Francis Younghusband under the name of the Congress of Faiths, as well as its American predecessor the so-called Parliament of Religions. More lately in Oxford one has had a most convinced and active promoter of such co-operation in the person of the late Mr. H. N. Spalding whose endowments in the field of university education both here and elsewhere, backed up by his own unremitting labors carried out in the face of failing health down to the last moments of his life, testified to his faith in the existence of a common spirituality at the basis of all the great religions and able even at the eleventh hour, as he always believed, to heal the deadly disease from which mankind is suffering. Again, one has read of conferences in North Africa attended by Muslims and Catholics, where a common faith in God and His Revelation as well as a common focus of opposition in the aggressive forces of militant atheism has served to draw together, under suitable safe guards, two old-time antagonists: the above represent but a few examples chosen at random from a list that is lengthening with every year that passes.[1]

Turning in quite another direction, account must be taken of the work of a number of writers of exceptional eminence who have taken their stand on both the fundamental unity and the universality of traditional knowledge as exemplified in the great religions despite all their differences of form, men like A. K. Coomaraswamy and René Guénon—to mention two of the principal names.[2] Neither of these writers was in any sense an eclectic and each tradition was, for him, something integral to be accepted on its own terms and expounded accordingly, failing which a claim to recognize a common principle in virtue of these very distinctions would be lacking in objective reality. A patchwork of beautiful citations drawn from all manner of traditional sources but so selected as to agree with the opinions, not to say the prejudices, of a particular author will no more constitute a "perennial philosophy" than an assemblage of the most expressive words out of half a dozen languages will add up to a super-language combining all their best qualities minus the drawbacks. The impotence of the eclectic approach to any subject springs from the fact that every form, to be such, must needs imply an exclusive as well as an inclusive aspect, the two jointly serving to express the limits that define the form in question. Thus whatever belongs in any sense to the formal order—as for instance any doctrinal expression, any language, or indeed any thought—will entail certain incompatibilities extending to qualities as well as to defects. In their formal aspects the oppositions between the various religions are not without some justification, though human prejudice and misrepresentation

[1] Some mention ought perhaps to be made of the serial broadcasts by speakers representing the various religions of the world which, in this country, have become a frequent and popular feature. Some of these lectures have been excellent as far as they went, others less so, for it is an undeniable fact that persons affected by anti-traditional tendencies are as a rule more given to publicizing their opinions than their more orthodox neighbours; heresy has always tended to be vociferous where true knowledge, as the Taoist sages so pertinently teach, is content to lie low and bide its time. Of quite unusual excellence (to quote a single example) was a talk given by the abbot of Ampleforth to mark the centenary of his abbey, one in which most of the principal religions were referred to in sympathetic terms, each being given credit for some particular quality characterizing its point of view. No one could suspect the reverend speaker of intending anything contrary to Catholic orthodoxy; yet it is fair to say that words like his would not have come easily from the mouth of a Christian prelate of but two generations ago. In its way, this is a sign of the times that cannot be dismissed as devoid of wider importance.

Highly significant, too, are the stirring words uttered by Pope Pius XI when dispatching his Apostolic Delegate to Libya: "Do not think you are going among infidels. Muslims attain to Salvation. The ways of Providence are infinite." By these words the traditional doctrine, far from being contravened, received a precise expression, one that displayed its truth, as it were, in a fresh dimension. (Quotation is from *L'Ultima*, Anno VIII, Florence 1954).

[2] The author cannot refrain from mentioning another work by a fellow-writer which, because of its originality as well as its clarity and beauty of expression, deserves more attention than it has received hitherto: this book is *The Richest Vein* by Gai Eaton (Faber & Faber, 1949; Sophia Perennis et Universalis [2nd ed.], 1995) and its author was a young officer just released from the Forces after the last war who, as the result of private reading and, as far as one can tell, without any direct traditional contacts at the time, has voiced the idea of traditional unity in virtue of, and not in opposition to, diversity of form. To one unfamiliar with the subject this book provides a useful introduction.

have often both aggravated and distorted their character; these oppositions cannot in any case be resolved by merely brushing them aside. What is, however, important to remember is that no opposition can be regarded as irreducible in an absolute sense (to treat it as such would be to turn it into a kind of independent divinity, an idolatrous act therefore) and the whole metaphysical problem consists in knowing the point where such a reconciliation of opposites can be brought about without evasion or any ill-judged compromise.

Among Orientals, other than Muslims,[3] for reasons that have already been explained in part, the idea of a "transcendent unity of religions" finds easy acceptance as shown, for instance, by the exceptional veneration paid to the person of Christ by many sincere Hindus and, in similar fashion, to the Prophet of Islam: this is especially true of those who follow the *bhaktic* way, the way to Union through Love, for whom an attitude of extreme receptiveness versus other forms is almost a commonplace: perhaps the most notable example during recent times of a *bhaktic* Saint who took up this standpoint was Sri Ramakrishna Paramahamsa, the great Bengali teacher of the second half of the nineteenth century, inasmuch as his appreciation of non-Hindu forms went beyond a merely theoretical approach, for the Saint in question actually *lived* both Islam and Christianity during certain periods of his life and thus was able to "verify" their essential agreement with his own Hinduism at a level where differences ascribable to form ceased to apply. In our own time and at a somewhat more external level the name of Mahatma Gandhi also requires to be mentioned, for whom belief in a common source of inspiration for all the great religions was one of his deepest convictions. By a strange paradox it was his own reaction against anything savoring of religious bigotry which led Gandhi into recommending that the new India should proclaim itself a "secular state," a phrase which, if it means anything at all, countenances the possibility of an effective functioning *minus* any acknowledgment of the Presence of God or of Man's dependence upon the divine Providence. It seems a pity that in this matter the constitutional pattern set by modernist Europe should have been hastily copied largely on sentimental grounds, instead of trying to find some solution more in accordance with the common mind of India, which despite all the profane upsurge of the times is still largely dominated by spiritual values. One asks whether it would not have been better to declare the newly constituted state to be religiously "all embracing" (thus excluding all parochialism) instead of "secular" which is a purely privative term and one that suffers from an inherently blasphemous flavor that no excuses can disguise.[4]

Through the foregoing discussion, sketchy though it has necessarily been in view of the much ground to be covered, it is hoped that sufficient evidence is now forthcoming to enable

[3] This is a statement that wants qualifying: for though Islam, under its more external aspects, occupies a position not dissimilar to that of Christianity, with much the same exclusiveness towards other doctrinal forms, this attitude is compensated by the existence in the Islamic tradition of an "internal dimension" represented by the Sufi Orders, whose point of view, though in no wise opposed to the teachings of ordinary faith at the individual level, gives to those teachings a deeper as well as a more ample scope, thus approximating in effect to the point of view of more purely metaphysical traditions such as the Hindu *Vedānta* and *Mahāyāna* Buddhism. It is this influence exerted at the heart of Islam which has given to the latter, despite its fiercer aspects, a certain elasticity in the presence of other traditions which historical Christianity has not displayed to an equal extent.

[4] It must not be supposed that we are trying to champion some kind of artificially combined religious form, a would-be esperanto of the Spirit: all that the term "all-embracing" might be expected to indicate is a primary recognition of religion as the indispensable mainspring of all valid activity, even political (which also was an article of faith with the Mahatma) and, secondly, the congruent rights of all the existing traditional forms. Admittedly, there is a certain looseness in such a constitutional provision, but it would have served the purpose.

the reader to "situate" the problem of effective communication between religions by showing that every such exchange, be it even confined to the realm of thought, will involve some application of the larger principle governing the relation between "forms" and "beyond forms," letter and Spirit. Admitting that individual existence will always imply the presence of the former though without prejudice to the ultimate supremacy of the latter (as containing the transcendent source of authority from which all lesser faculties derive), it is obvious that at any point short of the supreme Enlightenment a certain degree of "tension" will be felt as between those two factors (so long, that is to say, as they are regarded through the spectacles of a more or less persistent dualism), and indeed all spiritual attitudes, all ascetic method, all *yogic* skill will be determined by the angle from which that tension is envisaged; the question of how much emphasis is to be laid in given circumstances upon individual and formal or supra-formal and universal elements respectively is a matter of "spiritual opportunism," varying in obedience to changing needs.

Where reliance upon formal elements is pronounced (even in a manner that is well-founded), bridging the gap to another form becomes correspondingly hard. This is the source of the Christian's habitual hesitations when faced with any evidence of a spirituality unclothed in the specifically Christian form, for his own outlook has been so powerfully molded according to a historical perspective on the basis of certain facts (and every fact belongs by definition to the world of forms) that he finds any act of transposition to another viewpoint exceptionally perilous: not that Christianity excludes such a transposition in itself, since those same historic facts upon which Christian faith reposes are, in virtue of their symbolism, realizable also on the universal plane where they provide the key to intellections far exceeding anything that a purely individual view is able to embrace. The danger to a faith relying too exclusively upon the factual element is this, namely that it leaves the minds of those concerned peculiarly vulnerable if, with or without good reason, serious doubt comes to be cast on the particular facts in which they put all their trust, as for instance the historicity of certain past events. When this happens, panic supervenes, and the flight from tradition easily becomes a rout. The modern world and its irreligiousness is the revenge of the Spirit upon those who attached to the formal elements of their tradition (important though these certainly are) that absolute character that belongs to the unembodied and total Truth. These people have been, as it were, abandoned to the facts they idolized; for that is what the profane point of view essentially consists of, namely an indefinite fragmentation of reality with no hope of unifying the consequent and ever-shifting oppositions.

If this is the burden of Western man, whose mind always shows the impress of its Christian formation even when believing itself to have shaken loose from its effects, the Oriental, for his part, is threatened by somewhat different dangers. For him questions of form do not, as we have seen, present any great difficulty and that is why he as a rule shows himself more venturesome in going forth to meet ideas issuing from unfamiliar traditions, without a corresponding risk of losing hold on his own. Moreover, having been schooled all his life in the thought that all forms are ephemeral—even the most hallowed—and that every separate fact is but another facet of the Cosmic Illusion, *Māyā,* he is much less prone to rest upon so unstable a foundation as the world of appearances. Where life and death themselves seem such relative states, both here and here after, the death of a fact, like its existence, causes far less disturbance than when it is treated as if endowed with an absolute reality of its own.

That is the strength of the Orient, observable not only in the life of Sages but also in that of quite humble people, subject as they are in other respects to ordinary human weaknesses. For habitual open-mindedness the danger of error will come, not as a result of a rigidity which it precludes, but rather through a too great readiness to accommodate itself, to the point of finding agreement where none really exists and of underrating the importance of forms in a time of crisis; the oft decried use of "dogmatic" definitions in the service of a religious orthodoxy can in such times amount to a solid protection, at least for the generality, though at the same time it will always remain something of a two-edged weapon. In the Eastern religions so long as the traditional structure remained substantially intact this danger of making too free with the formal element was hardly likely to arise; but in very modern times, with the sudden impact of Western profanity upon Eastern minds at a moment when many of the native traditions were already suffering from the degeneration which time must bring to every form itself born temporally, a serious breakdown at the surface level rapidly took place, evinced in many cases by a clamorous depreciation of all formal, that is to say doctrinal, ritual and artistic elements such as had supplied people through the ages with their day-to-day nourishment for the soul—all this in the name of a neo-spiritual "idealism" which, in most cases, amounted to nothing more than ethical sentimentalism and specious universalism, after the Western modernist model. Both in India and elsewhere much weakening has occurred as a result of these tendencies, which that very open-mindedness we have been discussing has, in present circumstances, helped to foster.

Before quitting our subject, allusion must be made to an oft-expressed opinion that with a view to better understanding between the religions of East and West *love* single-handed might forge the necessary link, and this suggestion is one which, more perhaps by its sound than its content, exerts a deceptive attraction upon many minds, both by reason of its obviously sentimental appeal when employed in such a context and also because its vagueness really commits one to nothing, leaving all the problems created by traditional differences where they were. Professions of peace and goodwill are cheaper today than in any previous age, and doubtless the fact that this has corresponded with a time when persecutions and wars, declared and undeclared, have reached a scale and extension without parallel in recorded history is no accident, so that both sets of phenomena can reasonably be traced to the same fundamental causes.

That goodwill, kindly feeling, is one of the conditions of success in every form of co-operation between humans is a truism, but this is by no means enough to ensure any but the most superficial success if only from the fact that a sentiment, however excellent in itself, remains by its nature a relatively unstable thing, which a very small shifting of the focus of attention may easily swing as far as its own opposite, in virtue of the law of polarity which governs the whole manifested universe, and this effect is often seen in wartime. Hence the repeated failures of the various peace movements which have been such a disappointing feature of our times, these having been due, in the writer's opinion, not so much to the absence of sincere goodwill in their promoters (even in "the politicians"!) as to its excess, itself due to an urge to make up for an intellectual lack felt, but not truly understood. Indeed it is a great and common error to suppose that Charity is something that can function unintelligently, for true Charity is grounded less upon kind feeling than upon the nature of things: fundamentally it demands a spiritual attitude, not simply a moral one. Charity is in fact intensely realistic and "practical"—"operative" in the sense given to that word by the old craft initiations—and is itself opposable to that very sentimentality with which it is so often confused. In an ultimate sense Charity rests upon the disappearance of ego-separativity in the face of God, with its accompanying abolition of all sense of otherness towards one's fellow beings, and this highest synthesis of the soul is only realizable in terms of both knowledge and love which at this point coincide: from which it follows that every attempt to reach understanding in the face of differences requires, as its force both motive and directive, the presence of Intelligence, which is something more than mere mind and which, if man were without it, would preclude all hope of reaching an effective conclusion, were it even in respect of the smallest of the problems consequent on existence, let alone the final problem set by existence itself.

Once it is accepted that an attitude not merely benevolent but also derived from a just appraisal of relevant factors is required by anyone who wishes to establish contact (whether only indirectly in the mind or in a more direct and complete sense) with "foreign spirituality"—and few serious-minded people escape this need under some shape or other today—then it becomes a matter of urgency that the operative principles should be presented in a form assimilable by an average intelligent person (we do not say "an erudite person," still less a "theological technologist"), accompanied by a commentary that will combine fairness and accuracy with insight and interpretative skill. It is for the sake of such inquirers, regardless of their angle of approach, that we will conclude this chapter by drawing attention to a pair of books which, in the writer's opinion, fulfill the required conditions in the highest degree—both works have been translated into English (from the French), under the respective titles of *Transcendent Unity of Religions* (Faber & Faber, 1953; Quest [2nd ed.], 1993) and *Gnosis: Divine Wisdom* (John Murray, 1959, World Wisdom [3rd ed.], 2006), their author being Frithjof Schuon.

There would be little point in filling one's own pages with an analysis of these two closely knit and also highly original works of practical theology—practical, because throwing light on some of the most urgent as well as complex questions affecting the spiritual life of individuals and groups; just enough must be said, however, in connection with the present discussion, to show why the appearance of these particular books has been so timely.

Of *Transcendent Unity* one can say that it marshals all the basic information needed in order that this pressing problem of religions and their relations to one another may be properly stated—wherever this is done one is already halfway to a solution. From the very outset, the author lays himself out to deal with the fundamental problem of letter and spirit, or otherwise expressed, of exoterism and esoterism.[5] Besides putting this great question with telling effect he points the way to an effective answer by showing that here is not a case of choice between two alternatives situated on the same plane but rather of recognizing that they refer to things belonging to different orders (thus implying a hierarchical, not a symmetrical relationship between them); a knowledge which once clearly possessed will allow of applying one and the same principle with unfailing discrimination to each case as it arises, without any confusion between the factors concerned. It is this knowledge in fact which confers mastery over forms and constitutes the primary qualification required of one who would build a bridge, for his own sake and for the sake of others, between religion and religion, even while the stream of formal distinction continues to flow in between. This is perhaps the most important, though by no means the only, message contained in the book, for much ground is covered in the course of it and many accessory aspects are dealt with in a manner not less illuminating, such as "the question of forms in art" and its bearing on the spiritual needs of mankind, and also certain matters touching the Christian tradition which occupy the two final chapters.

[5] Incidentally he helps to clear the latter term of the reproach that has become attached to it as a result of its tendentious and fanciful employment by various pseudo-mystical and occultist schools such as always make their appearance in times of widespread bewilderment, these times being no exception. Correctly used, the twin terms "exoteric" and "esoteric" are in their way extremely useful ones, as corresponding to two fundamental aspects of reality, and therefore to necessities, spiritual and practical.

In comparison with the earlier of the two works, charged as it is with a wealth of illustrative material from which conclusions disengage themselves at a sure but gradual pace, *Gnosis: Divine Wisdom* makes easier reading, being in fact extremely concise in its presentation as well as more "poetical" in tone. As far as our present subject is concerned, some twenty-odd pages[6] suffice to cover most of the ground in a manner that is never less than masterly: one would gladly have reproduced those pages in their entirety by way of a final summing up. The rest of the book is taken up with different aspects of spiritual life, including, as in the previous case, one whole section on the Christian tradition which, by its appeal at once intelligent and moving, is well calculated to put heart into many a flagging aspiration. It is especially in the opening pages of *Gnosis*[7] that the author touches the most tender point in the continual misunderstanding existing among the religions, which to a visiting outsider might indeed seem very strange given both the actual facts and the apparent intelligence and good faith of many of the people concerned—not that the contrary of these qualities does not enter in at times, for the methods used in religious controversy have often been far from edifying: the point he makes in those first pages is that, in many cases if not in all, misunderstanding has been bound up with a proneness to compare elements not strictly comparable, than which there can be no more fatal cause of confusions.

In the spiritual field the fact is that differences of expression often mask an identity of content, while verbal resemblances may, on the contrary, accompany essential differences. In our time René Guénon was probably the first to point this out clearly: this truth once seen, one becomes wary alike of superficial assimilations and oppositions. Before proceeding to compare two doctrinal formulations arising from a different background one must first master the true language of each, its essential assumptions as also the things left unsaid, otherwise the conclusion will betray one. For this work of "spiritual translation" a fully awakened power of discernment is an indispensable qualification and this means an intuitive, not a merely rational quality. One cannot do better than quote Frithjof Schuon himself in his opening lines which already contain the key of all that is to follow:

> One of the chief reasons for the mutual incomprehension which rises, like an impermeable partition, between the religions, seems to us to reside in the fact that the sense of the absolute in each case is situated on a different level, so that points of comparison are most often illusory ones. Formally similar elements figure in such differing contexts that they change function from one case to another and consequently also change nature: thus it is, because the infinity of the possible precludes all exact repetition.

A clearer picture of the whole situation could not be given.

[6] We are referring especially to the first few pages of Chapter I and to the sections on "Revelation" and "Natural Mysticism."

[7] As with the word "esoterism" in the other book, here the author is at pains to rid "gnosis," a word that should be sacrosanct if ever there was one, of the prejudice that has in course of time gathered round its use, chiefly from its association in many minds, and often for mutually exclusive reasons, with "gnosticism" and the early heresies of that name. Here this term is restored to its normal connotation, indicating in spirituality its sapiential essence, unitive Knowledge.

Considered together these two books are characterised by the maintenance, at every turn, of a sharp distinction between what in any question belongs to its essence and its more accidental and therefore variable factors. The reader is continually being put in a position of having to face his difficulties in all their complexity and irrespective of what may be his own personal leanings; if the experience causes discomfort, this will have to be endured, for the author never makes any kind of concession to intellectual hedonism. At times our author can indeed be very severe in his judgments, but never uncharitable. As for his use of language, whether the theme under treatment be simple or subtle, expression remains that of every day speech, but used purely and with accuracy;[8] no reader of his need fear that his task will be rendered heavier by a text loaded with ultra-technical phraseology and "long words" such as shallow minds delight in; close attention he is asked to pay, but nothing besides.

If it be asked now what, in the present writer's view, is the chief distinguishing feature of these books, his answer is that they exemplify, in a pre-eminent degree, a possession of "the gift of tongues," the ability, that is to say, both to speak and understand the various dialects through which the Spirit has chosen to communicate itself to men in their diversity and therefore, in practice, also the ability to communicate clearly with one's fellows across the religious frontiers. In other words it exemplifies the power to penetrate all traditional forms as well as to render them mutually intelligible for the sake of those who, not by evading but rather by faithfully observing the claims of form where they properly belong, will make of this obedience not a shuttered but an open window, one through which light and air are able to penetrate and from which the imprisoned bird can start forth on an unhindered flight.

[8] This statement refers primarily to the French text which however also translates well into English: those able to read the books in the original are naturally advised to do so. For their information the titles and publishers are given, namely *De l'Unité Transcendante des Religions* (Gallimard) and *Sentiers de Gnose* (La Colombe).

Religio Perennis

Frithjof Schuon

One of the keys to understanding our true nature and our ultimate destiny is the fact that the things of this world are never equal to the true range of our intelligence. Our intelligence is made for the Absolute, or else it is nothing; among all the intelligences of this world the human mind alone is capable of objectivity, and this implies—or proves—that the Absolute alone confers on our intelligence the power to accomplish to the full what it can accomplish and to be wholly what it is.[1] If it were necessary or useful to prove the Absolute, the objective and transpersonal character of the human Intellect would be a sufficient testimony, for this Intellect is the indisputable sign of a purely spiritual first Cause, a Unity infinitely central but containing all things, an Essence at once immanent and transcendent. It has been said more than once that total Truth is inscribed in an eternal script in the very substance of our spirit; what the different Revelations do is to "crystallize" and "actualize", in different degrees according to the case, a nucleus of certitudes that not only abides forever in the Divine Omniscience, but also sleeps by refraction in the "naturally supernatural" kernel of the individual, as well as in that of each ethnic or historical collectivity or in the human species as a whole.

Similarly, in the case of the will, which is but a prolongation or complement of the intelligence: the objects it commonly sets out to achieve, or those that life imposes on it, do not measure up to the fullness of its range; only the "divine dimension" can satisfy the thirst for plenitude in our willing or our love. What makes our will human, and therefore free, is the fact that it is proportioned to God; in God alone it is kept free from all constraint, hence from everything that limits its nature.

The essential function of human intelligence is discernment between the Real and the illusory or between the Permanent and the impermanent, and the essential function of the will is attachment to the Permanent or the Real. This discernment and this attachment are the quintessence of all spirituality; carried to their highest level or reduced to their purest substance, they constitute the underlying universality in every great spiritual patrimony of humanity, or what may be called the *religio perennis*;[2] this is the religion to which the sages adhere, while basing themselves always and necessarily on the formal elements of divine institution.[3]

*   *   *

[1] "Heaven and earth cannot contain Me (Allah), but the heart of My faithful servant containeth Me" (*hadīth qudsī*). Similarly Dante: "I perceive that our intellect is never satisfied if the True does not enlighten it, outside which no truth is possible" (*Paradiso* 4:124-26).

[2] These words recall the *philosophia perennis* of Steuchus Eugubin (sixteenth century) and the neo-scholastics; but the word *philosophia* suggests rightly or wrongly a mental elaboration rather than wisdom and therefore does not convey exactly the sense we intend. *Religio* is what "binds" man to Heaven and engages his whole being; as for the word *traditio*, it is related to a more outward and sometimes fragmentary reality, besides suggesting a retrospective outlook; a new-born religion "binds" men to Heaven from the moment of its first revelation, but it does not become a "tradition"—or have "traditions"—until two or three generations later.

[3] This is true even in the case of the pre-Islamic Arab sages, who lived spiritually on the heritage of Abraham and Ishmael.

Metaphysical discernment is a "separation" between *Ātmā* and *Māyā*; contemplative concentration or unifying consciousness is on the contrary a "union" of *Māyā* with *Ātmā*. Discernment is separative,[4] and it is what "doctrine" refers to; concentration is unitive, and it is what "method" refers to; "faith" is connected to the first element and "love of God" to the second.

To paraphrase the well-known saying of Saint Irenaeus, the *religio perennis* is fundamentally this: the Real entered into the illusory so that the illusory might be able to return into the Real. It is this mystery—together with metaphysical discernment and contemplative concentration that are its complement—which alone is important in an absolute sense from the point of view of *gnosis*; for the gnostic—in the etymological and rightful sense of that word—there is in the last analysis no other "religion". It is what Ibn Arabi called the "religion of Love", placing the accent on the element "realization".

The twofold definition of the *religio perennis*—discernment between the Real and the illusory and a unifying and permanent concentration on the Real—implies in addition the criteria of intrinsic orthodoxy for every religion and all spirituality: in order to be orthodox a religion must possess a mythological or doctrinal symbolism establishing the essential distinction in question, and it must provide a path that guarantees both the perfection of concentration and its continuity; in other words a religion is orthodox if it provides a sufficient, if not always exhaustive, idea of the Absolute and the relative, and thus of their reciprocal relationships, and a spiritual activity that is contemplative in its nature and effective with regard to our ultimate destiny. For it is notorious that heterodoxies always tend to adulterate either the idea of the Divine Principle or the manner of our attachment to it; they offer a worldly, profane, or, if one prefers, a "humanist" counterfeit of religion, or else a mysticism containing nothing but the ego and its illusions.

* * *

It may seem disproportionate to treat in simple and as it were schematic terms a subject as complex as that of spiritual perspectives, but since the very nature of things allows us to take into consideration an aspect of simplicity, the truth would be no better served by following the meanders of a complexity not called for in this case. Analysis is one function of the intelligence, and synthesis is another; the association of ideas commonly made between intelligence and difficulty, or between ease and presumption, obviously has nothing to do with the true nature of the Intellect. It is the same with intellectual vision as it is with optical vision: there are things which must be examined in detail if they are to be understood and others which are better seen from a certain distance and which, appearing simple, convey their real nature all the more clearly. Although truth can expand and differentiate indefinitely, it is also contained in a "geometrical point"; grasping this point is everything, whatever the symbol—or symbolism—that in fact brings about intellection.

Truth is one, and it would be vain to want to seek for it in one particular place alone, for the Intellect, containing as it does in its substance all that is true, the truth cannot but be manifested wherever the Intellect is unfolded in the atmosphere of a Revelation. Space can be represented by a circle as well as by a cross, a spiral, a star, or a square; and just as it is impossible for there to be only one figure to represent the nature of space or extension, so it is also impossible for there

[4] This is what the Arabic word *furqān* signifies, namely, "qualitative differentiation", from *faraqa*, to separate, discern, to branch off; it is well known that *Furqān* is one of the names of the Koran.

to be only one doctrine giving an account of the Absolute and of the relations between the contingent and the Absolute; in other words, believing that there can be only one true doctrine is like denying the plurality of the geometrical figures used to indicate the characteristics of space or—to choose a very different example—the plurality of individual consciousnesses and visual points of view. In each Revelation, God says "I" while placing Himself extrinsically at a point of view other than that of earlier Revelations, hence the appearance of contradiction on the plane of formal crystallization.

The objection might be raised that the various geometrical figures are not strictly equivalent in their capacity to serve as adequations between graphic symbolism and spatial extension and thus that the comparison just made could also be used as an argument against the equivalence of traditional perspectives; to this we reply that traditional perspectives are not meant so much to be absolute adequations—at least *a priori*—as to be paths of salvation and means of deliverance. Besides, even though the circle—to say nothing of the point—is a more direct adequation of form to space than is the cross or any other differentiated figure, and even though it therefore reflects more perfectly the nature of extension, there is still this to be considered: the cross, the square, or the spiral express explicitly a spatial reality that the circle or the point expresses only implicitly; the differentiated figures are therefore irreplaceable—otherwise they would not exist—and they are in no sense various kinds of imperfect circles; the cross is infinitely nearer the perfection of the point or the circle than are the oval or trapezoid, for example. Analogous considerations apply to traditional doctrines as regards their differences of form and their merits as an equation.

* * *

That said, let us return to our *religio perennis*, considered either as metaphysical discernment and unifying concentration or as the descent of the Divine Principle, which becomes manifestation in order that manifestation may return to the Principle.

In Christianity—according to Saint Irenaeus and others—God "became man" that man might "become God"; in Hindu terms one would say: *Ātmā* became *Māyā* that *Māyā* might become *Ātmā*. In Christianity, contemplative and unifying concentration is to dwell in the manifested Real—the "Word made flesh"—in order that this Real might dwell in us, who are illusory, according to what Christ said in a vision granted to Saint Catherine of Siena: "I am He who is; thou art she who is not." The soul dwells in the Real—in the kingdom of God that is "within us"—by means of permanent prayer of the heart, as is taught by the parable of the unjust judge and the injunction of Saint Paul.

In Islam the same fundamental theme—fundamental because it is universal—is crystallized according to a very different perspective. Discernment between the Real and the non-real is affirmed by the Testimony of Unity (the *Shahādah*): the correlative concentration on the Symbol or permanent consciousness of the Real is effected by this same Testimony or by the Divine Name which synthesizes it and which is thus the quintessential crystallization of the Koranic Revelation; this Testimony or this Name is also the quintessence of the Abrahamic Revelation—through the lineage of Ishmael—and goes back to the primordial Revelation of the Semitic branch. The Real "descended" (*nazzala, unzila*); it entered into the non-real or illusory, the "perishable" (*fānin*),[5] in becoming the Koran—or the *Shahādah* that summarizes it, or the

[5] The word *fanā'*, sometimes translated as "extinction" by analogy with the Sanskrit *nirvāna*, has the same root and literally means "perishable nature".

Ism (the "Name") which is its sonorous and graphic essence, or the *Dhikr* (the "Mention") which is its operative synthesis—in order that upon this divine barque the illusory might return to the Real, to the "Face (*Wajh*) of the Lord that alone abides" (*wa yabqā Wajhu Rabbika*),[6] whatever the metaphysical import attributed to the ideas of "illusion" and of "Reality". In this reciprocity lies all the mystery of the "Night of Destiny" (*Laylat al-Qadr*), which is a "descent", and of the "Night of Ascension" (*Laylat al-Mi'rāj*), which is the complementary phase; contemplative realization—or "unification" (*tawhīd*)—pertains to this ascension of the Prophet through the degrees of Paradise. "Verily"—says the Koran—"prayer guards against the major (*fahshā*) and the minor (*munkar*) sins, but the mention (*dhikr*) of *Allāh* is greater".[7]

Nearer to the Christian perspective in a certain connection, but much more remote in another, is the Buddhist perspective, which on the one hand is based on a "Word made flesh", but on the other hand knows nothing of the anthropomorphic notion of a creator God. In Buddhism the two terms of the alternative or of discernment are *Nirvāna*, the Real, and *Samsāra*, the illusory; in the last analysis the path is the permanent consciousness of *Nirvāna* as *Shūnya*, the "Void", or else it is concentration on the saving manifestation of *Nirvāna*, the Buddha, who is *Shūnyamūrti*, "Manifestation of the Void". In the Buddha—notably in his form Amitabha—*Nirvāna* became *Samsāra* that *Samsāra* might become *Nirvāna*; and if *Nirvāna* is the Real and *Samsāra* is illusion, the Buddha is the Real in the illusory, and the *Bodhisattva* is the illusory in the Real,[8] which suggests the symbolism of the *Yin-Yang*. The passage from the illusory to the Real is described in the *Prajnāpāramitā-hridaya-sūtra* in these terms: "Gone, gone—gone for the other shore, attained the other shore, O Enlightenment, be blessed!"

* * *

It is in the nature of things that every spiritual outlook juxtaposes a conception of man with a corresponding conception of God; this leads to three ideas or three definitions: first, of man himself; second, of God as He reveals Himself to man as defined in a specific way; and third, of man as determined and transformed by God according to a given perspective.

From the point of view of human subjectivity, man is the container, and God is the contained; from the divine point of view—if one can express it this way—the relationship is reversed, all things being contained in God and nothing being able to contain Him. To say that man is made in the image of God means at the same time that God assumes something of that image *a posteriori* and in connection with man; God is pure Spirit, and man is consequently intelligence or consciousness; conversely, if man is defined as intelligence, God appears as "Truth". In other words God, desiring to affirm Himself under the aspect of "Truth", addresses Himself to man insofar as man is endowed with intelligence, just as He addresses Himself to man in distress to affirm His Mercy or to man endowed with free will to affirm Himself as the saving Law.

The "proofs" of God and religion are in man himself: "Knowing his own nature, he also knows Heaven", says Mencius, in agreement with other analogous and well-known maxims. We must extract from the elements of our own nature the key-certainty that opens up the

6 *Sūrah* "The Merciful" [55]:27.

7 *Sūrah* "The Spider" [29]:45.

8 See "Le mystère du Bodhisattva" (*Études Traditionnelles*, May-June, July-August, September-October, 1962). [Translator's note: For an English translation of this article, see "Mystery of the Bodhisattva" in *Treasures of Buddhism* (Bloomington, Indiana: World Wisdom Books, 1993), pp. 107-34.]

way to certainty of the Divine and Revelation; to speak of "man" is to speak implicitly of "God"; to speak of the "relative" is to speak of the "Absolute". Human nature in general and human intelligence in particular cannot be understood without the religious phenomenon, which characterizes them in the most direct and most complete way possible: grasping the transcendent—not the "psychological"—nature of the human being, we thereby grasp the nature of revelation, religion, tradition; we understand their possibility, their necessity, their truth. And in understanding religion, not only in a particular form or in a specific word-for-word way, but in its formless essence, we also understand the religions, that is to say, the meaning of their plurality and diversity; this is the plane of *gnosis*, of the *religio perennis*, where the extrinsic antinomies of dogma are explained and resolved.

* * *

On the outward and therefore contingent plane—which nonetheless has its importance in the human order—there is a concordance between the *religio perennis* and virgin nature and by the same token between it and primordial nudity, that of creation, birth, resurrection, or the high priest in the Holy of Holies, a hermit in the desert,[9] a Hindu *sādhu* or *sannyāsin*, an American Indian in silent prayer on a mountain.[10] Nature inviolate is at once a vestige of the Earthly Paradise and a prefiguration of the Heavenly Paradise; sanctuaries and garments differ, but virgin nature and the human body remain faithful to the initial unity. Sacred art, which seems to move away from that unity, in reality simply serves to restore to natural phenomena their divine messages, to which men have become insensitive; in art, the perspective of love tends toward overflowing and profusion whereas the perspective of *gnosis* tends toward nature, simplicity, and silence; such is the opposition between Gothic richness and Zen sobriety.[11] But this must not lead us to lose sight of the fact that outward frameworks or modes are always a contingent matter and that all combinations and all compensations are possible, especially since in spirituality every possibility can be reflected in every other according to the appropriate modalities.

A civilization is integral and sound to the extent it is founded on the "invisible" or "underlying" religion, the *religio perennis*, that is, to the extent its expressions or forms are transparent to the Non-formal and that they tend toward the Origin, thus conveying the recollection of a lost Paradise, but also—and with all the more reason—the presentiment of a timeless Beatitude. For the Origin is at once within us and before us; time is but a spiral movement around a motionless Center.

Translated by Mark Perry

[9] Such as Mary of Egypt, in whose case the non-formal and wholly inward character of a love effected by God partakes of the qualities of *gnosis*, so much so that one could call it a "*gnosis* of love" (in the sense of *parabhakti*).

[10] Simplicity of clothing and its color, white in particular, sometimes replace the symbolism of nudity within the framework of sartorial art; on every plane the disrobing that is inspired by the naked Truth counterbalances a worldly "culturism". In another respect, however, a sacred robe symbolizes the victory of the Spirit over the flesh, and its hieratic richness—which we are far from criticizing—expresses the inexhaustible profusion of Mystery and Glory.

[11] But it is very apparent that the most sumptuous sacred art is infinitely nearer to *gnosis* than the ignorant and affected stripping of ornamentations of those of our contemporaries who profess to be "making a clean sweep". For only a simplicity that is qualitative, noble, and conformable to the essence of things, reflects and transmits the perfume of non-formal wisdom.

Not Fusion But Mutual Understanding

René Guénon

All the Eastern civilizations, despite the very great difference of the forms that they are dressed in, may be compared with each other, because they are all essentially traditional in character; each tradition has its own ways of expression, and its own modalities, but, wherever there is tradition, in the true and deep sense of the word, there is necessarily agreement on the principles. The differences lie solely in the outward form, in the contingent applications, which are naturally conditioned by circumstances, above all by racial characteristics, and which, for a given civilization, may even vary within certain limits, since that is the domain which is left open to adaptation. But where there is no longer anything but outward forms, which reflect nothing of any deeper order, there can hardly be any longer anything but differences with regard to the other civilizations. There is no longer any agreement possible as soon as there are no longer any principles, and that is why the lack of actual attachment to a tradition seems to us the very root of the Western deviation. That is also why we declare in so many words that, if the intellectual elite comes one day to be constituted, the essential end which it will have to work for is the return of the West to a traditional civilization; and we will add that if there has ever been a properly Western development in this sense, we have the example of it in the Middle Ages, so that it would be on the whole a question, not of copying or reconstituting purely and simply what existed then (a task that would obviously be impossible, for, whatever certain people may maintain, history does not repeat itself, and there are merely analogous things in the world, not identical things), but of drawing inspiration from it for the adaptation made necessary by the circumstances. That is, word for word, what we have always said, and it is not without express intention that we reproduce it here in the same terms that we have already used;[1] this seems to us clear enough to leave no room for any doubt. However, there are some who have shown the strangest misunderstanding on this score, and who have thought fit to attribute to us the most fantastic intentions, for example that of wanting to restore something comparable to the Alexandrian "syncretism." We will come back to that directly, but let us make it quite clear to begin with that when we speak of the Middle Ages, we have particularly in mind the period beginning with Charlemagne's reign and going down to the end of the thirteenth century —which is rather remote from Alexandria! It is indeed curious that when we maintain the fundamental unity of all the traditional doctrines, we can be taken as meaning that the task in question is a "fusion" between the different traditions, and that people should fail to see that agreement about the principles in no way presupposes uniformity. Does not this seem to be yet another outcome of that very Western fault of not being able to go further than outward appearances? In any case, we do not think it a waste of words to revert to this question and to lay further stress on it, so as to save our intentions from being any longer misrepresented in this way; and, besides, apart from this consideration, the question is not without interest.

In virtue of the principles being universal, as we have said, all the traditional doctrines are identical in essence; there is and can only be one metaphysics, however differently it may be expressed, insofar as it actually is expressible, according to the language at one's disposal, which moreover merely serves as a symbol and never as anything more; and this is so quite simply

[1] *Introduction to the Study of the Hindu Doctrines.*

because the truth is one, and because, being in itself absolutely independent of our conceptions, it imposes itself alike on all those who understand it. Two veritable traditions, then, can never in any instance be in contradiction with each other. If there are doctrines that are incomplete (whether they have always been so or whether part of them has been lost), and that may be more or less far-reaching, it is nonetheless true that up to the point where they stop they remain in agreement with the others, even though their living representatives should be unaware of it. For all that lies beyond, there can be no question either of agreement or of disagreement; but only the systematic mind could call in question the existence of this "beyond," and apart from this biased negation, which is a little too like those that are second nature to the modern mind, all that the incomplete doctrine can do is to admit itself incompetent with regard to what goes beyond it. In any case, if two traditions were found to be in apparent contradiction with one another, the right conclusion would be, not that one was true and that the other was false, but that at least one of them was not fully understood; and on a closer examination it would be seen that there was in fact one of those mistakes of interpretation which the differences in expression, for anyone not sufficiently used to them, may very easily give rise to. As for us, more-over, we must say that in point of fact we do not find such contradictions, while on the contrary we see in a very clear light, beneath the most diverse forms, the essential unity of doctrine. What amazes us is that those who assume on principle the existence of one "primordial tradition," originally common to all mankind, do not see the consequences implied in this affirmation or do not know how to draw them from it, and that they are sometimes just as rabidly anxious as others to discover oppositions which are purely imaginary. We are only speaking, of course, of the doctrines that are truly traditional, or, if it be preferred, "orthodox"; there are means of recognizing these doctrines among all the others without any possible mistake, just as there are also means of determining the exact degree of understanding that any one doctrine corresponds to; but that does not concern us at the moment. To sum up what we think in a few words, we can say this: every truth is exclusive of error, not of another truth (or, to express ourselves better, of another aspect of the truth); and, we repeat, all exclusivism other than that is nothing more than the mark of a systematic outlook, which is incompatible with the understanding of the universal principles.

Since the agreement is essentially on principles, it can only be truly conscious for those doctrines that have in them at least a part of metaphysics or of pure intellectuality; it is not conscious for those strictly limited to a special form, for example that of religion. However, this agreement exists nonetheless really in such a case, in that the theological truths may be considered as an adaptation of certain metaphysical truths to a special point of view; but to show this, the transposition must be made which gives back to these truths their deepest meaning, and only the metaphysician can make it, because he places himself beyond all the particular forms and all the special points of view. Metaphysics and religion are not, and never will be, on the same plane; it follows, furthermore, that a purely metaphysical doctrine and a religious doctrine cannot enter into rivalry or conflict, since their domains are clearly different. But, on the other hand, it follows also that the existence of a solely religious doctrine is not enough to allow the establishment of a deep mutual understanding like the one we have in view when we speak of intellectual relations being renewed between East and West. That is why we have insisted on the necessity of carrying out in the first place work of a metaphysical order, and it is only then that the religious tradition of the West, revived and restored in its fullness, could come to be of use for this end, thanks to the addition of the inner element which it now lacks, but which might very well succeed in superposing itself without there being any outward change. If a mutual understanding is possible among the representatives of the different traditions—and we know that there is nothing against it in principle—this understanding can only be brought about from above, in such a way that each tradition will always keep its full independence, with the forms that belong to it; and the masses, while sharing in the advantages of this understanding, will not be directly conscious of it, for that is something which only concerns the elite, and even "the elite of the elite," according to the expression used by certain Islamic schools.

It is obvious how remote all this is from all those schemes of "fusion" which we consider to be utterly impracticable. A tradition is not a thing that can be invented or artificially created. However well or badly elements borrowed from different traditions be put together, the result will never be more than a pseudo-tradition without value and without bearing, and such fantastic ideas should be left to the occultists and the Theosophists. To act as they do means ignorance of what a tradition truly is and failure to understand the real and deep meaning of these elements that they strive to fit together into a more or less incoherent assemblage. In fact, it is all no more than a sort of "eclecticism," and there is nothing that we are more resolutely against, precisely because we see the deep agreement beneath the diversity of the forms, and because we see also, at the same time, the reason for these many forms in the variety of the conditions that they must be adapted to. The very great importance of studying the different traditional doctrines lies in the scope that it gives for verifying this agreement and harmony which we affirm here; but there can be no question of making this study the source of a new doctrine: such an idea, far from conforming to the traditional outlook, would be absolutely against it. No doubt, when the elements of a certain order are lacking, as is the case in the modern West for all that is purely metaphysical, they must be looked for elsewhere, wherever they actually exist; but it must not be forgotten that metaphysics is essentially universal, so that it is not the same thing as it would be in the case of elements that have reference to a particular domain. Besides, the Eastern forms of expression would never have to be assimilated by any but the elite, which would then have to set about the task of adaptation; and the knowledge of the doctrines of the East would make it possible, by a judicious use of analogy, to restore the Western tradition itself in its entirety, just as it may make it possible to understand the vanished civilizations; these two cases are altogether comparable, since it must be admitted that, for the most part, the Western tradition is now lost.

Where we have in view a synthesis of a transcendent order as the only possible starting-point for all the further realizations, some people imagine that there can only be question of a more or less confused "syncretism"; however, those are things that have nothing in common, and there is not even the least connection between them. In the same way, there are some who cannot hear the word "esoterism" (which we do not abuse, as will be admitted) without thinking immediately of occultism or of other things of the same kind, in which there is not a trace of true esoterism. It is incredible that the most unjustified claims should be so easily admitted by those very people who would have most interest in refuting them. The only effective means of fighting occultism is to show that there is nothing serious in it, that it is only an altogether modern invention, and that esoterism, in the true sense of the word, is in reality something quite different from it. There are also some who, by another confusion, think that "esoterism" may be glossed by "gnosticism"; here the conceptions in question are genuinely older, but for all that the interpretation is neither more exact nor more justified. It is rather hard to know now the precise nature of the somewhat varied doctrines which are classed together under the term "gnosticism," and among which there would no doubt be many distinctions to make;

but, on the whole, they seem to have contained more or less disfigured Eastern ideas, probably misunderstood by the Greeks, and clothed in imaginative forms which are scarcely compatible with pure intellectuality; it would assuredly cost little effort to find things more worthy of interest, less mixed with heteroclite elements, of a much less dubious value, and much more surely significant. This leads us up to a few remarks about the Alexandrian period in general: that the Greeks were then in fairly direct contact with the East, and that their outlook was thus opened to conceptions against which it had until then been shut, seems to us beyond all question; but the result seems unfortunately to have remained much nearer to "syncretism" than to true synthesis. We have no wish to depreciate unduly such doctrines as those of the Neoplatonic school, which are in any case incomparably superior to all the productions of modern philosophy, but when all is said and done it is better to go back directly to the Eastern source than to take any intermediate steps, and, besides, that has the advantage of being much easier, since the Eastern civilizations still exist, whereas the Greek civilization has not really had any direct successors. The Eastern doctrines, once known, may serve as a means for better understanding the Neoplatonic ones, and even ideas more purely Greek than those, for despite some considerable differences the West was then much closer to the East than it is today; but the inverse would not be possible, and anyone who sought to approach the East through Greece would lay himself open to many mistakes. Besides, the wants of the West can only be supplied by addressing oneself to what actually still exists. There can be no question here of archeology, and the things we have in mind have nothing to do with the pastimes of scholars. If the knowledge of antiquity can play a part, it is only insofar as it will help to understand certain ideas properly, and confirm still further that doctrinal unity which is the meeting ground of all civilizations, with the exception of the modern one alone, which, having neither doctrine nor principles, is outside the normal ways of humanity.

If no attempt at fusion between the different doctrines is admissible, still less can there be any question of substituting one doctrine for another; not only is there no disadvantage in there being many traditional forms, but on the contrary there are very definite advantages in it; even though these forms are, at bottom, fully equivalent, each one of them has its point, if only because it is better fitted than any other to the conditions of some particular setting. The tendency to make everything uniform comes, as we have said, from prejudices instilled by those who preach "equality"; to seek to apply it here would therefore amount to making a concession to the modern outlook, and this concession, even if involuntary, would be nonetheless real, and could only have most deplorable consequences. Only if the West showed herself definitely powerless to go back to a normal civilization could an alien tradition be imposed upon her; but then there would be no fusion, because there would no longer be left anything that was specifically Western; and there would be no substitution either, for, to reach such an extremity, the West would have to have lost even the last vestiges of the traditional outlook—all except for a small elite without which, unable even to receive this alien tradition, she would sink inevitably into the worst barbarism. But, we repeat, it is not too late to hope that things will not go so far and that the elite will be able to establish itself and carry out its task fully, so that the West may not only be saved from chaos and dissolution, but find once more the principles and means of a development that is natural to her, while being at the same time in harmony with that of the other civilizations.

As for the part to be played by the East in all this, let us, to make things clearer, sum it up once more as precisely as possible; we can also make clear, in this connection, the difference between the period of the elite's constitution and that of its effective action. In the first period it is by the study of the Eastern doctrines, more than by any other means, that those who are destined to belong to this elite will be able to acquire and develop in themselves pure intellectuality, since they cannot possibly find it in the West. It is also only by this study that they will be able to learn what a traditional civilization is in its various elements, for it is only a knowledge as direct as possible that has any value in such a case, and there is no place for mere book-learning, which is of no use by itself for the end that we have in view. For the study of the Eastern doctrines to be what it ought to be, certain individuals will have to serve as intermediaries, in the way that we have explained, between the possessors of these doctrines and the Western elite in formation; that is why, for the latter, we speak only of a knowledge as direct as possible, and not absolutely direct, at least to begin with. But subsequently, with the way prepared by this work of assimilation, nothing need stop the elite itself (since it is from it that the initiative must come) from appealing in a more direct way to the representatives of the Eastern traditions; and the latter would be brought to take an interest in the lot of the West by the very presence of this elite and would not fail to answer this appeal, for the one condition that they insist on is understanding (and this one condition is moreover imposed by the very nature of things). We can state definitely that we have never seen any Easterner keep up his habitual reserve when he finds himself face to face with someone whom he thinks capable of understanding him. It is in the second period that actual and visible help of this kind could be given by the Easterners. We have said why that presupposes an elite already constituted, that is, in fact, a Western organization capable of entering into relations with the Eastern organizations which work in the order of pure intellect, and of receiving from them, for its action, the help that is to be had from forces which have accumulated from time immemorial. In such an event the Easterners will always be, for the people of the West, guides and "elder brothers"; but the West, without claiming to be on a footing of absolute equality with them, will nonetheless have the right to be considered as an independent power as soon as she possesses such an organization; and the Easterners' deep distaste for anything that smacks of proselytism will be sufficient guarantee of her independence. The Easterners are not in the least bent on absorbing the West, and they will always much prefer to help on a Western development in conformity with the principles, however little possibility they see of this; it is precisely for those who are to belong to the elite to show them this possibility, proving by their own example that the intellectual degradation of the West is not past all cure. The thing to be done, then, is not to impose on the West an Eastern tradition whose forms would not correspond to the people's mentality, but to restore a Western tradition with the help of the East, first with indirect help, then direct, or, in other words, inspiration in the first period and actual support in the second. But what is not possible for Westerners in general will have to be so for the elite: before it can hope to carry out the necessary adaptations, it must first have penetrated and understood the traditional forms that exist elsewhere; it must also go beyond all forms, whatever they may be, to grasp what constitutes the essence of all tradition. It is in virtue of this that, when the West is once more in possession of a regular and traditional civilization, the elite will be bound to play its part still further: it will then be the means by which the Western civilization will communicate permanently with the other civilizations, for such a communication can only be established and kept up by what is highest in each of them. In order that it may not be simply at the mercy of events, there must be men present who are, for their own part, detached from all particular forms, fully conscious of what is behind the forms, and who, placing themselves in the domain of the most transcendent principles, may take part in all the traditions without distinction. In other words, the West would finally have to reach the stage of having representatives in what is symbolically termed the "center of the world" or its equivalent (which should not be taken literally as indicating any fixed place whatsoever); but this question is concerned with things too remote and, for the moment and no doubt for some time to come, too inaccessible for there to be any advantage in insisting on it.

Since the first step toward rousing Western intellectuality from its slumber must be the study of the doctrines of the East (we mean a real and deep study, with everything that it includes concerning the personal development of those who undertake it, and not an outward and superficial study after the manner of the orientalists), we must now explain why one of these doctrines is, in general, to be approached rather than the others. It might in fact be asked why we take India as our mainstay rather than China, or why we do not think more is to be gained from basing our work on what is closest to the West, that is, on the esoteric side of the Islamic doctrine. We will confine ourselves, moreover, to considering these three big divisions of the East; all the rest is, either of lesser importance, or, like the Tibetan doctrines, so unknown to the Europeans that it would be very difficult to speak to them intelligibly about them before they had understood things less completely foreign to their usual way of thinking. As for China, there are similar reasons for not fixing on her to begin with; the forms in which her doctrines are expressed are really too far removed from the Western mentality, and the methods of teaching in use there are such as might immediately discourage the most gifted Europeans; very few indeed are those who could bear up under work directed along such lines, and, if the prospect of a very rigorous selection should in any case be kept in mind, one should nonetheless avoid as much as possible difficulties that would merely depend on contingencies, and which would arise rather from the temperament inherent in the race than from a real lack of intellectual faculties. The forms of expression of the Hindu doctrines, while being also extremely unlike all those that Western thought is used to, are to be assimilated with relatively greater ease, and they have in them greater possibilities of adaptation. We might say, taking the East as a whole, that India, being in the middle, is neither too far from the West nor too near her for our present purpose. In fact, there would also be disadvantages in taking what is nearest as a basis, and though these would be of a different kind from the ones that we have just been pointing out, they would nonetheless be quite serious enough; and perhaps there would not be many real advantages to make up for them, as Westerners are almost as ill-informed about the Islamic civilization as they are about the more Eastern ones, and the metaphysical part of it in particular, which is what interests us here, escapes them altogether. It is true that this Islamic civilization, with its two aspects, esoteric and exoteric, and with the religious form which the latter is clothed in, comes nearest to being like what a traditional Western civilization would be; but the very presence of this religious form, by which Islam takes as it were after the West, might arouse certain susceptibilities which, however little justified they were, would not be without danger. Those who are incapable of distinguishing between the different domains would wrongly imagine there to be a rivalry between the religions; and there is certainly, among the Western masses (in which we include most of the pseudo-intellectuals), much more hatred against all that is Islamic than against what concerns the rest of the East. Fear enters a good deal into the motives of this hatred, and this state of mind is only due to lack of understanding, but, so long as it exists, the most elementary forethought demands that it shall not be altogether ignored. The elite on its way to being formed will have quite enough to do in the way of overcoming the hostility which it will run up against on different sides, without pointlessly adding to this hostility by making room for false suppositions which stupidity and malignity combined would not fail to give credit to; there will probably be some in any case, but, when they can be foreseen, it is better to take steps against their materializing, if at least it is possible to do so without incurring other consequences that would be still worse. That is why we do not think it advisable to take as our mainstay Islamic esoterism; but, naturally, that does not mean that this esoterism, being truly metaphysical in its essence, has not the equivalent to offer of what is to be found in the other doctrines; all this, then, we repeat, is merely a question of opportuneness, which only arises because it is as well to select the most favorable conditions for work, and does not involve the principles themselves.

Moreover, if we take the Hindu doctrine as the center of the study in question, that does not mean that we intend to refer to it exclusively; it is important on the contrary to bring out, at every favorable opportunity, the agreement and equivalence of all the meta-physical doctrines. It must be shown that beneath expressions that vary there are conceptions that are identical because they correspond to the same truth; sometimes even there are analogies that strike one all the more because they have bearing on very particular points, and also there is a certain community of symbols among the different traditions. These are things that it would be impossible to overemphasize, and there is no question of "syncretism" or "fusion" in establishing these real likenesses and this sort of parallelism which exists among all the civilizations that are traditional, and which can only be surprising to men who believe in no transcendent truth both beyond and above human conceptions. For our part, we do not think that civilizations like those of India and China need necessarily have been in direct communication with one another in the course of their development; that does not prevent them from having, side by side with very marked differences that are to be explained by ethnic and other conditions, features in which they are noticeably alike; and here we are not speaking of the metaphysical order, where the equivalence is always perfect and absolute, but of the applications made to the order of contingent things. Of course, one must always keep in mind the possibility of something belonging to the "primordial tradition"; but since this is by definition previous to the special development of the civilizations in question, its existence does not take away any of their independence. Besides, the "primordial tradition" must be considered as having essentially to do with the principles, and in this domain there has always been a certain lasting communication, established from within and from above, as we have just been saying; but that also does not affect the independence of the different civilizations. However, in the face of certain symbols which are the same everywhere, there is clearly nothing for it but to acknowledge them to be a manifestation of this fundamental traditional unity which is so generally unrecognized today, and which the "scientists" are at great pains to discount as something particularly annoying; the existence of such points in common cannot be mere chance, especially as the ways of expression are, in themselves, apt to vary indefinitely. In short, unity, for whoever has eyes to see it, is everywhere, underlying all diversity; it is there in consequence of the universality of the principles. That the truth should impress itself in the same way on men who have no direct connection with one another, or that real intellectual relations should be kept up between the representatives of different civilizations, is only made possible by this universality; and, if it were not consciously admitted by one or two at least, there could be no question of any truly stable and deep agreement. What all normal civilizations have in common are the principles; if these were lost sight of, each civilization would have scarcely anything left but the special characteristics by which it differs from the others, and even the likenesses would become purely superficial since the true reason for them would not be known. We do not mean that it is absolutely wrong to cite, in explanation of certain general likenesses, the unity of human nature; but it is usually done in a very vague and altogether inadequate way, and moreover the mental differences are much greater and go much further than those who only know one type of humanity can imagine. This unity itself cannot be clearly understood and given its full significance without a true knowledge of the principles, apart from which it is somewhat illusory; the true nature of the species and its deep reality are things that no mere empiricism could account for.

But let us revert to what led us up to these considerations: there cannot be the slightest question of "specializing" in the study of the Hindu doctrine, since the order of pure intellect is just what eludes all specialization. All the doctrines that are metaphysically complete are fully equivalent, and we can even say that they are necessarily identical at bottom; it only remains, then, to decide which is the one that would lend itself most to the sort of exposition required, and we think that, in a general way, it is the Hindu doctrine; that is the reason, and that alone, why we take it as a basis. But if it should happen that certain points are treated of by other doctrines under a form that seems easier to assimilate, there can clearly be no harm in having recourse to those doctrines; in fact it would be yet another way of bringing to light that agreement which we have just been speaking of. We will go further: tradition, instead of standing in the way of the adaptations called for by circumstances, has on the contrary always provided the principle which all necessary adaptations could be based on, and these are absolutely legitimate through their keeping to the strictly traditional line, or, in other words, to what we have also termed "orthodoxy." So, if new adaptations are called for, as is all the more natural on account of the difference in the setting, there is no harm in formulating them by drawing inspiration from those that exist already, while taking also the mental conditions of this setting into account, provided that it is done with the required forethought and competence, and that the traditional outlook has already been grasped in all its depth with all that it includes; this is what the intellectual elite will have to do sooner or later, in everything for which no earlier Western form of expression can be found. It is clear how remote this is from the standpoint of scholarship: the origin of a particular idea does not interest us in itself, for this idea, in being true, is independent of all the men who have expressed it under this form or that; historical contingencies are irrelevant. But since we do not claim to have reached by ourselves and without any help the ideas which we know to be true, we think that it will be as well for us to say who passed them on to us, especially since by so doing we shall be pointing out to others which way they can turn so as to find them for themselves; and, in fact, it is to the Easterners alone that we owe these ideas. As to the question of age, if only considered in a historical way, it is not of very great interest either; only when connected with the idea of tradition does it take on quite another aspect, but then, if it be understood what tradition really is, this question loses its point at once through the knowledge that from the beginning everything was implied principially in what is the very essence of the doctrines, so that it merely had to be deduced from the principles later by a development which, in its foundation if not in its form, could not admit of any innovation. There is no doubt that a certainty of this kind is scarcely communicable; but, if some people possess it, why should not others attain to it as well, especially if the means are given them insofar as they can be given? The "chain of the tradition" is sometimes renewed in a very unexpected way; and men have thought that they had conceived certain ideas spontaneously whereas they had in fact received help that was effective in spite of not being consciously felt by them; still less should such help fail those who put themselves expressly in the required disposition for obtaining it. Of course, we are not denying here the possibility of direct intellectual intuition, since we maintain on the contrary that it is absolutely indispensable and that without it there is no real metaphysical conception;

but it must be led up to, and whatever latent faculties an individual may have, we doubt if he can develop them by himself; at the very least a certain event is necessary to make way for this development. This event, which may vary indefinitely according to the particular cases is never accidental except in appearance; in reality, it is brought about by an action whose ways of working, although they inevitably escape all outside observation, may be grasped by those who understand that "spiritual posterity" is no empty phrase. However, it should be said that cases of this sort are always exceptional, and that if they occur in the absence of all unbroken and regular transmission carried out by organized traditional teaching (one or two examples of such cases might be found in Europe, as also in Japan), they can never entirely make up for this absence, firstly because they are few and far between, and secondly because they lead to the acquisition of knowledge which, whatever its value, is never more than fragmentary. It should also be added that the means of coordinating and expressing what is conceived in this way cannot be given at the same time, so that the benefit remains almost exclusively a personal one. True, that is already something, but it must not be forgotten that even from the point of view of this personal profit, a partial and incomplete realization, like that which may be had in such a case, is a poor result compared with the veritable metaphysical realization that all the Eastern doctrines assign to man as his supreme goal (and which, let us say in passing, has absolutely nothing to do with "quietist sleep" as is imagined by some people that we have come across, through a grotesque interpretation that is certainly not justified by anything we have said of it). Besides, where realization has not been preceded by a sufficient theoretic preparation, many confusions may arise, and there is always the possibility of losing one's way in one of those intermediate domains where there is no security against illusions; it is only in the domain of pure metaphysics that such security is to be had, and, since it is then acquired once and for all, there can no longer be the least danger in entering any other domain whatsoever, as we have already pointed out.

The truth of facts may seem almost negligible compared with the truth of ideas; however, even in the contingent order, there are degrees to be observed, and there is a way of looking at things, by linking them up with their principles, which gives them an importance such as they altogether lack by themselves; what we have said about the "traditional sciences" should be enough to make this clear. There is no need to become involved in questions of chronology, which are often insoluble, at least by the ordinary historical methods; but there is some point in knowing that such and such ideas belong to a traditional doctrine, and even that such and such a way of presenting them is equally traditional in character; we think it unnecessary to insist on this any more, after all the considerations that we have already put forward. In any case, although the truth of facts, which is merely supplementary, must not make one lose sight of the truth of ideas, which is the essential, it would be wrong to refuse to take into account the additional advantages to be had from knowing a fact, since, despite their being, like it, contingent, they are not always to be disdained. To know that certain ideas have been given us by the Easterners is to know a true fact; this is less important than to understand these ideas and to acknowledge inwardly that they are true, and if they had come to us from elsewhere, we would see not the slightest reason for waving them aside a priori; but since we have found nowhere in the West the equivalent of these Eastern ideas, we think it as well to say so. Of course, it would be possible to have an easy success by putting forward certain conceptions as if one had, as it were, invented them from start to finish, and by keeping their real origin secret; but we cannot admit such behavior, and besides, it would amount in our eyes to robbing the conceptions of their true bearing and their authority, since in this way they would be reduced to seeming no more than a "philosophy," when really they are something quite different; here once more we are touching on the question of the individual and the universal, which is at the bottom of all such distinctions.

But let us keep, for the moment, to what is contingent: to maintain boldly that it is in the East that pure intellectual knowledge may be acquired, while striving at the same time to reawaken the intellectuality of the West, is to help promote, in the only effective way, the renewal of relations between East and West; and we hope that it will now be understood why this possibility is not to be neglected, since that is the chief object of all that we have said so far. The restoration of a normal civilization in the West may be only a contingency; but, we repeat, is that a reason for losing all interest in it, even if one is above all a metaphysician? And besides, apart from the importance that such things have in their own relative order, they may be the means of realizations that are not limited to the domain of contingency, and that, for all those who take part in them directly or even indirectly, will have consequences before which all transitory things efface themselves and vanish. The reasons for all this are many, and the deepest of them are perhaps not those that we have laid most stress on, since we could not think of expounding here the metaphysical theories (and even cosmological ones in certain cases, as, for example, where the "cyclic laws" are concerned) without which they could not be fully understood; we intend to do so in other works which will follow in due course. As we said at the beginning, we cannot possibly explain everything at once; but we state nothing gratuitously, and we are conscious of having, for want of many other merits, at least that of only talking about what we know. If then there are some who are surprised at certain considerations that they are not used to, we hope that they will take the trouble to give them their more attentive reflection, and perhaps they will then see that these considerations, far from being useless or superfluous, are precisely some of the most important, or that what seemed to them at first sight to take us away from our subject is on the contrary what concerns it most directly. There are indeed things that are connected in a way quite different from what is usually thought, and the truth has many aspects that most Westerners scarcely suspect; that is why we should always be more afraid of seeming to limit things too much by the expression that we give them than of implying possibilities that are too great.

Translated by Henry D. Fohr

On Religion

Jagadguru Sri Chandrasekharendra Saraswati Swamigal

You must look upon the world as belonging to the Lord, and it is your duty to so conduct yourself as to conform to this belief. This constitutes the *dharma* (code of conduct, set of duties) of humanity. Acts dictated solely by selfish interests will push one into unrighteousness. A man must learn to be less and less selfish in his thoughts and actions; he must always remember the Lord and must ever be conscious that He is the master of all this world. This view is the basis on which all religions have evolved.

No religion teaches us to live according to our whims and fancies; no religion asks us to acquire wealth and property for our personal needs alone. If a man believes that he alone is important, that he is all, he will live only for himself. That is why all religions speak of an entity called God and teach man to efface his ego or I-feeling. "Child," they tell him, "you are nothing before that Power, the author of this universe. It is He—that Power—who has endowed you with intelligence. Your intelligence, your intellect, must guide you on the path of *dharma*, righteousness. For this purpose you must look up to this Power for support."

The great importance attached to *bhakti* or devotion in all religions is founded on this belief, the need for divine support for virtuous conduct.

Ordinarily it is not easy to develop faith in, or devotion to, God expressed in abstract terms. For the common people devotion must take the form of practical steps. That is how ritual originated. *Sandhyāvandana* (morning and evening prayers), *namāz* (Persian word for Islamic prayers) and other forms of prayer are examples of such ritual. The religions teach people their duties, how they must conduct themselves in this world, and how they must devote themselves to God in the very midst of their worldly life.

"Love everyone." "Live a life of sacrifice." "Serve mankind." Such are the teachings of the various religions. If a man lives according to these tenets, it is believed that his soul will reach God after it departs from his body. Those who subscribe to *Advaita* or non-dualism declare that the soul will become one with the Godhead. According to another system of belief, after reaching the Lord, the soul will serve Him and ever remain happy as the recipient of His compassion. There is no need to quarrel over the nature of the final state. "By following one path or another we attain the Lord. And that will be the end of all our sorrows, all our frustrations, and all our failures in this world. There will now be nothing but bliss, full and everlasting." No more than this do we need to know for the present.

If the *Paramātman* (Transcendent Unity of God—the Great Transcendent Self) is to draw us unto Himself we must, without fail, perform our duties to Him as well as to the world. It is these duties that constitute what is called *dharma*. *Dharma* it is that serves us when we dwell in our body and when we cease to dwell in it. It serves us in life and after life. When we are in this world we must do that which would take us to a desirable state after we depart from it. We take an insurance policy so that our relatives will be able to take care of themselves when we are gone. But is it not far more important to ensure that we will be happy in our afterlife? *Dharma* is afterlife insurance. But in this life too it is *dharma* that gives us peace and happiness.

There need be no doubt or confusion about the *dharma* we ought to follow. We are all steeped in the *dharma* that our great men have pursued from generation to generation. They have inwardly realized eternal beatitude and we know for certain that they lived without any care, unlike people in our own generation who are always discontented and are embroiled in agitations and demonstrations of all kinds. All we need to do is to follow the *dharma* that they practiced. If we tried to create a new *dharma* for ourselves it might mean trouble and all the time we would be torn by doubts as to whether it would bring us good or whether it would give rise to evil. It is best for us to follow the *dharma* practiced by the great men of the past, the *dharma* of our forefathers.

Man is subject to all kinds of hardships and misfortunes. To remind ourselves of this, we eat the bitter flowers of the neem on New Year's Day—that is, on the very first day of the year we accept the bitternesses of life. During the Pongal ceremony, which is celebrated almost towards the close of the year, we have sugarcane to chew. If we have only sweetness in the beginning we may have to experience bitterness towards the end. We must not have any aversion for the bitter but welcome it as the medicine administered by Mother Nature or by *dharma*. If we do so, in due course, we will learn to regard any experience, even if it be unpleasant, as a sweet one.

Dharma—and *dharma* alone—is our protecting shield.

One's religion is nothing but the *dharma* practiced by one's forefathers. May all adhere to their *dharma* with unwavering faith and courage and be rewarded with everlasting bliss.

***Punya* (Virtuous Action)**

Nobody wants to be known as a sinner, but all the same we keep transgressing the bounds of morality and disobeying the divine law. We wish to enjoy the fruits of virtue without being morally good and without doing anything meritorious.

Arjuna says to Bhagavān Krishna (Lord Krishna): "No man wants to commit sin. Even so, Krishna, he does evil again and again. What is it that drives him so?" The Lord replies: "It is desire. Yes, it is desire, Arjuna."

Only by banishing desire from our hearts may we remain free from sin. How is it done? We cannot but be performing our works. Even when we are physically inactive, our mind remains active. All our mental and bodily activity revolves round our desires. And these desires thrust us deeper and deeper into sin. Is it, then, possible to remain without doing any work? Human nature being what it is, the answer is "No".

"It is difficult to quell one's thinking nor is it easy to remain without doing anything," says Tāyumānavā-svamigal (*swami*). We may stop doing work with the body, but how do we keep the mind quiet? The mind is never still. Apart from being unstill itself, it incites the body to action.

We are unable either to efface our desires or to cease from all action. Does it then mean that liberation is beyond us? Is there no way out of the problem? Yes, there is. It is not necessary that we should altogether stop our actions in our present immature predicament. But, instead of working for our selfish ends, we ought to be engaged in such work as would bring benefits to the world as well as to our inward life. The more we are involved in such work, the less we shall be drawn by desire. This will to some extent keep us away from sin and at the same time enable us to do more meritorious work. We must learn the habit of doing work without any selfish motive. Work done without any desire for the fruits thereof is *punya*, or virtuous action.

We sin in four different ways. With our body we do evil; with our tongue we speak untruth; with our mind we think evil; and with our money we do so much that is wicked. We must learn to turn these very four means of evil into instruments of virtue.

We must serve others with our body and circumambulate the Lord and prostrate ourselves before him. In this way we earn merit. How do we use our tongue to add to our stock of virtue?

By saying, by repeating, the names of the Lord. You will perhaps excuse yourself saying: "All our time is spent in earning our livelihood. How can we then think of God or repeat His Names?" A householder has a family to maintain; but is he all the time working for it? How much time does he waste in gossip, in amusements, in speaking ill of others, in reading the papers? Can't he spare a few moments to remember the Lord? He need not set apart a particular hour of the day for his *japa* (recitation of a *mantra*—a Divine formula). He may think of God even on the bus or the train as he goes to his office or any other place. Not a penny is he going to take with him finally after his lifelong pursuit of money. The Lord's name, Bhagavan *nāma*, is the only current coin in the other world.

The mind is the abode of *Īśvara* (the *Paramātman* with attributes) but we make a rubbish can of it. We must cleanse it, install the Lord in it and be at peace with ourselves. We must devote at least five minutes every day to meditation and resolve to do so even if the world crashes around us. There is nothing else that will give us a helping hand when the whole cosmos is dissolved.

"Come to me, your only refuge. I shall free you from all sins. Have no fear." This assurance that Śri Krishna gives to free us from sin is absolute. So let us learn to be courageous. To tie up an object you wind a string round it again and again. If it is to be untied you will have to do the unwinding in a similar manner. To eradicate the habit of sinning you must develop the habit of doing good to an equal degree. In between there ought to be neither haste nor anger. With haste and anger the thread you keep unwinding will get tangled again. *Īśvara* will come to our help if we have patience, if we have faith in him, and if we are rooted in *dharma*.

The goal of all religions is to wean away man—his mind, his speech, and his body—from sensual pleasure and lead him towards the Lord. Great men have appeared from time to time and established their religions with the goal of releasing people from attachment to their senses, for it is our senses that impel us to sin. "Transitory is the joy derived from sinful action, from sensual pleasure. Bliss is union with the *Paramātman*." Such is the teaching of all religions and their goal is to free man from worldly existence by leading him towards the Lord.

The Purpose of Religion

We know for certain that ordinarily people do not achieve eternal happiness. The purpose of any religion is to lead them towards such happiness. Everlasting blessedness is obtained only by forsaking the quest for petty pleasures. The dictates of *dharma* help us to abandon the pursuit of sensual enjoyments and endeavor for eternal bliss. They are also essential to create a social order that has the same high purpose, the liberation of all. Religion, with its goal of liberation, lays down the tenets of *dharma*. That is why the great understand the word *dharma* itself to mean religion.

To Be a True Man

The first step in this process of enlightenment is to make a man truly a man, by ensuring that he does not live on an animal level. The second step is to raise him to the heights of divinity. All religions have this goal. They may represent different systems of thought and philosophy. But their concern ought to be that man is not condemned as he is today to a life of desire and anger. All religions speak in one voice that man must be rendered good and that he must be invested with the qualities of love, humility, serenity, and the spirit of sacrifice.

Devotion Common to All Faiths

What is special about *sanātana dharma* (primordial, eternal code of conduct) or Hinduism as it has come to be called? Alone among all religions it reveals the one and only Godhead in many different divine forms, with manifold aspects. The devotee worships the Lord in a form suited to his mental make-up and is thus helped to come closer to the Lord with his love and devotion. These different forms are not the creation of anyone's imagination. The *Paramātman* has revealed himself in these forms to great men and they have had close contact, so to speak, with the deities so revealed. They have also shown us how we too may come face to face with these divinities, given us the *mantras* (Divine formulas) to accomplish this, and also prescribed the manner in which the divine forms, whose vision they have had, are to be adored.

Bhakti or devotion is common to all religions whatever the manner of worship they teach. It is not exclusive to our faith in which different deities are reverenced.

The Unity of Religions

All religions have one common ideal: worship of the Lord; and all of them proclaim that there is but one God. This one God accepts your devotion irrespective of the manner of or that religion. So there is no need to abandon the religion of your birth and embrace another.

The temple, the church, the mosque, the *vihāra* (a Buddhist monastery; a residence for meditation) may be different from one another. The idol or the symbol in them may not also be the same and the rites performed in them may be different. But the *Paramātman* (Transcendent Unity) who grants grace to the worshipper, whatever be his faith, is the same. The different religions have taken shape according to the customs peculiar to the countries in which they originated and according to the differences in the mental outlook of the people inhabiting them. The goal of all religions is to lead people to the same *Paramātman* according to the different attitudes of the devotees concerned.

One big difference between Hinduism and other faiths is that it does not proclaim that it alone shows the path to liberation. Our Vedic religion alone has not practiced conversion and the reason for it is that our forefathers were well aware that all religions are nothing but different paths to realize the one and only *Paramātman.* The Vedas proclaim: "The wise speak of the One Truth by different names." Śrī Krishna says in the Bhagavad Gītā: "In whatever way or form a man worships me, I increase his faith and make him firm and steady in that worship." This is the reason why Hindus have not practiced—like adherents of other religions—proselytization and religious persecution. Nor have they waged anything like the crusades or *jihāds* (Arabic word for holy war).

All religions that practice conversion employ a certain ritual. For instance, there is baptism in Christianity. Hinduism has more ritual than any other religion, yet its canonical texts do not contain any rite for conversion. No better proof is needed for the fact that we have at no time either encouraged conversion or practiced it.

That the beliefs and customs of the various religions are different cannot be a cause for complaint. Nor is there any need to make all of them similar. The important thing is for the followers of the various faiths to live in harmony with one another. The goal must be unity, not uniformity.

Qualities of Religious Teachers

I believe that the growth or expansion of a religion is in no way related to its doctrines. The common people do not worry about questions of philosophy. A great man of exemplary character and qualities appears on the scene—a great man of compassion who creates serenity everywhere—and people are drawn to him. They become converts to his religion in the firm belief that the doctrines preached by him, whatever they be, must be good. On the other hand, a religion will decline and decay if its spokesmen, however eloquent they are in expounding its concepts, are found to be guilty of lapses in character and conduct. It is difficult to give an answer to the question why people flock to religions that have contradictory beliefs. But, if we examine the history of some religions—how at one time people gloried in them and how these faiths later perished—we shall be able to know the reason. At the same time, it would be possible for us to find out how in the first place they attracted such a large following. If you find out how a religion declined you will be able to know how it had first grown and prospered.

The decay of a religion in any country could be attributed to the lack of character of its leaders and of the people constituting the establishment responsible for its growth.

We need not be critical of those who indulge in conversion. We need not nurture enmity towards them. What is the reason for them to draw others to their religion by force or temptation? Is it not because of their belief that their religion represents the highest truth? They may engage themselves in conversion in good faith thinking, "Only if our religion is accepted by others, can they have ultimate release. In order to do them such great good, there is nothing wrong in using force or temptations".

If religions that resort neither to force nor to the power of money have grown, it is solely because of the noble qualities of their teachers. Outward guise alone is not what constitutes the qualities of the representative or spokesman of a religion. Whatever the persuasion to which he belongs he must be utterly selfless, bear ill-will towards none, in addition to being morally blameless. He must live an austere life, and must be calm and compassionate by nature. Such a man will be able to help those who come to him by removing their shortcomings and dispelling the evil in them.

Producing men of such noble qualities from amongst us is the way to make our religion flourish. It is not necessary to carry on propaganda against other religions. The need is for representatives, for preceptors, capable of providing an example through their very life of the teachings of our religion. It is through such men that, age after age, *sanātana dharma* has been sustained as a living force. Hereafter too it will be through them that it will continue to remain a living force.

Religious Pluralism and the Transcendent Unity of Religions

Roland Pietsch

Religious Pluralism

Religious pluralism, as an existing phenomenon, has been interpreted indifferent ways. The position of modern sociology, which has developed this concept, is to comprehend religious pluralism as a characteristic of modernity. In this context modernity is understood as an outcome of secularization. Sociology, especially that of Peter L. Berger and Thomas Luckmann, generally defines pluralism as a situation in which there is competition in the institutional ordering of comprehensive meanings for everyday life. Historically, such competition generally succeeds a situation in which it was more or less absent. That is, pluralism is the consequence of a historical process of de-monopolisation. The global historical force producing pluralism is secularization, by which we mean the progressive autonomization of social sectors from the domination of religious meanings and institutions.

In analyzing the social-structural dimension of pluralism it is possible to distinguish between the latter's effect on the relationship between institutional religion and other social institutions, and the effect on institutional religion itself. The social structure has its correlates in subjective consciousness. Religious pluralism, to wit, entails religious subjectivization. This means that the old religious contents lose their status of objective facticity in individual consciousness. This change is already given in the reflective attitude that the consumer comes to take as he is presented with a multiplicity of products. He must choose between them and is thereby forced to hesitate, to compare, and to deliberately evaluate. In this process the traditional religious affirmations about the nature of reality lose their taken-for-granted quality. They cease to be objective truth and become matters of subjective choice, belief, and preference. Other meaning-systems come to take the place of the objective facticity that was previously occupied by religious tradition.[1]

This purely sociological portrayal of religious pluralism is not aware of religion's truth. Ultimately, it only expresses the existing crisis-of-meaning imbued in modernity itself. Hence, without doubt, religion can best and most adequately be understood from the point of view of religion itself. Accordingly, this is also true for the plurality and diversity of religions. Concerning the idea of religious pluralism, as seen by the various religions, there exist great differences. Judaism, as the first of the monotheistic religions, does not acknowledge any other religion as a matter of principle, whether that religion had been existing before it or emerged afterwards. Christianity as the second monotheistic religion sees Judaism to a certain degree as a prefiguration of Christian revelation. But it does not acknowledge Islam that arose later. Eventually, Islam acknowledged both Judaism and Christianity as true revelations, though they only reached completion in and through the religion of Islam. In praxis this resulted in Christianity holding a monopoly in Christian countries for centuries. In most Islamic countries the religion of Islam was and is—apart from some small minorities—the sole religion. This

[1] Peter L. Berger and Thomas Luckmann, "Secularization and Pluralism" in *Internationales Jahrbuch fur Religions-soziologie/ International Yearbook for the Sociology of Religion*, vol. 2, 1966, pp. 73-81.

meant that Christianity lost its monopoly.

> With the collapse of the Europe-centered view of the world and the rapid development of international interaction in various fields of human life, Christians have come again to experience intensely the reality of religious pluralism. In this connection they have come to recognize the existence of non-Christian religions and the integrity of non-Christian systems of belief and values, not only in foreign lands, but in Europe and America as well. Hence, religious pluralism now appears to many Christians to be a serious challenge to the monotheistic character of Christianity. On the other hand, Buddhism, throughout its long history, has existed and spread throughout Asia within a religiously pluralistic situation: in India, it coexisted with Brahmanism, Jainism and many diverse forms of Hinduism; in China with Confucianism and Taoism; and in Japan with Shinto and Confucianism. Thus to most Buddhists the experience of "religious pluralism" has not been the serious shock it has been to most Christians.[2]

And certainly not the shock it would be for the representatives of both other monotheistic religions. The Christian shock was peculiar and corresponds not so much to the two other monotheistic religions as it does to the non-monotheistic religions. Meanwhile Christian theologians tried to deal with this shock by way of a theology of religious pluralism. The central question asked by such a theology was whether religious pluralism should be accepted as a reality, *de facto*, in our present world or if it should, on the contrary, be viewed theologically as existing *de jure*.

> In the first case, the plurality of religions . . . is seen as a factor to be reckoned with, rather than welcomed. . . . In the other case, the same plurality is welcomed as a positive factor which witnesses at once to the superabundant generosity with which God has manifested himself to humankind in manifold ways and to the pluriform response which human beings of diverse cultures have given to the Divine self-disclosure. Seen from God's side, the question is whether religious pluralism is only permitted by God or, on the contrary, positively willed by Him. Or rather—if one prefers to avoid both these terms—the question is whether theology is able to assign to the plurality of religious traditions a positive meaning in God's overall design for humankind or not.[3]

The Catholic theologian Schillebeeckx responds to this problematic question by noticing that even in the Christian self-understanding. . .

> The multiplicity of religions is not an evil which needs to be removed, but rather a wealth which is to be welcomed and enjoyed by all. . . . The unity, identity and uniqueness of Christianity over and against the other religions . . . lies in the fact that Christianity is a religion which associates the relationship to God within the

[2] Masao Abe, "A Dynamic Unity in Religious Pluralism: a Proposal from the Buddhist Point of View," in Masao Abe, *Buddhism and Interfaith Dialogue*, ed. Steven Heine (Honolulu, 1995), pp. 17-18.

[3] Jacques Dupuis, S. J., *Toward a Christian Theology of Religious Pluralism* (New York, 1997), p. 386.

> context of a historical and thus a very specific and therefore limited particularity: Jesus of Nazareth. This is the uniqueness and identity of Christianity, but at the same time, its unavoidable historical limitation. It becomes clear here that . . . the God of Jesus is a symbol of openness, not of confinement. Here Christianity has a positive relationship to other religions, and at the same time the loyal Christian affirmation of the positive nature of other world religions is honored.[4]

The question here is where do the origins of religious pluralism lie? An answer can be that the principle of plurality is mainly based on the superabundant richness and diversity of God's self-manifestation to mankind. The religion of Islam acknowledges the principle of the plurality of religions to an even greater extent than does Christianity, simply because it accepts all the previous monotheistic revelations and completes them. In this sense it does not need to be explained much, whereas what calls for further discussion is Islam's problematic relationship with Hinduism and Buddhism. The solution to such a problem and similar problems can be found to lie in taking up an esoteric or transcendental point of view. The point of departure for the teachings of the transcendent unity of religions, as they have been formulated by their most important representative Frithjof Schuon, can, as paradoxical as it may seem, be found in the actual diversity of mankind and the corresponding limitations that such diversity and multiplicity call for.

The Transcendent Unity of Religions

The multiplicity of religions has its origin in the single divine Truth that has manifested itself in manifold ways to mankind throughout its history. These divine revelations occurred at different times, in different places, and to different human collectivities. Thereby they assumed different shapes. Thus, "what determines the differences among forms of Truth is the difference among human receptacles. For thousands of years already humanity has been divided into several fundamentally different branches, which constitute so many complete humanities, more or less closed in on themselves; the existence of spiritual receptacles so different and so original demands differentiated refractions of the one Truth."[5]

This principle bears great meaning for there is no doubt that the Truth is one. In this context the revelations of the one divine Truth can be viewed as formalisations of this truth. And the formalisations are not completely identical with this Truth-in-itself, because, "Truth is situated beyond forms, whereas Revelation, or the Tradition that derives from it, belongs to the formal order, and that indeed by definition; but to speak of form is to speak of diversity, and thus of plurality."[6]

As a matter of course the principle of a multitude of revelations is "not accessible to all mentalities and its implications must remain anathema to the majority of believers. This is in the nature of things. Nevertheless, from a traditionalist viewpoint, anyone today wishing to understand religion as such and the inter-relationships of the various traditions must have a firm purchase on this principle."[7]

4 Edward Schillebeeckx, *Church: The Human Story of God* (London, 1993), p. 164.

5 Frithjof Schuon, *Gnosis, Divine Wisdom* (London, 1979), p. 29.

6 Frithjof Schuon, *ibid.*

7 Kenneth Oldmeadow, *Traditionalism: Religion in the Light of the Perennial Philosophy* (Colombo, 2000), p. 70.

In this regard it has to be emphasized that every single revelation is the origin of a religion. And every religion is self-sufficient and comprises all that is necessary for man's salvation. But at the same time every religion is limited as a form. Frithjof Schuon has explained this coherence as follows:

> A religion is a form, and so also a limit, which, "contains" the Limitless, to speak in paradox; every form is fragmentary because of its necessary exclusion of other formal possibilities; the fact that these forms—when they are complete, that is to say when they are perfectly "themselves"—each in their own way represent totality, does not prevent them from being fragmentary in respect of their particularization and their reciprocal exclusion.[8]

Given the diversity of revelations the question arises who the messengers were who received the respective revelation and passed it on. A first conclusion is that: "The great Messengers, if they are assuredly one by their principle, in their gnosis and in the Logos, are not however of necessity equal on the phenomenal plane, that of manifestation on earth; what are equivalent are the Messages when each is taken in its entirety. It is necessary, in any case, not to confuse the phenomenal or cosmic with the spiritual reality; it is the latter which is one, and the former which is diverse."[9]

To understand the correlation between the diversity of revelations and the respective messengers, it has to be clarified that the revelation received by the respective messenger is the foundation of a religion. The peculiar imprint that characterizes every single religion indeed depends on when and where the respective messenger fulfilled his challenge and in what particular manner. According to this Seyyed Hossein Nasr, a follower of Frithjof Schuon, could write: "When one says *the* Prophet it means the prophet of Islam... when one says *the* Incarnation it refers to Christ who personifies this aspect. And although every prophet and saint has experienced "enlightenment," *the* Enlightenment refers to the experience of the Buddha which is the most outstanding and universal embodiment of this experience."[10]

But how can a religion be understood and interpreted in this meaning? Essentially there are two elements which build the foundation of a religion: Namely doctrine and method, that is to say, "a doctrine which distinguishes between the Absolute and the relative, between the absolutely Real and the relatively real . . . and a method of concentrating upon the Real, of attaching oneself to the Absolute and living according to the will of Heaven, in accordance with the purpose and meaning of human existence."[11]

When we speak of a doctrine, which distinguishes between the Absolute and the relative, the question about its orthodoxy arises. "In order to be orthodox a religion must possess a mythological or doctrinal symbolism establishing the essential distinction between the Real and the illusory, or the Absolute and the relative . . . and must offer a way that serves both the perfection of concentration on the Real and also its continuity. In other words a religion is orthodox condition that it offers a sufficient, if not always exhaustive, idea of the absolute and

[8] Frithjof Schuon, *Understanding Islam* (London, 1976), p. 144.

[9] Frithjof Schuon, *Gnosis, Divine Wisdom*, p. 14.

[10] Seyyed Hossein Nasr, *Ideals and Realities of Islam* (London, 1966), p. 67.

[11] *Ibid.*, p. 67.

the relative, and therewith an idea of their reciprocal relationships."[12] Concerning a religion's inner or outer orthodoxy Frithjof Schuon speaks clearly and precisely: "For a religion to be considered intrinsically orthodox—an extrinsic orthodoxy hangs upon formal elements which cannot apply literally outside their own perspective—it must rest upon a fully adequate doctrine . . . then it must extol and actualize a spirituality that is equal to this doctrine and thereby include sanctity within its ambit both as concept and reality; this means it must be of Divine and not philosophical origin and thus be charged with a sacramental or theurgic presence."[13]

Indeed, traditional orthodoxy means, as Schuon says:

> . . . being in accord with a doctrinal or ritual form, and also, and indeed above all, with the truth which resides in all revealed forms; thus the essence of every orthodoxy is intrinsic truth... and not merely the internal logic of a doctrine that may turn out to be false. What makes the definition of orthodoxy rather troublesome is that it presents two principal modes, the one essential or intrinsic, and the other formal or extrinsic: the latter is the being in accord with a revealed form, and the former the being in accord with the essential and universal truth, with or without being in accord with any particular form, so that the two modes sometimes stand opposed externally. To give an example, it can be said that Buddhism is extrinsically heterodox in relation to Hinduism, because it makes a departure from the basic forms of the latter, and at the same time intrinsically orthodox, because it is in accord with that universal truth from which both traditions proceed.[14]

In order to provide a deeper insight into the difference between intrinsic and extrinsic orthodoxy the relationship between exotericism and esotericism will be briefly explained. First, an explanation of exotericism: "Exotericism never goes beyond the "letter." It puts its accent on the Law, not on any realisation, and so puts it on action and merit. It is essentially a "belief" in a "letter," or a dogma envisaged in its formal exclusiveness, and an obedience to ritual and moral Law. And, further, exotericism never goes beyond the individual; it is centred on heaven rather than on God, and this amounts to saying that this difference has for it no meaning."[15] The famous American scholar Huston Smith has clarified this definition of exotericism with the following words: "For the exoteric, God's personal mode is His only mode; for the esoteric this mode resides in one that is higher and ultimately modeless. . . . For the exoteric the world is real in every sense; for the exoteric it has only a qualified reality. . . . For the exoteric God is primarily loved; for the esoteric He is primarily known; though in the end the exoteric comes to know what he loves and the esoteric to love what he knows."[16]

What characterizes esotericism "to the very extent that it is absolute, is that on contact with a dogmatic system, it universalizes the symbol or religious concept on the one hand, and interiorizes it on the other; the particular or the limited is recognized as the manifestation of the

[12] Frithjof Schuon, *Light on the Ancient Worlds* (London, 1966), p. 138.

[13] Frithjof Schuon, *Islam and the Perennial Philosophy* (London, 1976), p. 14.

[14] Frithjof Schuon, *Language of the Self* (Madras, 1959), p. 1.

[15] Frithjof Schuon, *Light on the Ancient Worlds*, p. 76.

[16] Huston Smith, "Introduction" in Schuon, *The Transcendent Unity of Religions* (New York, 1975), p. xxvi.

principle and the transcendent, and this in its turn reveals itself as immanent."[17] And further: "If the purest esotericism includes the whole truth—and that is the very reason for its existence—the question of "orthodoxy" in the religious sense clearly cannot arise: direct knowledge of the mysteries could not be "Moslem" or "Christian" just as the sight of a mountain is the sight of a mountain and not something else."[18]

The exoteric point of view is "doomed to end by negating itself once it is no longer vivified by the presence within it of the esotericism of which it is both the outward radiation and the veil. So it is that religion, according to the measure in which it denies metaphysical and initiatory realities and becomes crystallized in literalistic dogmatism, inevitably engenders unbelief; the atrophy that overtakes dogmas when they are deprived of their internal dimensions recoils upon them from outside, in the form of heretical and atheistic negations."[19] Hence it is necessary to refer to religion's spirituality or religion's esoteric dimension.

A religion is indeed "not limited by what it includes but by what it excludes; this exclusion cannot impair the religions' deepest contents—every religion is intrinsically a totality—but it takes its revenge all the more surely on the intermediary plane . . . the arena of theological speculations and fervors . . . [hence] extrinsic contradictions can hide an intrinsic compatibility or identity, which amounts to saying that each of the contradictory theses contains a truth and thereby an aspect of the whole truth and a way of access to this totality."[20] In contrast, the exoteric claim to the exclusive possession of a unique truth, or of Truth without epithet, is "an error purely and simply; in reality, every expressed truth necessarily assumes a form, that of its expression, and it is metaphysically impossible that any form should possess a unique value to the exclusion of other forms; for a form, by definition, cannot be unique and exclusive, that is to say it cannot be the only possible expression of what it expresses."[21] The diversity of religions does not demonstrate the incorrectness of the various doctrines of the supernatural. It rather shows that revelation lies beyond the formal, whereas human comprehension has a formal nature. According to this the essence of every religion—or enlightenment—is always the same. The diversity on the contrary arises from human nature.

Conclusion

This concise and fragmentary comparison of religious pluralism and the transcendent unity of religions aimed at two things: First, to deepen the understanding of every single religion. And second, through the realisation of the esoteric and spiritual dimension of this religion, to recognize the transcendent unity of all true religions. To understand every single religion however not only requires in-depth studies, but above all demands the acceptance of the authentic self-conception of the religion.

The realisation of the metaphysical doctrine goes even further. It means to follow a spiritual path that ultimately leads to immediate love and gnosis of the divine Truth itself.

An outstanding example for such a spiritual path is the life and work of Ibn 'Arabi, who wrote in his famous *Tarjuman al-Ashwaq*, out of his own mystic and theosophic experience,

[17] Frithjof Schuon, *Esoterism as Principle and Way* (London, 1981), p. 37.

[18] Frithjof Schuon, *Understanding Islam*, p. 139.

[19] Frithjof Schuon, *The Transcendent Unity of Religions*, p. 9.

[20] Frithjof Schuon, *Islam and Perennial Philosophy*, p. 46.

[21] Frithjof Schuon, *The Transcendent Unity of Religions*, p. 17.

the following marvellous verses:

> My heart has become capable of every form,
> a pasture for gazelles,
> a convent for Christian monks,
> a temple for idols,
> the pilgrim's Ka'ba,
> the tables of the Torah,
> the book of the Koran.
> I follow the religion of love
> whatever way Love's camels take.[22]

[22] Ibn ʻArabi, *Tarjuman al-Ashwaq*, ed. by R. N. Nicholson (London, 1911), pp. 19/67.

II
PERSPECTIVES

The Paths of the Ancient Sages: A Sacred Tradition Between East and West

Peter Kingsley

The year: 1191. At Aleppo in Syria a man called Shihab al-Din Yahya al-Suhrawardi was executed on direct orders from the great Islamic ruler, Saladin. He was 38 years old.

His death and short life might appear to have nothing to do with ancient Greece, or with the person known to us as Pythagoras. But appearances are often misleading.

Suhrawardi has been known in Persia since his death as "The Sheikh of the East," or simply as "He who was killed." While still alive he taught and wrote about how he had uncovered a continuous line of esoteric tradition: a tradition that started in the East, passed from there to the early Greek philosophers, then was carried from Greece to Egypt where it traveled a long way up the Nile and eventually was transmitted from southern Egypt back to Persia.

For him this tradition wasn't just a matter of history. On the contrary, he presented himself as its living representative in his own time. And he explained that he was the person responsible for bringing it to its fulfillment by returning it, full circle, to its roots in the East.

The few people in the West who study Suhrawardi nowadays tend to believe his vision of the past is strictly symbolic; that his interpretations of history aren't to be taken literally, or seriously. Suhrawardi himself, though, was very serious about what he said. And so were his successors—people who down to the present day claim they have perpetuated intact an esoteric tradition based not on theorizing or reasoning about reality, but on direct experience gained through spiritual struggle and very specific techniques of realization.

For them this tradition was alive, incredibly powerful. Suhrawardi described it as an eternal "leaven"—likely to create a tremendous ferment or restless dissatisfaction with the way things are but also capable of transforming whatever it touches, of raising people who are ready into another level of being. And just as yeast acts subtly but irresistibly, transforming from the inside, unrestrainable precisely because it's so subtle, the theologians in his time reckoned that the only way to try and stop his teaching from growing would be to kill him. But of course in killing him they stopped nothing.

And Suhrawardi, like his successors among Persian Sufis, was quite precise about his ancestors. He mentions two early Greek philosophers in particular: Pythagoras and a man from Sicily called Empedocles. He also states the name of the particular town in southern Egypt where the tradition eventually arrived. And he gives the name of the man responsible for carrying it out of Egypt in the ninth century—nearly one and a half thousand years after Pythagoras and Empedocles.

As we will see, he knew what he was saying. But first we need to start at the beginning.

* * *

Those who specialize in the history of classical Greece naturally tend to dislike any talk about contacts with the ancient East. It can be disconcerting to find that the area you have given your life to studying is nothing but one tiny square on a far vaster chess board, that the details you have been analyzing for so long are just the marks left behind by chess pieces being moved from somewhere you don't know about to somewhere you don't understand.

Western philosophy is presented nowadays as strictly a Greek phenomenon, explainable in Greek terms alone. Claims made by ancient sources that the earliest philosophers traveled to distant places in search of wisdom are dismissed as romantic fantasies, dreamed up by Greek writers long after the time of the people they were writing about.

The trouble is that, in the case of Pythagoras, the reports about him traveling far and wide go back more or less to the time when Pythagoras was alive. Historians like to speak about what they call the "Oriental mirage"—the exotic illusion conjured up by Greeks that their culture owed a great deal to the East. But the real mirage is the "Greek mirage": the illusion that the Greeks grew up in a self-enclosed world on their own.

The reality is this: the ancient world was one vast, interrelated whole. Everything was intimately and subtly interconnected. You only have to look at what happened in Pythagoras's own lifetime and you find Babylonian astrological traditions being introduced into Egypt by Persian Magi. Further to the east, the same traditions were being carried by Magi to India. Almost everywhere you look nowadays it's stated that Alexander the Great was responsible for opening up the East—centuries after Pythagoras. But that's just a myth. The routes Alexander's army followed had been used by Persian traders, and teachers, long before Alexander was even born.

Then there's the case of Pythagoras himself. His home was an island called Samos, just off the mainland from what's now the Mediterranean coast of Turkey. It so happens that the people of Samos were among the specialists of specialists in long-distance trade. They had a reputation for traveling and trading that was almost mythical in its dimensions. And there is nothing mythical or unreal at all about the archaeological discoveries that show how the great temple of Hera on Samos became a storehouse for objects imported from Syria and Babylonia, from the Caucasus, Central Asia, India.

Of all the places that people from Samos did trade with, there's one in particular that they had close ties with. This was Egypt. They built their own depots and places of worship along the Nile, together with other Greeks. For them Egypt wasn't just some foreign or exotic land. It belonged to the world they knew and lived and worked in.

And that's only part of the story. According to an old tradition, Pythagoras's father was a gem engraver. What Pythagoras' father did, Pythagoras himself would have learned as a matter of course. But for a Greek gem engraver of the time, in the middle of the sixth century BC, life would have meant learning skills introduced from Phoenicia and bringing in materials from the East. We happen to know about other famous gem engravers on Samos at the time when Pythagoras was alive. They trained in Egypt, worked for kings of Anatolia, produced some of the finest works of art right in the heart of ancient Persia—because Samos was an island that, from century to century, had the closest of ties with Persia.

* * *

The realities of history are full of ironies and paradoxes at every turn. With Pythagoras the paradoxes start multiplying from the moment he decided, in around 530 BC, to leave Samos and settle in Italy.

The island where he had grown up had contacts with Egypt; and one would suppose that in leaving Samos for the West he was leaving those contacts behind. But he didn't leave anything behind. Italy was saturated with influences from Egypt. The most extraordinary finds have been made, there and in Sicily, like Egyptian magical objects dating from the seventh century

BC that show the goddess Isis suckling her son Horus. Their similarities to the imagery of Persephone suckling her son Dionysus—imagery that depicts the crucial moment in Orphic mysteries of initiation, when the initiate dies to be reborn as Persephone's child—are by no means a coincidence.

Orphic tradition blossomed in Italy. Early Pythagorean tradition absorbed its language and techniques, made them its own. And in origin they're plainly Egyptian.

This is particularly clear in the case of the famous Orphic gold plates that originally were buried together with initiates in south-Italian tombs. They're pieces of folded gold foil, inscribed with directions for finding one's way in the world of the dead and with promises for obtaining immortality. They describe the guardians in the underworld that challenge the soul, prevent it from finding the refreshment it needs. But then they remind the soul how to announce its real identity by stating that it belongs with the gods.

And here we come to the other man mentioned by Suhrawardi alongside Pythagoras: the great philosopher Empedocles. Empedocles lived in the fifth century BC and played the major role of transmitting Pythagoras' teachings in Sicily. He used the language of the gold plates in the poetry he wrote, and through what he says he shows that the process of dying to be reborn doesn't just refer to dying physically. Initiates had to die before they died—face the underworld before their physical death.

The similarities in detail between the magical sayings on the gold plates and Egyptian texts in the *Book of the Dead* are obvious. But what hasn't been realized is that this isn't just a case of parallels between texts from Italy and texts from Egypt: the missing links have also been discovered.

They're strange discoveries, like stepping stones carefully marking out a curve of influence that stretches from Egypt across to Italy. Strips of gold foil have been found in tombs at Carthage, on the coast of what now is Tunisia; and on the island of Sardinia. They were put there during the seventh, sixth and fifth centuries BC. The strips were made by Phoenicians—but they're engraved with Egyptian images. And they were rolled up, like amulets, inside tubes often sculpted with pictures of Egyptian gods.

You won't find much mention of these strips of gold foil in Phoenician tombs. Most modern historians have little respect for Phoenicians, disregard them as inferior to the Greeks. Evidence that Pythagoreans in Italy included Phoenicians among their number, or were taught by Phoenicians, is neglected. And no significance is seen in how one particular man—the man who most blatantly gives the lie to the modern fantasy that ancient Pythagoreans were impractical dreamers—is said to have learned mechanics and engineering from a Phoenician in Carthage.

The man's name was Archytas. He was Plato's greatest friend among the Pythagoreans; and he along with his disciples transmitted to Plato the wisdom preserved in the famous Platonic myths. But already in Plato's own circle the tendency to glorify the Greeks, especially the Athenians, at everyone else's expense quickly covered over the facts. It was Plato's secretary who wrote down the famous statement that "whatever Greeks receive from barbarians they improve on, carry to perfection."

And it was precisely the people who were in a position to know best who went so far in creating our Western sense of superiority that now we find ourselves proudly clutching at straws.

* * *

Traditions have their ebbs and flows, just as cultures do. People go, whether they understand why or not, exactly where they're needed.

Egyptian ideas had for a long time been carried to Italy, but eventually the opposite movement started—from Italy back to Egypt. It began in a big way when Alexander the Great had the city called Alexandria built at the mouth of the Nile during the late fourth century BC. People in southern Italy and Sicily gave themselves all kinds of reasons for doing what they had to do: emigrating to Egypt.

Pythagoreanism itself had always been a flexible tradition. Its personal demands on anyone who wanted to become a Pythagorean were immense. But, paradoxically, to be a Pythagorean meant belonging to a system that encouraged initiative and creativity: that kept changing, consciously adapting to the needs of different people and places and times.

So when Pythagoreans started arriving in Egypt they didn't simply set up shop as Pythagoreans. They also started merging their teachings with a tradition that was eminently Egyptian. This was the tradition that belonged to the god Thoth—or, as he came to be called by Greeks in Egypt, Hermes Trismegistus.

The Hermetic texts, or "Hermetica," that began being produced in Greek were initiatory writings. They served a very particular and practical purpose inside the circles of Hermetic mystics. And many of the methods they describe, as well as a great deal of the terminology they use, are specifically Pythagorean in origin.

But the Hermetica are far more than adaptations of Pythagorean themes. They are also the most obvious manifestation of Pythagoreanism returning to Egypt.

Until not long ago, the occasional references to Egyptian gods and religion in the Hermetic writings were dismissed as superficial veneer: as touches of local color added to the Greek texts to give them the illusion that they contained the authentic wisdom of Egypt. But the Hermetic literature is Egyptian to its core. Even the name "Poimandres" or "Pymander," the title often given to the Hermetica as a whole, is Egyptian through and through. It's simply a Greek version of *P-eime nte-re*, "the intelligence of Re." And the god who was known in Egypt as the "intelligence" of the sun god, Re, was Thoth—the Egyptian Hermes.

Already in the early 1990s it was possible to start mapping out the details of how much the Hermetica owed to Egypt. The resulting picture was startling enough. But then something extraordinary happened.

In 1995 two historians quietly announced the existence of a *Book of Thoth*, written in Demotic Egyptian. Just like the Greek Hermetica, it's a dialogue between a teacher and disciple. The teacher is Thoth "the three times great"—the exact equivalent of Hermes Trismegistus. He talks, like in the Greek Hermetica, about the process of rebirth: about the need to become young when you're old, old instead of young.

The *Book of Thoth* is purely Egyptian, with not a trace or sign of any foreign influence. But its general correspondences with the Greek Hermetic texts, and its parallels with them down to the most specific expressions and details, prove without any doubt that here we have a lost Egyptian prototype of the Hermetica only known to us before through their Greek translations and adaptations.

These were the Egyptian traditions that Pythagoreanism started merging with to become those Greek Hermetica. And you could say that in doing so it was at last coming home.

* * *

The Greek Hermetic writings weren't the end of Pythagoreanism's return to Egypt. On the contrary, they were just the beginning.

Already in the second century BC Greek-speaking Egyptians who lived on the Nile Delta had started receiving Pythagorean traditions on one hand and, on the other, shaping what was to become known as the art of alchemy. Northern Egypt was simply the starting point for a whole process of transmission from West back to East.

Over the centuries a combination of Pythagoreanism and alchemy was carried hundreds of miles along the Nile, down towards the Ethiopian frontier. And it was carried to one town in particular. The Greeks called it Panopolis; later it would become known as Akhmim. It's been said that outwardly this town in the middle of the desert "has no history." That's quite correct. Its history and significance belonged in another dimension.

The most famous of Greek alchemists, Zosimus, lived in the third century AD. He came from Panopolis. Already in his time there were small groups of alchemists either living in the town or staying in contact with the alchemists who lived there. These groups weren't just concerned with transforming physical objects. They were also preserving and perfecting techniques for the transformation of themselves.

It was here, when the real meaning of early Greek philosophy had already become lost in the West, that the alchemists kept those philosophers' teachings alive—especially the teachings of Pythagoras and the Pythagoreans. And they would go on preserving the significance of their teachings intact, from generation to generation, for hundreds of years.

It's still possible to trace how the teachings of Empedocles in particular were transmitted from Sicily down to Egypt and into the Hermetica, into Egyptian magical traditions, and in alchemical circles all the way down to Akhmim. In 1998 the remains of a papyrus, discovered at Akhmim, which had contained huge amounts of Empedocles' poetry were published for the first time. This was much more than a chance discovery.

During the ninth century AD, seven hundred years after Empedocles' teachings had been copied onto this papyrus, an alchemist in Akhmim wrote a work that was to have the profoundest influence on virtually every aspect of medieval alchemy. His name was Uthman Ibn Suwaid, and he wrote the work in Arabic.

It became known in the Islamic world as *The Book of the Gathering*; translated into Latin it came to be called the *Turba philosophorum*, or *Gathering of the Philosophers*. The book described a series of meetings between ancient Greek philosophers at four "Pythagorean conferences," all of them dedicated to getting to the heart of the alchemical art. The meetings were presided over by Pythagoras himself. And in the text one of the speakers at the gathering, Empedocles, outlines genuine aspects of the historical Empedocles' teaching—about the fundamental importance of fire at the center of the earth—which until recently had been, when not just forgotten, completely distorted in the West.

The significance of these details is immense. What Empedocles wrote and taught during the fifth century BC played a crucial role in shaping Western philosophy, Western science, the history of Western ideas. But the simple fact is that a true understanding of what Empedocles had taught didn't survive in the West. All that was left there of his teaching—about the mysteries of the world around us, about the nature of the soul—was empty theorizing and hollow ideas. The lived reality had moved elsewhere.

It's strange, now, to look at the surviving evidence in Arabic texts about the existence of groups of alchemists who called themselves "Empedocles circles," or "Pythagoras circles." You find "Empedocles circles" mentioned again in descriptions of Islamic esoteric groups who saw

Empedocles as their guide: who "regard themselves as followers of his wisdom and hold him superior to all other authorities." Here were people who in spite of their culture, religion, language, took as their inspiration and teacher a man who had lived one and a half thousand years before them.

* * *

And this is where we come back to Suhrawardi, "Sheikh of the East."

It was Suhrawardi who gave the name of the man who passed the essence of Pythagoras' and Empedocles' teachings to the Sufis: Dhu 'l-Nun.

Dhu 'l-Nun came from Akhmim. He was fiercely attacked by Islamic theologians; put on trial. He narrowly escaped with his life. And this man, who aroused so much opposition through what he taught, would come to be known as "the head of the Sufis" for the simple reason that practically every line of Sufis in existence looks back in one way or another to him.

He soon came to be considered the crucial figure in "a line of secret gnostic teaching" that he transmitted to the great Sufi Sahl al-Tustari and then—through Sahl—to Sahl's disciple al-Hallaj and into the early Sufi orders. But Dhu 'l-Nun was also famous for his involvement with alchemy, and for deriving his wisdom from the alchemical traditions preserved at Akhmim.

This connection between alchemy and the beginnings of Sufism has often been put aside as something of an embarrassment. And yet, as a few historians have realized, the evidence for the connection goes back too far into the past to be discounted so easily.

But even that isn't all, because there is one other piece of evidence that strangely has been missed.

This is the fact that the earliest witness to Dhu 'l-Nun's involvement with alchemy lived hardly any later than Dhu 'l-Nun himself. He was Ibn Suwaid, the alchemist from Akhmim who wrote the Pythagorean *Book of the Gathering*—and who, alongside the other alchemical books he produced, wrote one specifically refuting the accusations leveled against Dhu 'l-Nun.

Apart from his connections with alchemy and Pythagoras, with Empedocles and Dhu 'l-Nun, Ibn Suwaid was linked with the beginnings of Sufism in more ways than one. He also wrote a work called *Book of the Red Sulphur.* That's highly significant. Red sulphur played a crucial role for alchemists because it represented the light in the depths of the underworld, the sun at midnight, the fire at the center of the earth. But it's significant, as well, because *Book of the Red Sulphur* was soon to become a standard book title among Sufis themselves. For them, red sulphur was the name used to describe the essence of the esoteric "inheritance" that was the ultimate goal of being a Sufi.

The tendency nowadays is to assume that when Sufis took over this alchemical language they changed its meaning by spiritualizing it, giving it a higher significance which it hadn't had before. But that's as accurate as the belief that Carl Jung in the twentieth century was the first person who ever gave alchemy an inner or symbolic meaning, who explained it as relating to human transformation.

The simple fact is that the oldest alchemical texts in the West which survive in anything approaching their full and original state talk explicitly about alchemy as the art of inner transformation—as the process of bringing the divine into human existence and taking the human back to the divine.

These texts have never been properly translated into English. They were written down in Greek during the third century by Zosimus, the famous alchemist from the town of Panopolis or Akhmim.

*   *   *

It's no surprise that Suhrawardi was killed.

His writings show he was a deep Muslim, profoundly inspired by the Quran. But the basic thrust of his teaching pointed in another direction. It was mainly through him that Empedocles and Pythagoras came to be seen, especially by certain Sufis in Persia, as among the greatest of Sheikhs who had ever lived.

Of course this way of viewing ancient philosophers has no place at all in the standard pictures of Sufism—any more than the idea of Empedocles or Pythagoras as teachers, responsible for transmitting an esoteric tradition based on genuine spiritual practice and realization, has any place in the standard pictures of ancient philosophy.

But that was bound to happen. For a long time in the West we've managed to forget the original meaning of the word "philosophy": love of wisdom, not the love of endlessly talking and arguing about the love of wisdom. And what's even sadder is the way we've managed to persuade ourselves that we haven't forgotten anything.

As one of Suhrawardi's successors—his name was Shahrazuri—stated very simply, the realities that Suhrawardi wrote about and died for are so fundamental they aren't easy to understand. In the West it was a long time ago that "the traces of the paths of the ancient sages disappeared"; "that their teachings were either wiped out or corrupted and distorted."

But, as Suhrawardi and his followers knew, these realities are never lost for good.

"What Hast Thou Done?": The Australian Aborigines and the Fate of the Nomads

Aminah Smith

What hast thou done? The voice of thy brother's blood crieth out unto Me from the ground. . . . And now art thee cursed from the earth. . . . And Cain went out from the presence of the Lord.

Genesis 4:10, 16

What men now understand by "civilization" is an essentially vicious and destructive force. . . . What is called "progress" is both suicidal and murderous.

Ananda Coomaraswamy

Given the man-made catastrophes of the twentieth century—world wars, the use of fearful new weapons, genocidal violence, widespread poverty and injustice, to name only a few—the claim that the disappearance of the nomadic peoples is perhaps the most tragic and fateful of modern disasters will perhaps strike many readers as surprising. The violent extermination of such people and cultures has received a good deal of attention but its underlying significance is rarely understood. The traditional activities of these peoples are understood as "cultural expressions," but a deeper study shows them to be life-preserving cosmic supports. According to diverse sources of wisdom, the position of the nomadic peoples is as central to humanity as the heart is to the body. Their going is not merely a matter for sentimental regret but a sign that humanity is in its Eleventh Hour. An allegorical account of this drama, which is only now reaching its climax, is found in the book of Genesis in the story of Cain's murder of Abel.[1] Here we discuss the dire implications of this parable with particular reference to the original people of Australia, whose religious tradition is possibly the most ancient of all.

The experience of the North American Indians, and particularly the metaphysical and cosmological doctrines implicit in their mythology and ritual life, has been recounted by a handful of commentators adequately equipped for such a task—one may mention Indian sages such as Black Elk and Thomas Yellowtail, and the Perennialist writers Frithjof Schuon and Joseph Epes Brown. In *The Spiritual Legacy of the American Indian* Brown wrote:

> Black Elk and his friend Little Warrior freely told me about their religion and gave me the keys to the spiritual meaning behind the forms of their rites and symbols. This new understanding made clear to me why these old men, and others among their people, manifested in their being and in every act a nobility, serenity, generosity, concentration, and kindness that we usually associate with the saints of the better-known religions.[2]

[1] See René Guénon, *The Reign of Quantity and the Signs of the Times* (Ghent: Sophia Perennis et Universalis, 1995), chap. XXI.

[2] Joseph Epes Brown, *The Spiritual Legacy of the American Indian* (Bloomington: World Wisdom, 2007), p. 24.

Few people are willing to afford this level of seriousness to the "spiritual legacy" of the Australian Aborigines. The population of these people is diminished, there are very few elders still alive, and their tradition remains one of the least understood and discussed. The shared language needed for this discussion is the *sophia perennis*, the highest wisdom of all ages and peoples, in the light of which diverse ways of life become intelligible. Modern European scholarship, generally ignorant of the *sophia perennis*, is responsible for much harm to the Nomads, and any attempt to understand these traditions "from the outside" is hazardous—yet we must try. The truth is that rather than being, as some have claimed, an undeveloped Stone Age prototype, Aboriginal civilization represents the human norm. Theirs is an exemplary expression of the *religio perennis*, the primordial religion from which all others spring, and in which the spiritual life of humanity has its roots.[3] Since their state is "central and correct," our relationship with the nomads is vitally important; they embody something which we cannot do without and which we urgently need to understand. Theoretical knowledge is not enough; without a *living* link to the sacred source of life, with which traditional peoples are in direct contact, humanity cannot survive; without it we have no future.

Cain and Abel

It has been stated that there are but two original vocations, farmer and herdsman—settler and nomad—and that all other vocations are modifications of these. In the myth of Cain and Abel, the two brothers represent the sedentary and the nomadic peoples respectively, these being the two original human modes. Yet we could go further and understand that these are the two fundamentally different spiritual conditions which are at play within the self. Cain, whose name means "created," was a farmer and a settler; his descendants built the first town and began to spread the way of life which has now claimed almost the entire surface of the planet, dominating rather than participating in nature.[4] By contrast, Abel, whose name means "breath," lived in the divine presence in nature: in this sense it can be said that Abel's way is the primal religion which needed no building or institution.[5] As a herdsman, Abel lived in constant contact with the animals and virgin nature (Genesis 4:5) just as the entire Aboriginal civilization did until very recent times.

After the murder of Abel, Cain was unable to escape the consequences of his transgression: the earth (receptive to Abel) had "opened to swallow the blood" but then "the blood in the earth cries out." The earth itself turns against Cain, prefiguring the divine verdict that he is doomed to "wander like a fugitive" (not like a nomad), and to be "an outcast from the earth." Modern man, the colonist, is thief and fugitive; as an outcast from the earth, he spends his life encased in clothes, cars, and buildings, seeking continual distractions from his inner state. Thus it is not only the physical earth from which he becomes estranged, but from his own

[3] The word religion, though problematic, is used advisedly. It is all too easy for Europeans to see nothing but otherness in the Aboriginal way of life, and while there is more to a primal mythological tradition than "religion" as many understand the word, it is essential that it is not imagined that there is less.

[4] See R. Davidson: "No Fixed Address" in *Quarterly Essay*, Issue 24, 2006 (Melbourne: Black Inc.), p. 9.

[5] In the sense that Abel never left the presence of God, his "death" symbolizes his inability to compromise his true nature—as such, his future could never be "of this world." In his essay "The Sacred Pipe" Schuon refers to the death of the Indians as a martyrdom because they would not give up their connection to the Truth. (This essay appears in *The Feathered Sun* [Bloomington: World Wisdom, 1990], pp. 44-70.) We feel this also applies to the Aboriginal people, and that their disappearance is not indicative of any weakness or inferiority on their part.

Self. The "environmental crisis," caused by sedentary man, is merely the physical counterpart to his spiritual alienation, prefigured biblically by God's statement to Cain, "Till the earth; it will yield thee nothing." This exhaustion of resources, on the spiritual level, refers to modern man's groping search for meaning in psychology, pseudo-spiritualities, and so on. Further, this increasingly peripheral human condition, in which humanity becomes enslaved by futile laboring and hurrying, is the antithesis of the "creative quietitude" (*wu wei*) of the Sage, of whom the *Tao Te Ching* says, "He is central and correct. . . . By doing nothing, he accomplishes all things."

Nothing is more characteristic of industrialized man (the ultimate slayer of Abel) than the increasingly marginal role religion plays in his life, if he is not altogether atheistic. The profession of atheism, or Godlessness, far from being the intellectual triumph of the superman, is merely the admission of an atrophied spiritual sense and, according to the Cain myth, is not a human achievement but a divine punishment. The hollowness of modern man, who now more frequently professes that "something is missing," is a haunting echo of the disappearance of that communal participation in the sacred truth of life which characterized all nomadic cultures and by virtue of which they were "blessed."

The "Murderous Machine"[6]

Modern rational methods of inquiry have not done justice to the fate of the nomads although it is one of the most significant hallmarks of our time. This is because these methods of inquiry are linked to the very apparatus which is responsible for annihilating the nomads (and countless other forms of life) in the name of science and "progress," and which continues to push genuine religion and spirituality into an ever more marginal and powerless position. From the "progressive" stance the past is viewed with contempt and the disappearance of its human relics is a "natural" event. Alarmingly, religious modernists echo this complacency about the extinction of the nomads, also claiming that it is natural and that God wills it because "their time has passed," implying that religion is subject to evolution. Their time did not merely pass; they were murdered, and this should always be made clear. Even if this destruction of the nomads is in some respects inevitable, for "it must needs be that offences come . . . woe to that man by whom the offence cometh!" (Matthew 18:7). Rationalism, atheism, and "progresso-evolutionism" are used to reduce the question of the nomads' disappearance to a merely social or "cultural" phenomenon. Predictably, the deeper aspects of the question are ignored by those for whom a fuller inquiry would be the most damning; nor can these deeper aspects be explored by those people for whom spirituality is a dead letter. However, while the obliteration of nomadic traditions by sedentary civilizations may be ignored, none can avoid the consequences. This is so because that which destroys nomads—an unnatural and increasingly profane way of life—is a self-destroying program.

People who have lost or betrayed their own spiritual traditions cannot understand those of others, and this alone is enough to account for the depreciation of the primal traditions. If the sedentary peoples were in a position to view the ancient traditions from the deeper perspectives of the religions with which they are already familiar, they would realize the importance of both; but the experts, whether religious or secular, are too often drastically restricted in their outlook

[6] The phrase comes from G. La Piana, quoted by A. Coomaraswamy in *Am I My Brother's Keeper?* (New York: Books For Libraries Press, 1967), p. 1.

and understanding—so much so that the limitations in question are celebrated as among the triumphs of modern civilization! The resulting attitude towards the nomadic traditions is dangerously irreverent; for, while one is free to think what one will, there is something that is beyond one's ability to choose: the fact of standing on holy ground, ground taken by force and desecrated against the will of its time-honored custodians (These are facts that can be demonstrated, but not without major digressions. People are prevented from knowing that the ground is holy and that Aborigines are deeply religious by a few popular and powerful ideologies, especially atheism, racism or Eurocentricism, and religious exclusivism), exposes the intruders to certain dangers of which they remain all too unaware. To those "with eyes to see and ears to hear" the ground itself remains as a symbol of certainty and of what cannot be avoided. In Aboriginal terms, this ground evokes the Dreaming, the eternal immutable spiritual Reality from which all life arises and to which it returns, without ever breaking from it. This Dreaming, akin to the Platonic Ideal, is the great Truth behind the "lie" of forms, of which the scientistic ideology of nature—which has built a grand illusion out of facts—is a parody. Modernity, excluding what is most human and most divine in us, rejects what is normal for all traditional civilizations, and particularly marked in the nomadic ones: certitude through metaphysical discernment.

In order to understand the nomadic traditions, the limitations—not to mention perversions—of the modern outlook must be overcome, for these have barred us from the direct appreciation of the symbolic and sacred. The primordial religious life is mythological and metaphysical, centered on direct knowledge of the hierophany that is nature. As Coomaraswamy remarked, "myth is the penultimate truth of which all experience is the temporal reflection... Myth embodies the nearest approach to absolute truth that can be stated in words." [7] This way of being is so different from the modern outlook that European contact with the nomads has produced anthropological fantasies which portray the nomads as "nature worshippers" or "godless savages"—there are numerous variations on the theme. The general failure to recognize in nomadic life the *religio perennis,* in its first and purest expression, has lead to embarrassing distortions of the truth. It is ironic that the civilizations most strictly governed by spiritual considerations should be considered devoid of religion. Yet it is symptomatic of our times that the best people will be murdered and mocked; it is part of the working out of the ages of which this present one is the darkest, as the well-known passage from the *Vishnu Purana* illustrates:

> Riches and piety will diminish daily, until the world will be completely corrupted. In those days it will be wealth which confers distinction, passion will be the sole reason for union between the sexes, and lies will be the only method for success in business. The earth will be valued only on account of the mineral treasures which it contains, . . . a simple ablution will be regarded as sufficient purification. . . . The observance of castes, laws, and institutions will no longer be in force . . . and the ceremonies . . . will be neglected. Man having been lead astray from orthodoxy, iniquity will prevail . . . and they will say: "Of what authority are the Vedas? Who are the Gods and the *brahmins*? What use is purification with water?" The dominant caste will be that of *shudras*. . . . Men, deprived of reason and subject to every infirmity of body and mind, will daily commit sins: everything which is

[7] Ananda Coomaraswamy, *Hinduism and Buddhism* (New Delhi, 1996), pp. 6, 33n.

impure, vicious, and calculated to afflict the human race will make its appearance in the Dark Age.[8]

These appalling operations are no better for having been predictable, yet they must be understood as part of the turning of a sacred wheel whose hub (and all that touches it) is by no means disturbed. The "murderous machine" of modernity, as part of the anti-tradition, must reach into all fields to pervert the natural order of things, yet it cannot reach the inviolable *sophia* herself; the "machine" of post-industrial Western civilization, wherever it operates, is unable to "process" the wisdom of the nomads and is limited to either ignoring or reducing it by describing outward forms of the nomads' behavior without penetrating their meanings. Although these meanings are beyond the reach of secular scholarship and outside the range of experience of most people they may still be approached, for the primordial religious experience is not foreign; it derives from *sophia perennis*, the pure intellectual content of all traditional formulations. In the case of the nomads, the perennial philosophy is not expressed in abstractions or even in highly systemized doctrines but in the symbolism of myth and ritual, and in immediately lived spiritual experience. Such is the cohesive unity and integrity of the nomadic traditional worldview that a machine whose only function is to take things to pieces, that "great profanation" that is empirical science, can do nothing but destroy it.

The Perennial Religion

At the depths of all religions, the same principles are found: outwardly we must conform to divine truths by praxis, and inwardly contemplate divine realities through engagement with their symbols. These symbols through which we may engage with divine Reality are innumerable: nature (including human nature: the breath and the cycles of the body, birth, bodily cycles, sex, and death), prayer, love, knowledge, and the arts are such "supports" for spiritual life. When the bare facts of the Aboriginal life are seen through a clear eye, free of the counterfeit philosophies of modernity, signs of the *religio perennis* are unmistakable: renunciation ("holy poverty"); reliance on the Divine; advanced etiquette towards humanity, creatures and nature; and many other signs of a refined spiritual life are evident to anyone familiar with *any* traditional framework. Also, at the theoretical level, it seems that Aboriginal formulations of philosophy and metaphysic are fully in accord with religious expressions the whole world over. The only conclusion is that a standard of wisdom and praxis characteristic of the mystics, saints and sages of the world is found here in an entire people.

Instead of the deep respect due to such people they have often been mocked for their "beliefs" (is this word not an insult?), which are regarded as superstitions. The doctrine of the land as Mother, for instance, is still largely seen as pure sentiment, and yet it is a very serious understanding, not limited to the sensory experience of the land we walk upon or the mother who bore us, but enmeshed with the metaphysical realities behind these symbols; a difficult doctrine indeed for those to whom even the physical ground or an earthly mother has no definite meaning. Likewise, the case of spiritual paternity, often considered to be one of the ridiculous superstitions of the Australian Aborigine, when subject to clear-minded examination is revealed to be a universal traditional belief, whose expression in Christian doctrine is "Call no man on

[8] *Vishnu Purana* 29, quoted in William Stoddart, *Introduction to Hinduism* (Oakton: Foundation for Traditional Studies, 1993), 75.

Earth thy father, for thy father is in Heaven" (Matt. 23:9). Of course, this is not to suggest that Aboriginal formulations can be accepted as *bona fide* wisdom only if they resemble Christian beliefs, but to propose that in this case, and countless others, the Aboriginal religion is seen to spring from the same sacred source as all other traditions and revelations. Furthermore, while it springs from the same source, it is closer to the fountainhead: the Aborigine, until prevented from doing so, *lives* these doctrines and does not merely talk about them; their lives, like the lives of saints, are symbolically resonant. Their life *is* their religion; religion is their life. These people have never suffered abstraction by literacy and similar "advances." If total absorption in one's religious life, to the point that nothing occurs outside of it, seems foreign to some, they need only recall Christ's first commandment, "Love the Lord thy God with all thy heart, all thy soul, and all thy mind." Perennial truths are transmitted, and fully enjoyed, through the ages with no need for a book or some manner of "religiosity" cut off from the rest of life. The nomad does not need a book on renunciation; in a sense he *is* a book on renunciation! In the same way, Jesus, upon taking up his spiritual calling, dwelt in the wilderness in holy poverty, caring for nothing but the favor of God.

The Aboriginal tragedy must be considered as a spiritual problem because it is a human problem, and humanity, as Rumi said, is not merely a device for "turning bread into dung." It is well-known that rationalism and "progress" has lead to post-modern uncertainty and rootlessness; what is less well understood is that this absence in the modern mentality of genuine ontological knowledge, or self-knowledge properly so called, is a direct *consequence* of destroying the nomads, who are the guardians of the "firm ground," both literally and symbolically. Without them, diabolical confusion reigns, and humanity reaches an inevitable impasse both spiritually and in its environment. As Guénon said of Cain and Abel: "he who is blessed dies, he who lives is accursed. Equilibrium is thus broken on both sides."[9] The same could be said for the spiritual and secular methods of enquiry respectively, the latter being part of the problem not the solution.

The Sacred Web

It is not often observed that the Aboriginal nomad strikingly resembles the *sadhu* or the Sufi, and matches the descriptions of John the Baptist and of Jesus with his "hair of wool and feet of brass," and that the Aboriginal people are at home in the same "poverty" and spiritual absorption that is the abode of these holy men. What are we to make of the fact that the Nomadic peoples share what these characteristics? This question should be pertinent for those who consider religion important, though it is not possible for this question to be asked by others. This is because,

> Whilst intellectual fashions amongst ethnologists and anthropologists have changed over the last two hundred years the one constant factor has been an intransigent reductionism which refuses to treat Aboriginal religion in its own terms or, indeed, in terms appropriate to any religious traditions. . . . Profane scholarship, immune to anything of a spiritual order, tries to force a living spiritual tradition into the sterile categories of a quasi-scientific reductionism—no matter whether the reductionism in question be Durkheimian, Freudian, or Marxist![10]

[9] René Guénon, *Reign of Quantity*, p. 183.

[10] Harry Oldmeadow, "Melodies From the Beyond" (online article; see *Eye of the Heart* archives).

The sub-religious or "humanist" view sees nothing in the Aboriginal tradition but "cultural expressions," when in fact it is metaphysical truth and direct mystical experience that are central here. The rest is merely "coloring," and it is this minor outward difference that makes it possible to distinguish one primordial tradition from another. In the case of some very ancient peoples, such as the Central Australians and the Bushmen of Africa, there is so little of this coloring that they do indeed resemble each other in almost every way, both inwardly and outwardly. In these cases there has been so small a descent from the Principle, from the holy source, that one tradition mingles (in expression and appearance) with another, even though they appear on opposite sides of the earth. They are like ice on the peak of the mountain, which has not yet thawed and descended in rivulets, each with a different history. In a sense, those directly connected to the *sophia perennis* are always "primordial people," whatever their religion, for change does not affect them. It is for this reason that there is so little difference between the Indian *sannyasin* in the mountains and the antipodean nomad on the plains. The same spirit moves each of them in performing their spiritual function, and they support each other as an unseen community.

It is only this web, visible to the heart's eye, which prevents humanity's fall into the abyss of non-existence. This community shelters humanity against the "cosmic gales of amnesia" through its steadfast remembrance of the Principle and the perennial philosophy, for theirs, as the Sufis say, is not only the *dhikr* (remembrance) of the tongue but of the heart. The ingratitude and foolishness of those who strike at this net and break it (though in an absolute sense it is inviolable), is certainly a signal event in our time, and its consequences are impossible to avoid by any practical or material means. As a saying attributed to the Prophet goes, "The community is like a body; when one part feels pain, the rest of it suffers." Evil rushes in through the broken parts of the sacred web of souls in communion with the highest good; strange as it may at first seem, it is only their presence in the world that prevents its obliteration. As another holy saying of Islam states, "It is only for you (Muhammad, in his role as "Perfected One") that I created the cosmos." What a loss it is when humanity shifts from its central position in the seat of honor, surrounded by the beauty and significance of natural phenomena, with the companionship of all "the animals of the soul," knowing the Self as the *kalian* of God, and raising children to philosophy rather than menial labor! Among Indians and Aboriginal people, it seems that there is a sense of despair not only because they could not preserve their culture but because a greater sacred circle has been broken, with all the beauty, happiness and knowledge that it had preserved for human beings. For traditional life, if nothing else, is a beautiful path through time. We recall the poignant words of Black Elk: "And I, to whom so great a vision was given in my youth—you see me now a pitiful old man who has done nothing, for the nation's hoop has broken and scattered. There is no center any longer, and the sacred tree is dead."[11]

"What Hast Thou Done?"

As the *I Ching* tells us, "If a man is not as he should be, he has misfortune and it does not further him to do anything." It is a spiritual deficiency that lead to the devastation of the nomadic traditions and the correction of that deficiency is a pressing task. It is not appropriate to take Indian or Aboriginal cultures as subjects for "disinterested research" and we patronizingly think

[11] John Neihardt, *Black Elk Speaks: Being the Life Story of a Holy Man of the Oglala Sioux* (Lincoln: University of Nebraska, 2004), p. 230.

of them as part of our cultural heritage. The intellectual acquisitiveness characteristic of the colonizing races is an extension of their ambition for land and possessions, and it drives them to want ownership of all information; amid the glut of facts it is forgotten that knowledge itself is sacred and if it is attained without the proper motive it will only cause the possessor harm. Better not to even discuss the *philosophia perennis* if one is not actually seeking wisdom or prepared to pay the price which its realization entails:

> Originally the word "philosophy" meant love of wisdom. Now it has just come to mean the love of endlessly talking and arguing about the love of wisdom—which is a complete waste of time. Philosophy is a travesty of what it once was, no longer a path to wisdom.[12]

Modern scholarship (for the most part *written*) is part of Cain's legacy and his offering with which God is less than pleased. While philosophy is universal, among modern scholars it no longer arises from its source, *Sophia,* but is a counterfeit arising from a set of violations by the people of Cain; higher thought is enslaved for low purposes. The betrayal of the nomads, the rape of the land, and the perversion of philosophy has all been done in the same motion, and literacy is perhaps the greatest weapon in that offensive. Literacy, particularly a fascination with it and an elevation of it as an end in itself, is characteristic of settled people; such people have the leisure time to be scholars because they no longer have full participation in an active and complete human civilization, which normally admits no experimentation and has no need of it. Like Cain, they build a town, or a castle in the air, and it is at the expense of their connection to the ground of their being. When the truth is admitted, that philosophy and wisdom, in all fullness, were with humanity from the very beginning, and that recent times have seen a progressive forgetting, it becomes impossible to underestimate or ignore the original custodians of this wisdom, the first true philosophers.

The connection of modern philosophy to the *philosophia perennis* is certainly tenuous; the recent perennialist movement, while understandably momentous for some in the West, is only a gesture towards this timeless wisdom and an exhortation to seek it. It is a serious error for Western scholars to assume that the last word on any grave matter must come from their own milieu when, manifestly, the opposite is normally the case: in the last two hundred years, they have largely been in the business of generating problems not solutions, problems which have displaced much of the Earth's population and hurt no one more than the nomadic peoples. This process of "civilization," which reached an inevitable crisis in recent modernity, began with the establishment of the first town by Cain, and it is part of the consequences of his betrayal of tradition. We say "betrayal" because, in spite of the scientific wonderworking and speech-making of modernity, the nomads are displaced, the water and air are poisoned, the creatures are suffering, and no one's children are safe from all manner of perils. The arrogance in denying or condoning these facts could very well be the worst of crimes, and this defect in Cain's spiritual condition could be said to be that "mark" by which all recognize Cain. This defect, expressed in his jealousy and murder of his brother, is epitomized by his question, "Am I my brother's keeper?" which evokes God's curse. When we turn to our brother for the sake of learning from him, to see a reflection of the self, it is a cure for this belligerence. Thinking of what we have done to the nomads, we cannot help but think of what we have done to

[12] Peter Kingsley, *Reality* (Inverness, CA: Golden Sufi Centre, 2003), p. 156.

ourselves, and it becomes clear that the purpose of real philosophical enquiry is bound up with Coomaraswamy's insight that "Western man is out of balance, and the question, Can he recover himself? is a very real one."[13] Erudition does not save, but the true intellect (*aql*) is a ray connecting us to the sun of Truth and it connects to what is above words.

The existence of humanity depends on participation in Reality, exemplified by the nomads who live at one with translucent nature. It has been said that "every Indian is something of a prophet"[14], and this we understand to mean that the primal religious experience is direct, a conduit for the knowing of God through the revelation of "His signs in the heavens, the earth and in the soul" (leitmotif of the Holy Quran). This is the primordial religion within which the full possibilities of humanity are realized and compared to which a religious experience that happens only at certain times and places is a diminution, albeit still authentic. It is in relation to the loss of these higher states, which are essential to humanity, that the disappearance of the saints or wisest people spells the end of humanity, as various traditions warn. The nomads also say this. An example from an American Indian speaker:

> We are small, but we are not a minority . . . for our brothers are all the natural world. . . . As long as the Indian nations exist, so will you. When we are gone, you too will go.[15]

Humanity ends with the Indian's disappearance because man is contingent and dependent on divine reality for his being. God's verdict upon Cain is that he will become peripheral, estranged from God and from "the ground"; that is, cut off from sacred experience and from the ground of being. Cain has lost access to that state of wholeness in which the separation of self, world, religion, time, and space, has not occurred. He has lost the faculty for an experience common to the nomads of Australia, an experience they call *Altyerre*, the Dreaming. An Aboriginal elder, unwilling to speak directly about the sacred reality, gave this elliptical comment about the sacred ceremony:

> If you go into the ring-place, things look different there, different from here.
> When you have finished there you will start crying.
> You don't want to go back in "outside"
> because *everything has to be left in the ring-place.*[16]

This apparently blissful experience of spiritual reality finds its full expression in the ritual life of these nomadic people, who are our link not only to sacred nature but also to its timeless origin, this "dreaming," which has often been misunderstood as an event in time. Just as regular returns to the state of sleep allow the waking state to be refreshed and to continue, immersion in the cosmogonic archetypes is a protection against the corruption of Time (or *maya*).[17] Taking part in Creation (through cosmogonic rites) stems "createdness" so that what remains somewhat

[13] Ananda Coomaraswamy, *Am I My Brother's Keeper?*, p. 64.

[14] Frithjof Schuon, "The Meaning of Caste," in *Language of the Self* (Bloomington: World Wisdom, 1999), p. 12.

[15] Oren Lyons, "Our Mother Earth," in *Seeing God Everywhere*, ed. B. McDonald (Bloomington: World Wisdom, 2003), p. 106.

[16] Bill Neidjie, *Story About Feeling* (Broome: Magabala Books, 1989), p. 103 (English rendition and italics mine).

[17] Huston Smith, *The World's Religions* (New York: HarperCollins, 1991), p. 367.

"unborn" cannot die; participation in the sacred and eternal is like wax that slows the burning of the wick. To be explicit, by regenerative ritual Aborigines and other nomadic peoples, as they have always claimed, maintain the world. They participate in that in which nature also participates, the eternal essences that give life to forms. Without this direct relationship with the divine Reality, humanity has no reason to exist or, to be more exact, no actual existence at all. It is this, and no less than this, which is occurring as the last of the nomadic peoples disappear from the face of the earth. To what extent does modern man feel the earth slipping away from under his feet, if indeed he can remember ever having felt it at all?

Finally, to the extent that life matters, its ending matters. The traditional "dreaming" of the Aborigines is giving way to a human state which, from a nomad's viewpoint, is a nightmarish restlessness wherein man is cut off from meaning and spiritual power. It is neither through mimicry of the outward ways of the nomadic cultures nor by abandoning humanity's great religious traditions that safe ground can be attained. Sacred traditions, especially those of the nomads, do not belong to the past but to the full experience of the present; the *philosophia perennis* is not eternal due to its extension through time, but chiefly because, through it, some members of humanity have always risen above history and its contingencies. As the perennialist writers often remind us, it is not to the past we must look, but to the sacred.[18] The deeper study of these crises that beset humanity brings us squarely back to the central fact: if harmony is to be restored, we must be reconciled with the Truth.

[18] Frithjof Schuon, "On the Margin of Liturgical Improvisations," in *The Sword of Gnosis*, ed. J. Needleman (Baltimore: Penguin Books, 1974), p. 353.

Make Your Choice

Chief Thomas Yellowtail (as told to Michael Oren Fitzgerald)

In the olden-days the Indians had their freedom and they followed their traditional ways. Then the whites made us settle on reservations. People had to live close together and we were not free to live in our traditional way. People also lost sight of the true meaning of these ways. It was not long until a lot of the powers and sacred things that had been given to the Indians were taken back. That is what we were told by prophecies before the time of settlement on the reservations. Many medicine men who had had good medicine, good powers, lost them. This all happened gradually over the last one hundred years, until today there are fewer men with less spiritual power and understanding. Those who still have spiritual gifts or medicine—and there are a few left—don't have as strong a power as in the days when the Indians were still free to roam the country and live in the traditional manner. As time went on, the Indians became more "civilized" and learned to live in the white man's ways, and so all of the spiritual powers were diminished. People lost sight of religion and prayer, so it seems that the old prophecies were correct. Back in the days when we were free, when our people knew more about Nature and important things, almost every man had medicine powers and the only life people knew was centered on the sacred. The real medicine man could do wonders in those days. It is really the modern world and "civilization" that is causing us to lose all these things. In olden times, the people had their values centered on spiritual concerns. The spiritual Powers, the givers of medicines, are taking those sacred things back from us because we do not know how to care for them correctly.

Modern Indians care little for spiritual things and traditional ways, so there are very few traditional people remaining with real medicine or understanding. Modern civilization has no understanding of sacred matters. Everything is backwards. This makes it even more important that young people follow what is left today. Even though many of the sacred ways are no longer with us, what we have left is enough for anyone, and if it is followed it will lead as far as the person can go. The four rites that we have left form the center of the religion: the sweat lodge for purification; the vision quest for the spiritual retreat; the daily prayer with the offering of tobacco smoke; and the Sun Dance itself.[1] With all this, any sincere person can realize his inner spiritual center.

It is important that the young people understand the difference between the traditional ways and the modern world we live in today. I have spoken before about the sacred support that was always present for the traditional Indians. With this support everywhere, from the moment you arose and said your first prayer, until the moment you went to sleep, you could at least see what was necessary in order to lead a proper life. Even the dress that you wore every day had sacred meanings, such as the bead work designs on the clothing, and wherever you went or whatever you did, whether you were hunting, making weapons, or whatever you were doing, you were participating in a sacred life and you knew who you were and carried a sense of the sacred with you. All of the forms had meaning, even the tipi and the sacred circle of the entire camp. Of course the life was hard and difficult and not all Indians followed the rules.

[1] These sacred rites are described in detail in *Yellowtail: Crow Medicine Man and Sun Dance Chief*, recorded and edited by Michael Oren Fitzgerald, University of Oklahoma Press, 1991.

But the support of the traditional life and the presence of Nature everywhere brought great blessings on all the people.[2]

The world we live in is quite different. Young people today can't read the signs of nature and they do not even know the names of the different animals. When a bird calls, or we see the prints left by an animal, most of our people will not know the name of the animal that stands close by. . . . What is worse, many young people do not even look, or sometimes even care, where they are walking and do not observe the beautiful things that *Acbadadea*, The Maker of All Things Above, has created. It almost makes me cry to see how some young people waste precious gifts. They will let food spoil or waste water and electricity. People do not seem to realize the value of the gifts they have been given; they think things will always be there when they need something. These same people will have a big surprise someday, because sooner or later they will be shown their errors.

Look at the way people travel and work nowadays. You always hear people say, "We are in the fast age." Everything has to be fast, according to the way people want to do things nowadays. If we are going a great distance, the destination or place we are going to isn't going to move; it is standing still, so there is no need to be in such a hurry. In addition to not being safe, there are other dangers in this fast way of life. It is a problem with their entire way of living. . . . People should ask themselves what it is that they are doing and why it is that they are doing it. So many people today don't even think; they just do something.

Many of the modern things that we have now have made everything worse. We didn't have television until a few years ago, and since the television has come into use, people have just fallen crazy for it. It is something that I don't care for myself. It makes people lazy and gives them strange ideas about life. For instance, it seems as if there isn't any modesty anymore. When people see something on television, they think it is right. They don't think for themselves; they let the television think for them. Television is something that is not good for the world. It is too bad that most people don't realize how something like television can ruin all of our true values.

It seems as if everything in today's world is set up so that everyone can keep going so fast that they never have to consider why they were given the miracle of life. It is too bad that people waste their life and their intelligence by becoming part of this fast society. If they just stopped for a moment and considered that they will all die and meet their Lord, I wonder what they would do?

One of the reasons our society is so fast is the machine. Machinery has changed the manner in which we live, and all of our values regarding this world. In olden-days, it required manual labor for just about everything. Everyone had a responsibility and everyone helped each other. There was no money to keep and to possess, so you couldn't acquire more things than your neighbor. The olden-day Indians moved about the countryside and they couldn't carry more than what they needed. The qualities that a man possessed within himself were important, not what outward possessions he had.

In those days, everyone knew what was expected of him and the Indian Way taught him just how to do it. Not all olden-day Indians lived up to the tribal goals, even though the sacred center was present. Today some people still pray, as they should, even though the sacred center is almost gone. But the goals of the society in those days and today are different and this is

2 In the vast expanses of Nature in which the traditional Indian roamed, he was in one sense without limits on this freedom; in another sense he was always confined to the strict role placed upon him by his religious universe. In every moment and in every place, everything reinforced the sacred obligations of his heritage.

something that everyone must understand. We have spoken about the manner in which we carry out our Sun Dance Religion and how everything has a meaning, a purpose. So it was with everything the olden Indians did, and so it should be today. You would begin to understand the mysteries of this world in which we have been placed and you would know what you must do to prepare yourself to meet death, to enter the world beyond that we cannot see.

Many of the Sun Dance ceremonies are difficult to endure; it is an ordeal to complete them. This is good and it helps us remember that there is a greater responsibility in life. Life is a gift that you are free to use as you see fit; but you also have to understand that your actions, your choices, are being observed by powers that you do not see. If everything is easy for us and if our concerns are only regarding our possessions, then we lose sight of what is important. In difficult times, we are always prepared to face death; it may come today. So it should be every day in everything we do. We must prepare ourselves today to meet *Acbadadea*, The Maker of All Things Above. People always think that there is plenty of time left to pray later. People who want to accumulate more wealth are always thinking, "I'll wait until later." The world today, and the way people do things, encourage people to be lazy in their spiritual duties.

Manual labor is not required anymore; it is all done by machinery. One man can now do a big field of hay all by himself. The hay is cut and baled by machines; they have even got machinery now that picks it up and brings it in. Without touching anything, the machine puts the bales there and they are already on the stack. Many men used to be required to work many days, but now it is practically done in one day with these machines. Sugar beet farming used to require several men; quite a few working people are all now eliminated by modern machinery. Men going around looking for farm jobs can hardly get any work now. No one needs them because the machinery they have takes care of all that.

Even in the cattle industry, it is the same way. There used to be some good cowboys who would take care of the work on the cattle ranch. A lot of them cannot find jobs anymore. There are machines now that take their place. So it looks as if we get to the time when many good men cannot find any work at all. That is not like it should be.

Nowadays men want to accumulate money and then they use the money to buy machines so that all the work can be done more quickly; then they can accumulate even more money. That is all the rich man thinks about. What about the men who want to work for a living? They have no jobs and nothing at all to do. People end up working against each other, as the people without money and machines start to hate the others. Many of the wars in the world today result from this problem.

Now what happens when one good Indian boy does go out and find a job with good, hard work? Everyone should be proud of him, but they are not. Jealousy is created by the fact that people are competing against one another. On our reservations today, people are jealous of each other. No one cooperates. People blame each other for all of the problems, and criticize people who do work hard and who try to help. . . . Maybe people can understand that what we see in this modern world is bad, that most of the values people have today are backwards. To follow the way of the machine world will not prepare you to meet your Maker either in this life or after death.

It is true that we cannot just go back to the olden-days either. What good does it do to wish you were an olden-day Indian? Why criticize your brother and try to find faults in everyone else? Will that make you a better person because you have decided that someone else has faults? Some Indians will face their problems with a bottle. This is very bad—drugs, too. It corrupts all of our youngsters. How can any of this solve problems. It just makes everything worse, because they don't try to make anything out of themselves. These same people expect that they will be given things by the tribe, the government. They think that it is the responsibility of others to take care of them. . . . They don't care at all about our children. All that matters is their own welfare today. These men will certainly receive their just reward when they meet their Maker.

We have spoken about the Sun Dance Religion and what it means for us today. You can see that everything is very different today and that many of the sacred things and sacred ways that were with our Indian people in the olden-days are lost. This was bound to come, for we did not deserve to keep them because we no longer had respect for them. But it does no good to blame any one person or country for our present-day situation. All these events were foreseen in sacred prophecies from all of the great religions.

No one person is to blame for our present state. Everyone who fails to live up to his spiritual duties causes further problems for everyone. Therefore, I tell people, "Don't criticize your neighbor; that will not help anyone. It is not good to fight Indian against Indian; it just makes matters worse. Work on yourself first; prepare yourself to meet your Lord."

Everyone can see how things have changed from the olden times, when sacred values were at the center of our life, up to the present day, when our society does not seem to have a sense of the sacred. So many young people wonder what may happen to this world that we are in, and what they should do if they want to follow a spiritual path. They may think, "Are there other people who want to follow a sacred way? Do I have an opportunity to lead a life in accordance with the traditional ways?"

If people continue on their present course, with no prayer and no respect for sacred things, then things will get worse and worse for everyone. Many prophecies from great religions all over the world speak of the end of time. The Crow have a prophecy about this time, too.

The Crow prophecy concerns an important Crow rite: the Beaver Dance or Tobacco Dance. It is the same thing, but is known by both names. It is a dance participated in by both men and women who are members of the Tobacco Dance Society. The society used to perform their ceremonies every year. We do not know of any other Indian tribe that has this same dance. You could call it a Crow Indian dance. The Tobacco Dance Society has an adoption dance to adopt new members into the society, so that the ceremonies can always be continued. Recently, very few new members have been adopted and the ceremonies are not held as often as they were in olden times. . . .

The plant they use in the ceremony is not really a tobacco. The Crow name for it is *Itchichea*. It is very holy. In olden-days, every year, they would plant the tobacco in a special ceremony in the spring, usually in May. They would harvest it in the fall and they would keep the plant and seeds and start the process over the next spring. Even when I was a young boy, they completed the planting and harvesting every year so that there would always be tobacco for special ceremonies and prayers. Today the Tobacco Society rarely plants and harvests the tobacco. Almost all of the old members are practically gone and very few new adoptions take place, so fewer people know about the correct way to perform the ceremony and care for the tobacco. I believe the last time they had a special planting ceremony was several years ago at my sister's place, just below where my brother lives now. They set up their tipis there and they held their ceremonies for a day or two. Then they came out and planted their tobacco plants. The plant grows all summer and they harvest it in the fall with another ceremony. I was not present at the time of the harvest ceremony of that planting, but I was told that the seed production and crop production were very poor. The plant is not a very strong plant and so it appears that it may be gone soon. There might not be any more of the plant left anywhere since this particular plant is only used by the Crow.[3]

The Crow Indian prophecy says that when this plant is gone, when it is not planted and harvested so that there is no reproduction of the seed, then finally, it will be the end of time and the world will end. It looks as if that time is near. I was not there that fall when they went to gather it, but they told me they did not get much production of seed that year. What they have on hand will finally get old and will not produce any more; it will not renew, and that will probably be the end.

There are prophecies from the other religions that also talk about the end of time.[4] The Hopi prophecies are very interesting to hear. I have met Thomas Banyacya several times, and he is very good at explaining the Hopi prophecies.[5]

[3] In May 1984, Yellowtail and I visited two of the oldest members of the Tobacco Society to inquire about recent ceremonies. Both informants verified Yellowtail's recollection that the last planting took place between 1976 and 1978. A severe frost killed all of the tobacco seed production that year, and the only known seed is from a previous planting. Two different society members are keeping this seed, but it is not known if the seed will germinate, and no plantings are scheduled at this time.

[4] The prophecies that Yellowtail discusses are not alone even among Plains Indians. For example, the Sioux have a symbolism of the buffalo and its four legs. Each year the buffalo loses a hair off one of the legs. The end of this cycle comes when the buffalo has no more hair on its legs. (The Hindu have an almost identical prophesy.) Moreover, the Indians feel that industrial civilization, since it ruptures the balance of Nature, cannot endure.

[5] This letter, signed by Thomas Banyacya on behalf of all Hopi Traditional Village Leaders, was sent to President Richard Nixon in 1970:

> We, the true and traditional religious leaders, recognized as such by the Hopi People, maintain full authority over all land and life contained within the Western Hemisphere. We are granted our stewardship by virtue of our instruction as to the meaning of Nature, Peace, and Harmony as spoken to our People by Him, known to us as *Massau'u*, the Great Spirit, who long ago provided for us the sacred stone tablets which we preserve to this day. For many generations before the coming of the white man . . . the Hopi People have lived in the sacred place known to you as the Southwest and known to us to be the spiritual center of our continent. Those of us of the Hopi Nation who have followed the path of the Great Spirit without compromise have a message which we are committed, through our prophecy, to convey to you.
>
> The white man, through his insensitivity to the way of Nature, has desecrated the face of Mother Earth. The white man's advanced technological capacity has occurred as a result of his lack of regard for the spiritual path and for the way of all living things. The white man's desire for material possessions and power has blinded him to the pain he has caused Mother Earth by his quest for what he calls natural resources. And the path of the Great Spirit has become difficult to see by almost all men, even by many Indians who have chosen instead to follow the path of the white man. . . .
>
> Today the sacred lands where the Hopi live are being desecrated by men who seek coal and water from our soil that they may create more power for the white man's cities. This must not be allowed to continue for if it does, Mother Nature will react in such a way that almost all men will suffer the end of life as they now know it. The Great Spirit said not to allow this to happen even as it was prophesied to our ancestors. The Great Spirit said not to take from the Earth - not to destroy living things. The Great Spirit, *Massau'u*, said that man was to live in Harmony and maintain a good clean land for all children to come. All Hopi People and other Indian Brothers are standing on this religious principle and the Traditional Spiritual Unity Movement today is endeavoring to reawaken the spiritual nature in Indian people throughout this land. Your government has almost destroyed our basic religion, which actually is a way of life for all our people in this land of the Great Spirit. We feel that to survive the coming Purification Day, we must return to the basic religious principles and to meet together on this basis as leaders of our people.
>
> Today almost all the prophecies have come to pass. Great roads like rivers pass across the landscape; man talks to man through the cobwebs of telephone lines; man travels along the roads in the

It is important for the young people to understand and follow their traditional religion. We must help to educate our young ones in the proper manner about our traditions. I always try to encourage the young to forget the other things that they have in mind: "Drop those things and try to learn something about your traditional Indian ways."[6] They should join these meetings that Indians are having and try to continue the use of the different ceremonies and of prayer according to the Indian heritage.

Some people might think, "It doesn't do any good to pray; it won't change anything." But there are many reasons to pray and those people are wrong. Only God knows when the end of this world will come, and when and how it comes will certainly depend on sincere prayers that are offered to Him in the correct way. Each man will pass from this earth in his own time. Some of the prophecies talk only about the end of time; others speak about the break-up of the modern world, as we know it and a return to the traditional ways of our ancestors. I can't say what will happen and whether we will find the spiritual ways of our ancestors in this world or another; but I do know that in either case we still have to make a choice, each one of us must choose at this present moment which path to follow. Each person's prayers can help everyone. The person who prays and remembers God will receive the greatest benefit for himself and for others.

Some people will not believe that they really have a choice in following a religion and in turning to prayer. This is a strange idea. Everyone has a free mind and at any moment each individual can choose to do one thing instead of another. Think about this. Even a child does not have to obey his parents; he can choose the punishment he will receive if he disobeys instead. So too, can each person choose whether to join a religion and way of prayer. There are different reasons why you should do this: Of course you can fear punishment just like the child who disobeys; or you can follow a sacred path because you know and love the sacred ways. Whatever your reason, you must choose one direction or another. . . . There is nothing more I can say except to raise my voice in prayer:

"During these next years, I need Your help to give me the knowledge and strength to carry our Sun Dance Religion to our people. I have been trying to speak out, so that all the young people will know what is expected of them. Help me to carry this message to their hearts. I am working with my grandson so that this message can be written down for many to see. Help us.

sky in his airplanes; two great wars have been waged by those bearing the swastika or the rising sun; man is tampering with the Moon and the stars. Most men have strayed from the path shown us by the Great Spirit. For *Massau'u* alone is great enough to portray the way back to Him.

It is said by the Great Spirit that if a gourd of ashes is dropped upon the Earth, that many men will die and that the end of this way of life is near at hand. We interpret this as the dropping of atomic bombs on Hiroshima and Nagasaki. We do not want to see this happen to any place or any nation again, but instead we should turn all this energy for peaceful uses, not for war.

We, the religious leaders and rightful spokesmen for the Hopi Independent Nation, have been instructed by the Great Spirit to express the invitation to the President of the United States and all spiritual leaders everywhere to meet with us and discuss the welfare of mankind so that Peace, Unity, and Brotherhood will become part of all men everywhere.

[6] Chief Fools Crow, Teton Sioux, commented on this same point: "I decided to go again to Bear Butte to fast and pray . . . and do you know what happened? *Wakan Tanka* and *Tunkashila* gave me the same answer I was given on my trip there in 1927. The Sioux should go back and pick up the good things that our grandfathers, grandmothers, aunts, uncles, fathers, and mothers had taught us. Our only hope was to fall back upon our traditional way of life. It was the only foundation we had that would give meaning and purpose to us. I brought this message back to the elders" (Thomas E. Mails, *Fools Crow* [Garden City: Doubleday, 1979]).

Our Apsaroke people need to see that their own religion is good and that it can help them if only they open their eyes and hearts. Everyone needs to make a choice—each should choose a religion. Help them to understand that they must make that choice before it is too late.

"You have told our people through our Apsaroke prophecies that the world will come to an end. The other religions that have been given to the white people also talk about the end of time. According to what we have been told, that time may be here soon. Help people see that they should select the religion of their choice. Then they must pray every day and live straight.

"There was a time when all the different denominations used to stay away from each other or there was a little rivalry between them. It should not be that way. They should unite and pray together. All the people on the reservation should unite regardless of their beliefs. You have given different ways to different people all over the world. As we know, this earth is round like a wagon wheel. In a wagon wheel, all the spokes are set into the center. The circle of the wheel is round and all spokes come from the center and the center is You, *Acbadadea*, The Maker of all Things Above. Each spoke can be considered as a different religion of the world, which has been given by You to different people and different races. All of the people of the world are on the rim of the wheel and they must follow one of the spokes to the center. The different paths have been given to us but they all lead to the same place. We all pray to the same God, to You. There are different places on the wheel so each way may look strange to someone following a different path. It is easy for people to say that their way is the best if they know all about their faith and it is good for them. But they should refrain from saying bad things about other ways that they don't know about. There should be no hard feelings about someone else if he is following a way that leads to You. Help us to see this wisdom.

"A person should learn all about a path to You before he joins. It is not good to just enter a faith and then drop it. I tell this to the young people: 'You must choose a religion, but before you enter one, you should know which one is the best for you. Take the time and find out all you can about the method of prayer and about what that religion tells you about The Maker of All Things Above. You should understand the rules and know what is expected of you. Find a path that provides you with the way you need to live a good life every day!' . . . *Acbadadea*, Medicine Fathers, help all young people to know these things.

"Some people don't want to know what religion requires of them. As soon as they don't like something—because it may not be easy or it may require some sacrifice—they leave in a hurry without asking themselves what You expect of them. They can't get anything out of a religion if they leave every time something hard is asked of them. If they ever do find a way that is so easy that they can always perform everything without any trouble, then they should know they have found a bad thing. That is the time they should leave that false religion. Maker of All Things Above, give people the wisdom to see these things and the strength to resist those who will not follow You.

"I have tried to speak my mind and my heart in the best way I know. Thank You for helping guide my words. Now I have completed my responsibility of speaking about the sacred ways of our Apsaroke people, and I feel good about this. Thank You for the help that You have given me already so that I could carry out Your wishes until now. Help me to keep working and praying so that this position as Sun Dance Chief can be fulfilled and my people will be able to live. . . . *Aho, Aho*!"

Sri Ramakrishna and Religious Tolerance*

Ananda Coomaraswamy

"They call Him by a multitude of names, Who is but One"; "A single Fire that burns on many altars"; "Even as He sheweth, so is He named"; these are affirmations taken from the sacrificial hymns of the *Rg Veda*. "As He is approached, so He becomes"; "It is because of His great abundance—or because He can be so variously participated in—that they call Him by so many names." By way of comment, we cite St. Thomas Aquinas, "The many aspects of these names are not empty and vain, for there corresponds to all of them one single reality represented by them in a manifold and imperfect manner" (*Sum. Theol.* 1.13.4 and 2). Nothing, perhaps, so strangely impresses or bewilders a Christian student of Saint Ramakrishna's life as the fact that this Hindu of the Hindus, without in any way repudiating his Hinduism, but for the moment forgetting it, about 1866 completely surrendered himself to the Islamic way, repeated the name of Allah, wore the costume, and ate the food of a Muslim. This self-surrender to what we should call in India the waters of another current of the single river of truth resulted only in a direct experience of the beatific vision, not less authentic than before. Seven years later, Ramakrishna in the same way proved experimentally the truth of Christianity. He was now for a time completely absorbed in the idea of Christ, and had no room for any other thought. You might have supposed him a convert. What really resulted was that he could now affirm on the basis of personal experience, "I have also practiced all religions, Hinduism, Islam, Christianity, and I have also followed the paths of the different Hindu sects. . . . The lake has many shores. At one the Hindu draws water in a pitcher, and calls it *jala*, at another the Muslim in leather bottles, and calls it *pani*, at a third the Christian finds what he calls 'water.'"

Such an understanding may be rare, but is absolutely normal in the East: as the *Bhagavad Gita* expresses it, "There is no deity that I am not, and in case any man be truly the worshipper of any deity whatever, it is I that am the cause of his devotion and its fruit. . . . However men approach Me, even so do I welcome them, for the path men take from every side is Mine." Similarly the *Bhaktamala* (cf. G. A. Grierson, ed., London, 1909): "No one is ignorant of the doctrines of his own religion. . . . Therefore let every man, so far as in him lieth, help the reading of the Scriptures, whether those of his own church, or those of another." And similarly also in Islam, "My heart has become capable of every form . . . it is a convent for Christian monks, a temple for idols, the place of pilgrimage at Mecca, the tables of the Torah, the book of the Koran: I follow the religion of Love, whichever way His camels take."

Such an understanding is rarer still, and one may say abnormal to the Western type of humanity. If the modern Christian does not quite endorse the conduct of Charlemagne's heroes at Saragossa—"The synagogues they enter and the mosques, whose every wall with mallet and axes they shatter: they break in pieces small the idols. . . . The heathen folk in crowds to the font baptismal are driven, to take Christ's yoke upon them. . . . Thus out of heathen darkness have five-score thousand been redeemed, and be now true Christians," it is at least quite certain that for every man that has died by religious persecution in India, ten thousand have died in Europe, and equally certain that the activity of Christian missions still quite frankly endorses a program

* Editor's Note: A lecture in New York in March, 1936, on the centenary of the sage's birth, reprinted in *Coomaraswamy: Selected Papers, Vol. 2: Metaphysics*, ed. Roger Lipsey.

of conversion by force—the force of money, not indeed paid out in cash, but expended on education and medical aid bestowed with ulterior motives. "Force," as Lafcadio Hearn once wrote, "the principal instrument of Christian propagandism in the past, is still the force behind our missions." No greater offenders are to be found than missionaries against the commandment, "Thou shalt not bear false witness against thy neighbor." I do not, however, at all wish to dwell upon this point of view, but rather to point out that although religious tolerance in Europe has never, as in Asia, been founded upon the belief that all religions are true, but rather founded on a growing indifference to all religious doctrines, an intellectual basis for a willing tolerance of other forms of belief is by no means wanting in Christianity. John, indeed, speaks of the "True Light that lighteth every man." Even St. Thomas admits that some of the Gentiles who lived before Christ's temporal birth may have been saved. For as Clement of Alexandria had long since said, "There was always a natural manifestation of the one Almighty God, amongst all right-thinking men." Eckhart speaks of "One of our most ancient philosophers who found the truth long, long before God's birth, ere ever there was Christian faith at all as it is now," and again much more boldly, "He to whom God is different in one thing from another and to whom God is dearer in one thing than another, that man is a barbarian, still in the wilds, a child."

Note that "Merlyn made the round table in tokenying of the roundenes of the world for by the round table is the world sygnefyed by ryghte. For all the world crysten and hethen repayren unto the round table . . . (that) by them which should be felawes of the round table the truth of the Sancgreal should be well knowen" (Malory, *Morte D'arthur*, XIV.2). The truth is with Blake when he says, "The religions of all nations are derived from each nation's different reception of the poetic genius[1] which is everywhere called the spirit of prophecy. . . . As all men are alike (though infinitely various), so all religions, and as all similars have one source." The Vedic and Christian traditions are never tired of employing "Truth," "Being," and "Beauty," as preeminently fitting, essential names of God. Now we are well aware that in this human world there cannot be a conceptual knowledge or expression of truth except in some way; just as there can be no perceptible beauty except of some kind. What is true in all truths, or what is beautiful in all beauties, cannot itself be any one of these truths or beauties. As Dionysius says, "If anyone in seeing God understood what he saw, he saw not God himself, but one of those things that are His." Belief in Revelation or Audition does not mean that the very words in which the truth is expressed in any case contain the truth, but rather that they point to it, for as St. Thomas says, "Everything has truth of nature according to the *degree* in which it imitates the knowledge of God"; "our intellect considers God *according to* the mode derived from creatures"; and finally, "the thing known is in the knower *according* to the mode of the knower." All concepts of God, even the most nearly adequate, are thus man-made; as we say in India, "He takes the forms that are imagined by His worshippers." Very surely He is not to be thought of as confined by or fully expressed by any of these forms, Who is Himself the single form of every form, and transcendent with respect to each and every form; it is from this point of view that many a Christian teacher has affirmed that "Nothing true can be said of God." The value of concepts, of any expression verbal or visible, *per verbum in intellectu conceptum*, is one of use; the concept is of value not as a thing in itself, but as dispositive to an essential vision, *not* in any likeness. The beauty of the formula, the verbal or visual icon, poignant as it may be

[1] Vedic *kavitva.*

in Christian gospel or Vedic liturgy, is not an end in itself but, referred to him who uses it, is an invitation. The purpose of any art, and no less of that highest art of theology, in which all other arts, whether literary or plastic, subsist *per excellentiam*, is to teach, to delight, and above all to move (Augustine's *docere, delectare, movere*). An exclusive attachment to any one dogma, any one group of verbal or visual symbols, however pertinent, is an act of idolatry; the Truth itself is inexpressible.

If the image is His whose image it is, the colors and the art are ours. Whoever claims that his own manner of understanding and statement is the only true one is moved not by the vision of God, but by spiritual pride. Such a believer, as Ibn Arabi says, "praises none but himself, for his God is made by himself, and to praise the work is to praise the maker of it: its excellence or imperfection belongs to the maker. For this reason he blames the beliefs of others, which he would not do if he were just. . . . If he understood the saying of Junayd, 'The color of the water is the color of the vessel containing it,' he would not interfere with others, but would perceive God in every form and every belief. He has opinion, not knowledge: therefore God said, 'I am in my servant's opinion of Me,' that is, 'I do not manifest myself to him save in the form of his belief.' God is absolute or unrestricted as He pleases; and the God of religious belief is subject to limitations, for He is the God who is contained in the heart of His servant." The Oriental Gnostic has no fault to find with any Catholic doctrine; judged by Vedic standards, one can say that Christianity is true and lovely, true so far as any formulation can be true, lovely in so far as any thing, as distinguished from One who is no thing, can be lovely.

Moreover, it can be positively affirmed that every notable Christian doctrine is also explicitly propounded in every other dialect of the primordial tradition: I refer to such doctrines as those of the eternal and temporal births, that of the single essence and two natures, that of the Father's impassibility, that of the significance of sacrifice, that of transubstantiation, that of the nature of the distinction between the contemplative and active lives and of both from the life of pleasure, that of eternity from aeviternity and time, and so forth. Literally hundreds of texts could be cited from Christian and Islamic, Vedic, Taoist, and other scriptures and their patristic expositions, in close and sometimes literally verbal agreement. To cite a trio of instances at random, whereas Damascene has to say that "He Who Is, is the principal of all names applied to God," in the *Katha Upanisad* we have "He is, by that alone is He to be apprehended"; whereas St. Thomas says, "These things are said to be under the sun which are generated and corrupted," the *Satapatha Brahmana* affirms that "Everything under the sun is in the power of death"; and whereas Dionysius speaks of That "which not to see or know is really to see and know," the *Jaiminiya Upanisad Brahmana* has it that "The thought of God is his by whom it is unthought, or if he thinks the thought he does not understand." All traditional teaching employs side by side the *via affirmativa* and the *via remotionis*, and in this sense is in agreement with Boethius that "Faith is a mean between contrary heresies." Sin is defined by the Thomist and in India in one and the same way as a "departure from the order to the end." All tradition is agreed that the last end of man is happiness.

On the other hand, while there can be only one metaphysics, there must be not merely a variety of religions, but a hierarchy of religions, in which the truth is more or less adequately expressed, according to the intellectual capacities of those whose religions they are. Nor do I mean to deny that there can be heterodox doctrines, properly to be condemned as heresies, but only that any and every belief is a heresy if it be regarded as the truth, and not merely as a signpost of the truth. Pantheism, for example, is equally a heresy from Christian, Islamic, and Hindu points of view; a confusion of things as they are in themselves with things as they are in God, of the essence of the participant with the participated Essence, is an egregious error, and yet not so great an error as to assume that the being of things as they are in themselves is altogether their own being. The distinction of essence from nature of the *Samkhya* system is true from a certain point of view, and yet false when regarded from the standpoint of a higher synthesis, as in the *Vedanta*, and similarly in Christianity, where from one point of view essence and nature are the universe apart, and yet in the simplicity of the First Cause are one impartite substance.

It is perfectly legitimate to feel that a given religion is more adequately true than another; to hold, for example, that Catholicism is more adequately true than Protestantism, or Hinduism than Buddhism. Real distinctions can be drawn: Christianity maintains, for example, that metaphysics, though the highest of the other sciences, is inferior to the sacred science of theology; Hinduism is primarily metaphysical, and only secondarily religious, hence the controversies as to the true significance of "deification," and hence it is that however much a Hindu may find himself in enthusiastic agreement with the angelic and celestial doctors (Thomas and Bonaventura), he is more at home with certain giants of Christian thought whose orthodoxy is suspect, I mean Eriugena, Eckhart, Boehme, Blake, and more at home with Plotinus than with the representatives of exoteric Christian orthodoxy; more at home with St. John than with St. James, more in sympathy with Christian Platonism than with Christian Aristotelianism, scarcely at all in sympathy with Protestant theologies, and far more in sympathy with Qabbalistic interpretations of Genesis and Exodus than with any historical approach. So that we do not for a moment mean to maintain the impropriety of all dogmatic controversy. We must bear in mind that even within the framework of a presumably homogeneous faith it is taken for granted that one and the same truths must be presented in various ways suited to the audience, and that this is not a matter of contradictory statement, but of "convenient means." What we do maintain is that all paths converge; that the Wayfarer, having already trodden a given path, will under all normal circumstances sooner reach that point at which all progress ends—"On reaching God, all progress ends"—than if he retrace his steps and start afresh.

What we must not forget is that no one can finally pronounce upon the truth of a given religion who has not lived it, as Ramakrishna lived both Christianity and Islam, as well as Hinduism; and that once convinced that only one's own truth is true, "It is," as Professor C. A. Briggs of Drew University lately remarked, "the easiest thing imaginable to take the concepts of other faiths, abstract them from their contexts, and demolish them." For example, how easily the Islamic definition of Christianity as a polytheistic religion could be deduced from the considered statement of St. Thomas, that "We do not say *the only God*, because deity is common to several" (*Sum. Theol.* 1.31.2c). In the same way, a pantheistic definition of Christianity could easily be deduced from St. Thomas' "A thing has being by participation. . . . We must consider . . . the emanation of all being from the universal cause, which is God" (*Sum. Theol.* 1.44.1 *ad* 1 and 45 1c).

*   *   *

What is then, in the last analysis, the value of comparative religion? Certainly not to convince us that one mode of belief is the preparation for another, or to lead to a decision as to which is "best." One might as well regard ancient or exotic styles of art as preparations for and aspirations towards one's own. Nor can the value of this discipline be thought of as one conducing to the development of a single universally acceptable syncretic faith embodying all that is "best" in every faith; such a "faith" as this would be a mechanical and lifeless monstrosity, by no means a stream of living water, but a sort of religious Esperanto. Comparative religion can demonstrate that all religions spring from a common source; are, as Jeremias says, the "dialects of a single spiritual speech." We cannot, therefore, take the formulae of one religion and insert them in another without incongruity. One can recognize that many formulae are identical in different religions; confront, for example, St. Thomas, "Creation, which is the emanation of all being from the not-being, which is no thing" (*Sum. Theol.* 1.45.1c) with the Vedic "Being is engendered from nonbeing" (*asatah sad ajayata, Rg Veda* X.72.3), and such comparisons can be validly employed (even by the most orthodox) as what St. Thomas calls "extrinsic and probable proofs" of the validity of a given dogma.

But of greater value than this is the clarification that results when the formulae of one tradition are collated with those of another. For, as we have already seen, every tradition is necessarily a partial representation of the truth intended by tradition universally considered; in each tradition something is suppressed, or reserved, or obscure which in another may be found more extensively, more logically, or more brilliantly developed. What then is clear and full in one tradition can be used to develop the meaning of what may be hardly more than alluded to in another. Or even if in one tradition a given doctrine has been definitely named, a realization of the significance of this definition may lead to the recognition and correlation of a whole series of affirmations in another tradition, in all of which the same doctrine is implicit, but which had previously been overlooked in their relation to one another. It is thus a great advantage to be able to make use of the expression *Vedic exemplarism*; or conversely, to speak of Christian *yoga* immediately brings out the analogy between St. Bernard's *consideratio*, *contemplatio*, and *raptus* with Sanskrit *dharana*, *dhyana*, and *samadhi*.

To many Christians, no doubt, Sri Ramakrishna's primary attachment to the cult of the Great Mother gives offense. Nothing is, indeed, more usual than to consider that Christianity, whether for better or worse, adheres to purely masculine interpretations of divine being; the Christian speaks of a Father, but not of a Mother in Heaven, whereas in India the ancient love of the Magna Mater maintains itself at the present day on equal terms with that of the Propator. And yet the doctrine of the maternity of the divine nature is repeatedly, however reservedly, affirmed in Christian theology, fundamentally in that of the "two natures," more explicitly in that of the temporal *and* eternal nativities, and in that of the Generation of the Son as a vital operation from conjoint principles—"Processio Verbi in divinis dicitur generatio . . . quae est operatio vitae . . . et propter hoc proprie dicitur genitum et Filius" (*Sum. Theol.* 1.27.2; cf. 1.98.2c, "In every act of generation there is an active and a passive principle."). It is inasmuch as "eternal filiation does not depend on a temporal mother" (*Sum. Theol.* III.35.5 *ad* 2) that Eckhart can speak of the "act of fecundation latent in eternity," and say that "it is God who has the treasure and the bride in Him," that the "Godhead wantons with the Word," and that "His birth in *Mary ghostly* was to God better pleasing than His nativity of her in the flesh." One sees that when St. Thomas speaks of "that Nature by which the Father begets" (*Sum. Theol.* 1.41.5), the reference is really to the Magna Mater, the Vedic Aditi, not to mention other names of the One Madonna, and sees what is really meant by the otherwise obscure assertion that notwithstanding primary matter "recedes from likeness to God, yet . . . it *retains* a certain likeness to the divine being" (*Sum. Theol.* 1.14.11 *ad* 3). Natura Naturata indeed "retains" a certain likeness to "Natura Naturans, Creatrix, Deus": Mother Earth to Mother Nature, Mary in the flesh to Mary ghostly. One need only consider Genesis 1:27, "To the image of God He created him; male and female He created them," in connection with Galatians 3:28, "according to the image of Him that created him, where there is neither male nor female," to realize that whereas Essence and Nature *in divinis* are one simple substance without composition, the very fact that the conjoint principles can be separately exemplified is proof that the Supreme Identity can be truly spoken of either as Father or as Mother, or as Father-Mother, just as in the Vedas the Divine "Parents" are indifferently "Fathers" (*pitara*) or "Mothers" (*matara*), or as "That One, spirated, despirated" (*tad ekam anit avatam, Rg Veda* X.129.2, where no gender is implied; cf. Eckhart's "Where these two abysms hang, equally spirated, despirated, there is the Supreme Being")

Thus we may go so far as to assert on behalf of a true "comparative religion," that however a religion may be self-sufficient if it be followed to the very end to which it is directed, there can hardly be supposed a way so plain that it could not here and there be better illuminated by other lights than that of the pilgrim's private lantern, the light of any lantern being only a refraction of the Light of lights. A diversity of routes is not merely appropriate to a diversity of travelers, who are neither all alike, nor start from one and the same point, but may be of incalculable aid to any traveler who can rightly read the map; for where all roads converge, there can be none of them that does not help to clarify the true position of the center of the maze, "short of which we are still in a duality." Hence we say that the very implications of the phrase "religious tolerance" are to be avoided: diversity of faith is not a matter for unwilling "toleration," but of divine appointment. And this will hold good even if we sincerely believe that other faiths are inferior to our own, and in this sense relatively "evil": for as Augustine says, "The admirable beauty of the universe is made up of all things. In which even what is called evil, well-ordered and in its place, is the eminent commendation of what is good" (*Enchiridion* XIII), whom St. Thomas quotes with approval, adding that "The universe, the present creation being supposed, cannot be better, because of the most beautiful order given to things by God" (*Sum. Theol.* 1.48.1 and 1.25.6 *ad* 3). As Augustine also says, "There is no evil in things, but only in the sinner's misuse of them" (*De doctrina christiana* III.12). As to the sinner's "misuse," who can assure us of that, with respect to which it has been said, "Judge not, that ye be not judged"?

In the matter of direction towards the Kingdom of Heaven "within you,"[2] the modern world is far more lacking in the will to seek, than likely to be led astray by false direction. From the Satanic point of view there could hardly be imagined a better activity than to be engaged in the "conversion of the heathen" from one to another body of dogmas: that, surely, was not what was meant by the injunction, "Go thou and preach the Kingdom of God"—or was He mistaken, when He said, "The Kingdom of Heaven is within you"?

[2] Sanskrit *hrdayakase, antarbhutasya khe.*

Coomaraswamy, St. Augustine, and the Perennial Philosophy

Stephen Cross

One of the key ideas in the writing of A.K. Coomaraswamy and his contemporary René Guénon is of course that of the Perennial Philosophy: the idea that the differences between the major religions, real enough at the level of externals, dissolve progressively as one penetrates towards the central content of the doctrines involved. It is at the highest levels of understanding and of spiritual experience that, in the phrase of Frithjof Schuon, the *transcendent unity of religions* is found. The idea is an important one because ever since the eighteenth century, and even before, the apparently irreconcilable claims of the major religions have provided rationalist critics with one of their principal arguments.

Coomaraswamy addresses this question in one of his best-known books, *Am I My Brother's Keeper?* Discussing the difficulties which arise from Christianity's claim to be in exclusive possession of the truth, he writes:

> The one outstanding, and perhaps the only, real heresy of modern Christianity in the eyes of other believers is its claim to exclusive truth; for this is treason against Him who "never left himself without a witness."[1]

Coomaraswamy then goes on to give examples of several Christian figures who seem to have been happy exceptions to this rule—St. Justin, and Meister Eckhart who "speaks of Plato as 'that great priest.'" He next quotes the following passage from St. Augustine, adding, "Had he not retracted these brave words, the bloodstained history of Christianity might have been otherwise written!"

> The very thing that is now called the Christian religion was not wanting among the ancients from the beginning of the human race, until Christ came in the flesh, after which the true religion, which had already existed, began to be called "Christian."

This passage comes from St. Augustine's *Retractationes*,[2] a book written at the close of his life, in which he painstakingly and with some humility goes through his earlier writings and corrects what now appear to him to be errors in these or carefully clarifies ambiguous points. However, the passage quoted by Coomaraswamy is not, as Coomaraswamy seems to have assumed, in the *Retractationes* because Augustine is now retracting it. On the contrary, it is there as a *fresh statement* which Augustine is now, at the end of his life, making, and the purpose of which is to clarify an earlier statement which he felt could give rise to misunderstanding. That earlier

[1] *Am I My Brother's Keeper?* (New York, 1947). Published in Great Britain under the title *The Bugbear of Literacy* (London, 1949), p. 56. The passages referred to occur in the essay "Paths That Lead to the Same Summit."

[2] *Retractationes*, 1.13.3; in Gustave Bardy (ed.), *Biblioteque Augustinienne*, vol. 12 (Paris, 1950). Bardy follows the authoritative Maurist edition of Augustine of 1700 A.D. Coomaraswamy refers to the same passage in his 1939 essay, "The Vedanta and Western Tradition," but without the comment.

statement occurs in a passage of *De Vera Religione*.[3] Here Augustine is explaining that the soul, crushed by the sins which envelop it, would be unable to rise towards the divine realities unless there was found within the human sphere something which would allow man to rise from the earthly life and to renew in himself the image of God. For this reason God, in his infinite mercy, has established a temporal means by which men may be recalled to their original perfection, and by which God comes to the help of each particular individual and of the human race as a whole. St. Augustine then adds: "That is in our times the Christian religion, to know and to follow which is the most secure and certain salvation."

It is this last sentence which Augustine wishes to clarify in the *Retractationes*, explaining that in it he has made use of the name (i.e. "Christian religion") but has failed to express the reality which lies behind that name: "It is said according to this name, not in accord with the thing itself, of which this is the name." Then comes the passage which Coomaraswamy quotes: "For the very thing that is now called the Christian religion was not wanting among the ancients from the beginning of the human race, until Christ came in the flesh, after which the true religion, which had already existed, began to be called 'Christian.'" To make things even clearer, Augustine next adds:

> When, in fact, following the resurrection and ascension into heaven, the Apostles began to preach and many persons came to believe, it was among the people of Antioch—so it is written—that the disciples were first called Christians. This is the reason why I said, "That is in our times the Christian religion"; not because in earlier times it did not exist, but because in later times this name was accepted.[4]

It appears from this that Coomaraswamy has misunderstood Augustine's position, and that far from having retracted the thesis of the Perennial Philosophy, Augustine's statement in the *Retractationes* constitutes an unequivocal assertion of it: the truth which is now expressed in the form of the Christian religion was known from the beginning of the human race.[5] It is hardly necessary to add that St. Augustine's works amongst which this appears carry the imprimatur of the Catholic Church.

St. Augustine's words are definite and unambiguous. The only way one can see in which they could be interpreted so as to be consistent with the exclusivism usually attributed to Christianity would be by arguing that in speaking of "the ancients" Augustine is referring only to the patriarchs of the Jewish tradition. One can only say that if such an argument were to be advanced the burden of proof would rest with those putting it forward. There is absolutely no indication in the passage as it stands, or in its context, that the meaning is confined to the Jewish tradition; on the contrary, the emphasis is upon *the human race*—a phrase which occurs both in the passage in *Retractationes* (*generis humani*), and again in the section of *De Vera Religione* upon which Augustine is commenting (*hominum generi*). St. Augustine was certainly not unaware of the many other religious traditions in addition to the Judeo-Christian one existing in the ancient Mediterranean world. In a work in which he is being careful to make everything as clear and exact as possible, and the whole purpose of which is to remove ambiguity, it is hardly conceivable that he would have expressed himself so loosely had he really intended to refer only to the Jewish tradition.

3 *De Vera Religione*, 10.19; in vol. 8 of Bardy's *Biblioteque Augustinienne.*

4 *Retractationes*, 1.13.3.

5 St. Augustine adopts a similar position in *The City of God* (*De Civitas Dei*); see Book 18, chapters 47 and 51.

As we have seen, Augustine's statement is not unique within Christianity. In addition to the "happy exceptions" mentioned above, Coomaraswamy also refers to the statement of St. Ambrose—which, he says, was subsequently endorsed by Aquinas—that "all that is true, by whomsoever it has been said, is from the Holy Ghost." Other examples could be found. Nevertheless, such views are inconsistent with the general position of Christianity as this has been widely understood - a position which is more in line with the passage in St. John's Gospel (10:8) in which those who came before the time of Jesus are referred to as "thieves and robbers." There has in consequence been a general tendency to pass over such statements as that of Augustine in silence, or to look upon them as the aberrations of otherwise great men, or, as with Eckhart, as the ideas of men whose orthodoxy is at least questionable. It is here that the importance of the passage in St. Augustine's *Retractationes* lies. For the Western church Augustine is one of the greatest formulators of Christian doctrine. He is second only to St. Paul in this respect, and his writings have always had immense authority. And let us repeat that Augustine's statement on the Perennial Philosophy is not some tentative and half-formulated idea, but a careful, deliberate, and even emphatic statement of a well considered position.

Finally, we may perhaps wonder how Coomaraswamy—a man whose scholarship is unquestionable—came to make such a slip. In all probability he came across the passage not in its original context, but quoted by some other author—quite possibly in F.S. Growse's *Mathura, a District Memoir*, a book which Coomaraswamy, with his strong interest in India, is likely to have read and in which the precise passage occurs in a footnote to chapter six—and finding that it came from Augustine's *Retractationes* assumed it was a passage which Augustine had subsequently withdrawn. This is an assumption which Coomaraswamy may perhaps have made the more readily since it fitted his own preconceptions with regard to the nature of Christianity. We may also note that the essays in *Am I My Brother's Keeper?* are written in a more popular vein than the later papers on which Coomaraswamy's enviable reputation as a scholar largely rests, and he may have been somewhat off his guard. Be that as it may, we may be sure that nobody would have been more happy than Coomaraswamy himself to discover the error. It was the inner core of truth, repeatedly confirmed by the experience of mystics throughout the world, and not the shell of conventions which in each particular culture has grown up around it, which was for him the true *tradition*. It is this traditional truth, mystical, universal and primordial, that we find St. Augustine affirming in his final work.

The Universality and Timeliness of Monasticism

Frithjof Schuon

Finding a common denominator for phenomena as varied as the different monasticisms of the West and the East does not appear at first an easy task, for in order to be able to define, one must have found a point of view that makes definition possible; now it seems to us that this point of view arises simply from the nature of things, seeing that it is impossible to provide an account of human nature without relating it back to its divine conditioning, or of the human phenomenon without connecting it either positively or negatively to God; for without God man is nothing. We can therefore say that the effort to reduce the complexity of life to a simple, but essential and liberating, formula comes from whatever is most complete and profound in the human condition, and that this effort has led, in the most diverse spiritual climates, to the sort of institutional sanctity that constitutes monasticism.

Man was created alone and he dies alone; monasticism seeks to preserve this solitude in its metaphysically irreplaceable aspect; it aims to restore to man his primordial solitude before God, or again it wishes to bring man back to his spiritual integrity and totality. A perfect society would be a society of hermits, if such a paradox may be permitted; now this is exactly what the monastic community seeks to realize, for monasticism is in a certain sense an organized eremitism.

The reflections that follow may seem to be truisms to some people, but they concern mental habits so ineradicable that it is difficult to underestimate their importance if one looks at things in depth. The point at issue is this: according to current opinion, monasticism is a matter of "vocation", but not in the proper sense of the word; when a man is simple enough to take religion literally and commits the indiscretion of allowing rather too spiritual opinions or attitudes to show through, people have no scruple telling him that he belongs "in a monastery", as if he were a foreign body with no right to existence outside the walls of an appropriate institution. The idea of "vocation", which in itself is positive, then becomes negative: a man is said to be "called" not insofar as he is in the truth and because he is so, but because he disturbs society by causing it to become involuntarily aware of what it is. According to this more or less conventional way of looking at things, an absence of vocation—or let us say worldliness—exists *de jure* and not merely *de facto*, which means that perfection then seems like an optional specialty, hence a luxury; it is reserved for monks, but one forgets to ask why it is not for everyone.

A monk will certainly never blame anyone simply for living in the world; this is self-evident, given the existence of secular clergy and lay saints; what is blameworthy is not living "in the world", but living in it badly and thus in a certain sense creating it. When someone reproaches a hermit or a monk for "fleeing" the world, he commits a double error: first, he loses sight of the fact that contemplative isolation has an intrinsic value independent of the existence of a surrounding "world"; second, he pretends to forget that there are forms of flight which are perfectly honorable: if it is neither absurd nor shameful to escape an avalanche if one is able to, it is no more so to run away from the temptations or even simply the distractions of the world, or from our own ego to the extent it is rooted in this vicious circle; and let us not forget that in disencumbering ourselves of the world we disencumber the world of our own sufferings. In our day people are very ready to declare that to flee the world is to shirk "responsibilities", a completely hypocritical euphemism that conceals behind "altruistic" or "social" ideas a spiritual laziness and a hatred of the absolute; people are happy to ignore the fact that the gift of oneself to God is always the gift of oneself to all. It is metaphysically impossible to give oneself to God without this resulting in something good for the environment; to give oneself to God—though it were hidden from all—is to give oneself to man, for this gift of self has a sacrificial value of an incalculable radiance.

On the other hand, to work for one's own salvation is like breathing, eating, sleeping; one cannot do these things for anyone else, nor help anyone else by abstaining from them. Egoism is taking away from others what they need; it is not taking for oneself something of which they know nothing or for which they have no desire.

Monasticism is not situated outside the world; it is the world that situates itself outside monasticism: if every man lived in the love of God, the monastery would be everywhere, and it is in this sense one can say that every saint is implicitly a monk or hermit. Or again: just as it is possible to introduce the "world" into the framework of monasticism, since not every monk is a saint, so also it is possible to transfer monasticism—or the attitude it represents—into the world, for there can be contemplatives anywhere.

* * *

If we define monasticism as a "withdrawal for God" while acknowledging its universal and inter-religious character—because a thirst for the supernatural is in the nature of normal man—how can we apply this definition to spiritual Muslims, who do not withdraw from society, or to Buddhists, who do cut themselves off but do not seem to have the idea of God? In other words—as far as Islam is concerned—how can there be a spirituality in a religion that rejects monasticism, or again why is monasticism excluded from a religion that nevertheless possesses mysticism, ascetic disciplines, and a cult of saints? To this we must reply that one of the reasons for Islam is precisely the possibility of a "monastery-society", if one may express it so: that is, Islam aims to carry the contemplative life into the very framework of society as a whole; within that framework, it succeeds in realizing conditions of structure and behavior that allow for contemplative isolation in the very midst of the activities of the world. It must be added that what corresponds to the monastery for the Muslim is above all an initiatic attachment to a brotherhood and submission—*perinde ac cadaver*—to a spiritual master, as well as the practice of supererogatory orisons together with vigils and fasts; the isolating element with respect to worldly people is strictness in observation of the *sunnah*; hence this strictness—which the surrounding society would not think of opposing in a Muslim country—is equivalent in practice to the walls of a monastery. It is true that dervishes assemble in their *zāwiyah*s for their communal practices and make retreats in them lasting sometimes for several months; a few live there and consecrate their whole lives to prayer and service of the *shaykh*; but the result is not monasticism in a strict sense, comparable to that of Christians or Buddhists. Be that as it may, the famous "no monasticism in Islam" (*lā rahbāniyah fī 'l-islām*) does not really mean that contemplatives must not withdraw from the world, but on the contrary that the world must not be withdrawn from contemplatives; the intrinsic ideal of monasticism or eremitism—namely, asceticism and the mystical life—is in no way in question. And let us not forget that "holy war" is accompanied in Islam by the same mystical development as in Christian chivalry, notably that of the Templars; it offers a way of sacrifice and martyrdom, which united Christians and Muslims—at the time of the crusades—in one and the same sacrificial love of God.

In the case of Buddhism the difficulty lies in the fact that this religion, while it is essentially monastic—and is so to a degree that cannot be surpassed—seems to ignore the idea of God; now it goes without saying that an "atheistic spirituality" is a contradiction in terms, and in fact Buddhism possesses completely the idea of a transcendent Absolute, just as it possesses the idea of a contact between this Absolute and man. If Buddhism does not have the idea of a "God" in the Semitic or Aryan sense of the word, it is nonetheless just as conscious in its own way of Divine Reality, for it is far from ignoring the crucial ideas of absoluteness, transcendence, perfection, and—on the human side—of sacrifice and sanctity; though "non-theist", no doubt, it is certainly not "atheist". The aspect of a "personal God" appears notably in the Mahayanic cult of the Buddha Amitabha—Japanese Amidism—where it is combined with a perspective of redemptive Mercy; Christian influences have been suggested, which is not only false, but even implausible from more than one point of view; it is forgotten that the fundamental nature of things can give rise to phenomena analogous at least in their forms wherever circumstances are favorable. This prejudice concerning "influences" or "borrowings" makes us think of the ethnographer who found among the Red Indians the myth of the flood and ingenuously concluded that missionaries had been in touch with them, whereas this myth—or rather this recollection—is found among almost all the peoples of the earth.

These last remarks give us the opportunity of saying a few words about the current confusion between syncretism and eclecticism, although this may take us away to some extent from our subject. Syncretism is never something substantial: it is an assembling of heterogeneous elements into a false unity, that is, a unity without real synthesis; eclecticism on the other hand is natural wherever different doctrines exist side by side, as is proven by the integration of Platonism or Aristotelianism into the Christian perspective. What matters in such a case is that the original perspective remain faithful to itself and accept foreign concepts only to the extent they corroborate its faithfulness by helping to shed some light on the fundamental intentions of its own perspective; Christians had no reason not to be inspired by Greek wisdom since it was at hand, just as Muslims could not prevent themselves from using Neoplatonic concepts in their mystical doctrine—at least to a certain extent—as soon as they became aware of them; but it would be a serious error to speak of syncretism in these cases by mistakenly recalling the example of such artificial doctrines as those of modern theosophy. There have never been borrowings between two living religions of essential elements affecting their fundamental structures, as is supposed when Amidism is attributed to the Nestorians.

The monasticism of Hindus and Taoists should also be mentioned as Asian examples, but they can scarcely be said to present difficulties comparable to those we have mentioned in connection with Islam and Buddhism; of course there is always the difficulty of religious differences in general, but this is a complex problem which our somewhat synthetic remarks about monasticism as a phenomenon of humanity need not take into account.

* * *

A world is absurd to the extent that the contemplative, the hermit, the monk appear in it as a paradox or "anachronism". Now the monk is timely precisely because he is timeless: we live in an epoch characterized by an idolatry of time and the monk incarnates all that is changeless, not through sclerosis or inertia, but through transcendence.

And this leads us to introduce certain issues that bring negatively into relief the burning timeliness of the monastic ideal—or simply the religious ideal, which in the final analysis amounts to the same thing. In the world of absurd relativism that we live in, anyone who says "our times" thinks he has said everything; to identify phenomena of any kind with "other times" or still more with "times gone by" is to get rid of them; and consider the hypocritical sadism concealed by such words as "bygone", "outdated", or "irreversible", which replace thought by a sort of imaginative suggestion—a "music of prejudice", we might say. People take note, for example, that some liturgical or ceremonial practice offends the scientistic or demagogic tastes of our age, and they are relieved when they recall that the usage in question dates from the Middle Ages, or perhaps that it is "Byzantine", because this allows them to conclude without further ado that it no longer has any right to existence; they completely forget that there is only one question to be asked, namely, *why* the Byzantines did such a thing; more often than not one finds that this "why" is located outside of time and that its reason for being is connected to timeless factors. Identifying oneself with an "age" and removing from things all, or nearly all, their intrinsic worth is quite a new attitude, one which is arbitrarily projected into what we retrospectively call "the past"; in reality our ancestors did not live in a time, speaking subjectively and intellectually, but in a "space", that is, in a world of stable values in which the flux of duration was only accidental so to speak; they had a marvelous sense of the absolute in things and of the rootedness of things in the absolute.

Our age tends more and more to cut man off from his roots; but in seeking to "start again from nothing" and to reduce man to the purely human it succeeds only in dehumanizing him, which proves that the "purely human" is only a fiction; man is fully man only in rising above himself, and he can do so only through religion. Monasticism is there to remind us that man is human only by virtue of his permanent consciousness of the Absolute and absolute values and that the works of man are nothing in themselves; the Desert Fathers, Cassian, Saint Benedict, and others have shown that before acting one must be and that actions are precious to the extent that the love of God animates them or is reflected in them and tolerable to the extent that they are not opposed to this love. The fullness of being, which depends on the spirit, can in principle dispense with action; action does not carry its end in itself: Martha is certainly not superior to Mary. Man is distinguished from the animals in two essential respects, first by his intelligence, which has a capacity for the absolute and thus for objectivity and a sense of the relative, and then by his free will, which is capable of choosing God and attaching itself to Him; the rest is only contingency, especially this profane and quantitative "culture", of which the early Church had no conception and which is now made into a mainstay of human value, in defiance of current experience and contrary to fact.

In our age man is defined not by reference to his specific nature—which is definable only in a divine context—but by reference to the inextricable consequences of an already secular Prometheanism: it is human works, or even the remote consequences of these works, which in the minds of our contemporaries determine and define man. We live in a scene-shifter's world in which it has become almost impossible to make contact with the primordial realities of things; prejudices and reflexes dictated by an irreversible slide intervene at every step; it is as if before the Renaissance or the Encyclopedists man had not been wholly man, or as if in order to be man it were necessary to have passed by way of Descartes, Voltaire, Rousseau, Kant, Marx, Darwin, and Freud, not forgetting—most recent of all—the lethal Teilhard de Chardin. It is sad to see how religious convictions are all too often enveloped in an irreligious sensibility or how such convictions are accompanied by reflexes directly opposed to them; apologetics tends more and more to take its stand on the wrong ground, on which its victory is in any case impossible, and to adopt a language that rings false and is able to convince no one, with the exception of an occasional propagandist success that is of no use whatsoever to religion as such; when apologetics ventures into demagogy it enters upon the road to suicide. Instead of keeping to the pure and simple truth—a truth that quite obviously cannot please everyone—people allow themselves to be fascinated by the postulates of the adversary, then by his self-assurance, dynamism, easy success, and efficient vulgarity; on the pretext of not wanting to "confiscate" the religious message, it is extrinsically and imperceptibly "falsified", though one carefully avoids believing in this danger and mentioning this word; at the very most, one speaks of the danger of "attenuating the message", a euphemism in which the bias is evident.

"Have dominion over the earth", says the Bible, and progressivists miss no chance of exploiting this sentence to justify the ever more totalitarian industrialism of our age and to extol a corresponding "spirituality"; in reality it is a very long time since man has obeyed this injunction of the Creator; in order to grasp its true intention and limits, it is necessary to remember the divine command to "take no thought for the morrow" and similar injunctions.[1] It is pure hypocrisy to make much of the Biblical sentence first quoted without situating it in its total context, for according to this logic it would also be right to attribute an absolute force to the words "be fruitful and multiply"[2] and abolish all chastity in Christianity or even to return to the polygamy of the Hebrews. This strange eagerness to follow the "commandments of God" might well lead, it seems to us, to many other scriptural discoveries besides that of a passage concerning agriculture, fishing, hunting, and stock-rearing and to many spiritual concerns other than the industrialization of religion.[3]

* * *

Inferiority complexes and mimetic reflexes are bad counselors: how often one meets with absurd reproaches leveled not only at the religion of the Middle Ages but also at that of the nineteenth century, which even then was still not "atomic", as if all men who lived before ourselves had been struck with an inexplicable blindness and as if it had been necessary to await the advent of a given atheistic philosopher to discover a light both decisive and mysteriously unknown to all the saints. It is too readily forgotten that, if human nature has a right to its shortcomings today, which no one disputes, it had the same right to them in the past; "progress" is most often a mere transference, the exchange of one evil for another; otherwise our age would be perfect and sanctified. In the human world as such, it is scarcely possible to choose a good; one is always reduced to choosing a lesser evil, and to determine which evil is the lesser we are obliged to refer to a hierarchy of values derived from eternal realities, and this is exactly what "our age" never does. In the Middle Ages one started from the idea that man is bad because he is a sinner, whereas in our century man is good since sin does not exist, the reversal being so complete that

[1] "For what is a man profited, if he shall gain the whole world, and lose his own soul?" (Matt. 16:26).

[2] "Be fruitful, and multiply, and replenish the earth, and subdue it; and have dominion over the fish of the sea, and over the fowl of the air, and over every living thing that moveth upon the earth" (Gen. 1:28).

[3] The partisans of this "forcing into step" must be answered by the Scriptures: "Whoso therefore will be a friend of the world is the enemy of God" (James 4:4). "And be not conformed to this world: but be ye transformed by the renewing of your mind, that ye may prove what is that good, and acceptable, and perfect, will of God" (Rom. 12:2). In our day it is the other way round: it is atheistic scientism, demagogy, the machine that decides what is good, what should be pleasing to God, what is perfect. "Woe unto you, when all men shall speak well of you! for so did their fathers to the false prophets" (Luke 6:26).

evil is above all whatever makes us believe in sin; modern humanitarianism, convinced that man is good, wants to protect man, but from whom? From man obviously, but what man? And if evil does not come from man, from whom does it come, given the conviction that nothing intelligent exists outside the human being nor especially above him?

There is the prejudice of science and the prejudice of society; monasticism, with its insistence on the "one thing needful" and with its collective pauperism, free from all envy—and perfectly concrete as far as individuals are concerned, though a monastery itself may be rich—offers in its own way the answer to these two pitfalls. What is a science that takes account neither of the transcendent and conscious Infinite, nor of the hereafter, nor of such basic phenomena as Revelation, miracle, pure intellection, contemplation, sanctity; and what is a social equilibrium that abolishes all real superiority and takes no account of the intrinsic nature of man nor of his ultimate destiny? People smile at the Biblical account of creation, but they know nothing of Semitic symbolism, which furnishes the key to things apparently naive; it is claimed that the Church has always been "on the side of the rich", and it is forgotten that from the point of view of religion there is only man, whether rich or poor—man, made of flesh and spirit, always exposed to suffering and doomed to die; and if the Church as an earthly institution has been forced to lean on the powerful who protected her, or were supposed to protect her, she has never refused herself to the poor and utterly compensates for her accidental and human imperfections by her spiritual gifts and numberless saints, not forgetting that permanent spiritual presence which is precisely what monasticism actualizes. The Catholic Church has been reproached for its "self-sufficiency": now the Church has every reason for being "self-sufficient" since she is what she is and offers what she offers; it is not for her to fret, nor undertake her own "self-criticism", nor "catch up with the times", as those who have no sense of her dignity wish. The Church has the right to repose in herself; her frontline troops are the saints; she has no need of officious demagogues with their mock "drama" and "death-throes". The saints are all she needs, and she has always had them.[4]

The success of atheistic materialism can be explained in part by the fact that it is an extreme position, all the more readily extremist given the tottering world that serves as its framework and the psychological elements to which it appeals. Christianity is also an extreme position, but instead of profiting from this fact it is concealed—this at least is the tendency that seems to prevail—and one adapts oneself to the position of the adversary, whereas it is precisely the extremism of the Christian message, if it is affirmed without disguise—but also without any makeshift "dynamism"—which has the gift of fascinating and convincing. A conscious or unconscious capitulation before the arguments of the adversary evidently originates in a desire to give him the impression that the Christian absolute realizes the same sort of perfection as the progressivist and socialist absolute, and those very aspects—although essential—of the Christian absolute which clash with the opposing tendencies are disowned, with the result that nothing is left with which to counter those tendencies except a half-absolute devoid of all originality; for both attitudes are false: saying that one has never had anything in view except social progress, which is a ridiculous falsehood wholly unrelated to the Christian perspective, or accusing oneself—while vowing to do better in the future—of having neglected this social progress, which is a betrayal pure and simple; what ought to be done is to put each thing in its place and insist at every turn on what man, life, the world, and society are from the religious

[4] And let us add in this regard that a Church which is not "triumphalist" is not a Church, any more than a dogma which is not "thunderous" is a dogma.

point of view. Christianity is an eschatological perspective, either considering things in relation to the hereafter or not considering them at all; to pretend to adopt some other way of looking at things—or to adopt it in fact—while remaining within religion is incomprehensible and disastrous nonsense. The timeliness of monasticism is that it incarnates—whether one likes it or not—precisely the sort of thing which is extreme and absolute in religion and which is of a spiritual and contemplative essence; earthly charity has no meaning save in connection with heavenly charity. "Seek ye first the kingdom of God, and his righteousness."

It is evident and inevitable that religion can and sometimes must adapt itself to new circumstances; but care must be taken not to decide *a priori* in favor of circumstances and not to look upon them as norms simply because they exist and please a majority. In proceeding to an adaptation it is important to adhere strictly to the religious perspective and the hierarchy of values it implies; inspiration must be sought on the basis of a metaphysical and spiritual criteriology, and one must not yield to pressures or allow oneself to be contaminated by a false evaluation of things. Do we not hear of a "religion orientated toward the social", which is either a pleonasm or else an absurdity, and even of a "spirituality of economic development", which—apart from its monstrosity—is a contradiction in terms? According to this way of thinking, error or sin need no longer be subordinated to the imperatives of truth and spirituality; on the contrary it is truth and spirituality that must be adapted to error and sin; and it is the opinion of the adversary that is the criterion of truth and falsehood, of good and evil.

* * *

But let us return for a moment to the modern scientific outlook since it plays so decisive a role in the contemporary mentality; we see absolutely no reason for swooning over space flights; the saints in their ecstasies climb infinitely higher, and we do not say this in an allegorical vein, but in a perfectly concrete sense that could be called "scientific" or "exact". In vain does modern science explore the infinitely distant and the infinitely small; in its own way it can reach the world of galaxies and that of molecules, but since it believes neither in Revelation nor in pure intellection, it is unaware of all the immaterial and supra-sensory worlds which envelop as it were our sensory dimension and in relation to which our dimension is no more than a sort of fragile coagulation, destined to vanish at its appointed time before the dazzling power of Divine Reality. Now to postulate a science without a metaphysics is a flagrant contradiction, for without metaphysics there can be neither standards nor criteria, no intelligence that penetrates, contemplates, and coordinates. Both relativistic psychologism, which knows nothing of the absolute, and evolutionism—which is absurd because contradictory, since the greater cannot come from the less—can be explained only by this exclusion of what is essential and total in intelligence.

In times past it was the object that was sometimes doubted, including the object that can be found in ourselves—an "object" being anything which the subject can be conscious of distinctively and separatively, be it a moral defect in the subject—but in our day no one fears the contradiction of doubting the knowing subject in what he is in his intrinsic and irreplaceable self; intelligence as such is called into question, even "examined", without anyone wondering "who" examines it—is there not talk about producing a more perfect man?—and without noticing that philosophic doubt is included in this same devaluation, that it falls with the fall of intelligence, and that at the same stroke all science and philosophy collapse. For if our intelligence is by definition ineffectual, if we are irresponsible or lumps of earth, philosophy is useless.

What we are being pressed to admit is that our spirit is relative in its very essence, that this essence contains no stable standard of measurement—as if the sufficient reason of the human intellect were not precisely that it should comprise such standards!—and that the ideas of the true and the false are therefore intrinsically relative, hence always vacillating; and since certain consequences of accumulated errors conflict with our innate standards and are unmasked and condemned by them, we are told that it is a question of habit and that we must change our nature, namely that we must create a new intelligence which finds beautiful what is ugly and accepts as true what is false. The devil is essentially incapable of recognizing that he is wrong unless such an admission is in his interest; it is thus error become habitual that must be right at all costs, even at the cost of our intelligence and in the final analysis of our existence; as for the nature of things and our faculty of adequation, this is all "prejudice".

It has been said and said again that monasticism in all its forms, whether Christian or Buddhist, is a manifestation of "pessimism"; thus through either convenience or carelessness, the intellectual and realistic aspect of the question is evaded and objective observations, metaphysical ideas, and logical conclusions are reduced to purely sentimental attitudes. A man who knows that an avalanche is an avalanche is accused of "pessimism", and one who thinks it is a mist is an "optimist"; to think serenely of death while scorning distractions is to see the world in dark colors, but to think of death with repugnance, or to avoid thinking of it at all, while finding all the happiness of which one is capable in passing things is "courage", it seems, and evinces a "sense of responsibility". We have never understood why those who put their hope in God, while having enough discernment to be able to read the "signs of the times", are accused of bitterness whereas others are credited with strong and cheerful natures because they mistake mirages for realities; and it is almost incredible that this false optimism, which is completely opposed to the Scriptures on the one hand and to the most tangible of criteria on the other, should win over men who profess to believe in God and the future life.

*   *   *

We now wish to describe in a certain way—though there would be a thousand other ways of doing so—how a man who has attached himself to God is spiritually situated in existence or how he takes his stand when faced with the dizzying abyss that is the world. The condition of the monk—for he is the main subject of our interest here, though the same considerations could be applied to contemplatives in general—constitutes a victory over space and time, or over the world and life, in the sense that he places himself by his attitude at the center and in the present: at the center in relation to a world full of phenomena and in the present in relation to a life full of events. Concentration of prayer and rhythm of prayer: these are in a certain sense the two dimensions of spiritual existence in general and monastic existence in particular. The monk withdraws from the world, fixing himself in a definite place—a place that is center because it is consecrated to God—and morally he closes his eyes and remains where he is, awaiting death like a statue set in a niche, as Saint Francis of Sales says; by this "concentration" the monk places himself beneath the divine axis, already partaking of Heaven by attaching himself concretely to God. In so doing the contemplative also withdraws from duration, for through prayer—that permanent actualization of consciousness of the Absolute—he is situated in a timeless instant: prayer—or the remembrance of God—is now and always, being "always now" and already belonging to Eternity. The life of the monk, by the elimination of disordered movements, is a rhythm; now rhythm is thc fixation of an instant—or the present—in duration just as immobility is the fixation of a point—or the center—in space; this symbolism, founded as it is on the law of analogy, becomes concrete by virtue of a consecration to God. Thus it is that the monk holds the world in his hands and dominates life as well: for there is nothing precious in the world which we do not possess even here, provided that this point where we are belongs to God and that, being here for God, we belong to Him; and in the same way, all our life is in that instant in which we choose God and not vanities.

In the temporal dimension that stretches ahead of us there are only three certainties: death, Judgment, and eternal Life. We have no power over the past, and we do not know the future; as far as the future is concerned we have only these three certainties, but we possess a fourth in this very moment, and it is everything: it is that of our actuality, our present freedom to choose God and thus to choose our whole destiny. In this instant, this present, we hold our whole life, our whole existence: all is good if this instant is good and if we know how to place our life within this blessed instant; the whole secret of spiritual faithfulness lies in dwelling in this instant, in renewing and perpetuating it by prayer, in holding on to it by means of spiritual rhythm, in enclosing completely within it the time that floods over us and threatens to drag us far away from this "divine moment". The vocation of the monk is perpetual prayer, not because life is long, but because it is only a moment; the perpetuity—or the rhythm—of the orison demonstrates that life is merely an ever-present instant, just as spatial fixation in a consecrated place demonstrates that the world is merely a point, a point however which belongs to God and is therefore everywhere and excludes no felicity.

This condensation of the existential dimensions—insofar as they are indefinite and arbitrary—into a blessed unity is at the same time what constitutes the essence of man; the rest is contingency and accident. This is a truth that concerns every human being; thus the monk is not a being apart, but simply a prototype or model, or a spiritual diagram, a point of reference: every man—because he is a man—should realize in one way or another this victory over the world which disperses and life which enslaves. Too many people think that they do not have time to pray, but this is an illusion that results from indifference, which—according to Fénelon—is the worst ailment of the soul; for the numerous moments we fill with our habitual dreams, including our all too often useless reflections, we take away from God and ourselves.

The great mission of monasticism is to show the world that happiness does not lie somewhere far away or in something located outside ourselves, in a treasure to be sought or in a world to be built, but precisely here where we belong to God. The monk represents, in the face of a dehumanized world, what our true standards are; his mission is to remind men what man is.

Translated by Mark Perry

The Transcendent Unity of Religions and Spiritual Practice

Charles Upton

The Transcendent Unity of Religions is not simply a doctrine; it is also a practice. It is important to understand this, since if our relationship to it remains limited to doctrine, it will sink to the level of abstraction, and lose its transcendent dimension. It will become mere exoteric ecumenism, or comparative religion, or a purely mental search for the metaphysical principles common to all traditions.

Frithjof Schuon and other Traditionalists usually explain the Transcendent Unity of Religions by means of what I call "the Traditionalist Spiderweb"—a symbol which is also found, for example, in Plotinus. As a young man, Schuon encountered, in his home town of Basle, Switzerland, a venerable Black marabout who was visiting from Senegal. During their talk, the old man drew a circle on the ground with radii connecting the circumference with the center. "God is the center," he said; "all paths lead to Him." This may have been the genesis of the Spiderweb in Schuon's mind; the full symbol, however—in both Schuon and Plotinus—includes a number of concentric circles which represent different planes of reality, different levels on "the Great Chain of Being." The circles, like those in the *Divine Comedy*, indicate the relative nearness or distance of a plane of Being from its central Principle, whereas the radii indicate incomparable quiddities ("whatnesses") which are precisely themselves and nothing else, irrespective of the level of Being on which they appear, just as the scent of a rose is precisely that scent and no other, whether we are catching only the faintest hint of it on the wind, or bathing in a pool full of rosewater. In Aristotelian terms, the radii symbolize *essence* and the concentric circles *existence*; the points where circle and radius intersect represent actual existing things, where essence ("whatness") and existence ("isness") are concretely united. A rock, for example, cannot be a rock if it lacks either the quality of rock-likeness, or the quality of really being there. In actual existing things—rocks, galaxies, human beings, spirits, angels—essence and existence are united only relatively, since it is possible to distinguish one radius or one concentric circle from another. Only in the Center, only in God Himself are essence and existence absolutely united, as in God's name "I Am That I Am," revealed to Moses in Genesis. To say "I Am That I Am" is the same thing as saying "*What* I am is none other than *the fact* that I am; as God, it is My unique and special Essence, shared by no other, to be Pure Being."

In terms of the Transcendent Unity of Religions, each radius is a single integral and revealed religious tradition. The fact that it radiates from the Center indicates that it has been revealed by God; the fact that all radii meet *only at the center* indicates that the unity of religions is not ecumenical ("worldly"), but transcendent. Religions come together, in other words, not by virtue of their relative comparability, but on the ground of their incomparable uniqueness. The field of comparative religion, the level on which we can say "Islam is like Christianity in this way but unlike in that; Hinduism is like Buddhism, or Islam, or Christianity, in these ways but unlike in those" is not that of the Transcendent Unity of Religions.

The Traditionalist Spiderweb can also be seen as a kind of "Traditionalist Stonehenge," a circle of separate and discrete doorways, each of which gives a unique view of the same Center, where, let us say, a great Light shines. It is only possible to look through one doorway at a single time. I can look sideways from my Muslim doorway, and see my wife Jenny kneeling in the light streaming through her Christian doorway, but that light will always be, for me, a reflected light. For her, Jesus is the Christ, the only-begotten Son of God. For me, as a Muslim, he is a great prophet, the Spirit and Word or God, born of a virgin and destined to return at the end of the age to slay the Antichrist; but he is not the Son of God, since according to the Koran, "He [Allah] neither begets nor is He begotten." So do we then disagree about the nature of Jesus? If we spent our time looking "sideways" in religion, we would have to disagree. Jesus would have to be either a great prophet, or the Son of God; he could not be both. But the essence of religion, which is the spiritual Path, does not move sideways. It travels only from whatever place on the circumference of our circle we happen to find ourselves, according to the imponderables of race, culture, religion, place of birth, individual psychology and personal destiny, and straight toward the Center, toward the One God. And that God is so great, so embracing of all conceptions of Him, and at the same time so fundamentally independent of all conceptions of Him, that every view of Him, if it is indeed directed toward the Center along an unbroken ray emanating from that Center, produces a unique and incomparable vision of God's Reality which, far from being relative to other views, is blessed and confirmed by the Absolute, and partakes of its nature; this is Schuon's doctrine of the "relatively Absolute." Each view of God—whether it be that of a revealed religion, or of an individual within that religion, or of a moment within the life of that individual—is unique and incomparable, since it is a vision of God the Incomparable, God the Unique. While I am contemplating that God, I have neither the time nor the perspective to compare my doctrine with that of another; while I am comparing and contrasting doctrine, I am not contemplating God.

God, however, is not only incomparable, for which read "transcendent"; He is also comparable, for which read "immanent." If God were not absolutely beyond all conception, He would not be Unique. He would be comparable, relative, able to be defined by something other or less than Him, and therefore not God. But if God were not also in a sense comparable to created things, we could form no conception of Him, and thus have no way to know Him. And since created things, in essence, are nothing else than conceptions of Him, symbolic manifestations of His Attributes, or Energies, or Names, then if God were incomparable while not at the same time having an aspect of comparability, there would be no universe. So once we understand God's Uniqueness, we can also understand how all created things are unique in themselves precisely because they reflect that Uniqueness. Furthermore, if we have the power to see things as they are in themselves, we also have the secondary power to compare them not with their common Source, but with each other, to see how they are alike in some ways and different in others. Here, however, is where we must heed Shakespeare's warning that "comparisons are odious." The power to compare existing things with each other rather than with their transcendent Source is the origin of abstraction—and the danger of abstraction, immensely convenient though it is, and even necessary to our lives according to the way the human mind works, is that we may begin to think that the abstract category is the origin of the unique particulars which comprise it, rather than the other way around. The nation, in a sense, produces the citizen; but it is much truer to say, and in line with a higher order of reality, that the citizen—or rather the human being, who is much more than his or her mere citizenship—produces the nation.

As we move away from the center of the Spiderweb, the tendency toward abstraction increases. Essences, symbolized by the radii, are still absolutely unique; but this truth becomes obscured as we move down through the concentric circles, toward lower levels of being. Higher levels of being reveal the uniqueness of the essences; lower levels obscure it. Consequently, on the material or socio-historical level of being, abstraction begins to confuse individuals, and cultures, and religions. A religion, on this level, is primarily defined by how it is like others or different from them. A culture becomes a set of quantitative parameters, a population, a mass of resources, a collection of laws and institutions, a gross national product. An individual becomes a statistical monad, fodder for the actuarial tables of an insurance company, a cipher. In Guénon's terms, motion toward the Center is toward Essence, or quality; motion toward the periphery is toward Substance, or quantity. (Substance as opposed to Essence, that is, not as opposed to the "accidents"; the philosophical term "Substance"—*ousia*—vis-à-vis its accidents, itself begins to take on the meaning of "Essence," whereas Guénon is using "Substance" more as synonymous with the Aristotelian/Thomistic *materia*, as opposed to *forma* which is nearly synonymous with "Essence.")

The Platonic Ideas or Names of God are often thought of as abstract categories, partly due to the fact that, on the plane of language, the most particular images are necessarily the most sensual. Language anchors our sense of the particular to the sensual level; the words we must use for higher-than-sensual realities become more and more abstract as we ascend the Great Chain of Being. This, however, is not true of the realities themselves: a Platonic Idea is not an abstract category, in other words, but *a higher level of particularity*. Many men may be the origin of the abstract category "man," but the *concrete Idea* "Man" is the origin and creator of many men. A Platonic Idea is not the abstract lowest common denominator of many particulars, but the concrete "highest common denominator" of the individuals which compose it, who, in relation to it, are relative abstractions. The Platonic Idea "Man" does not contain only whatever is common to all human beings—which, because there are two sexes, would have to exclude genital organs, as it would exclude arms, legs and eyes as well because there are also amputees and eyeless persons, and so on—but rather everything that "Man" in all his variations could ever manifest, and all this in a single form. This is why, among other things, the original human form in Plato's *Timaeus* is an androgyne, and also a sphere: the spherical form represents in this case the simultaneous and synthetic realization of all human possibilities. And because Ideas are not pale abstractions but higher orders of particularity, realities which are *more concrete* than matter, not less, the Persian mystical philosophers, such as Suhrawardi—in line with their Jewish, Christian and Zoroastrian brethren—were led to a vision of the Platonic Ideas as vast, powerful and conscious beings: in other words, as *angels*. According to Judeo-Christian angelology, for example, the archangel Michael is not an abstract symbol of spiritual warfare; he is a individual, conscious being of vast wisdom and power who is the commanding general of this warfare—not because of *what* he is but because of *who* he is. Nonetheless, he remains the very essence and Idea of spiritual warfare, "incarnate" on the archangelic plane. There is ultimately no contradiction between the personal and the archetypal orders of reality, since both are attempts to express the quality of essences, and essences are incomparable; they are incapable of being fully defined in terms other than themselves.

(I said above that the words we use to describe higher-than-sensual realities—realities more concrete than sense experience—must become increasingly abstract to the degree that their objects become more and more concrete. The exception to this is when we use words not as *descriptions* but as *names*. "Spiritual warfare" is an abstract concept; "Holy Michael" is a concrete person. Consequently, the most concrete and reality-charged words in existence are the Names of God, which are used in various traditions to invoke—in other words, to recognize—His presence. His Names are not primarily our descriptions of Him, but rather His acts of Self-manifestation to us.)

Abstraction, however, has an "ascending" function as well, by which it too can serve the vision of the Transcendent Unity of Religions. Comparative religion, if pursued thoroughly and in depth, reveals two things: 1) That the doctrines of the different religions all draw closer to each other as the esoteric centers of these religions are approached, and 2) that perfect unanimity, on the level of doctrine, is never in fact achieved. The Muslim Sufi Ibn al-'Arabi and the Christian sage Meister Eckhart are much closer to one another than, say, the doctrines of the Church Councils within Christianity and the *ulema* within Islam; nonetheless, Eckhart remains thoroughly Christian, Ibn al-'Arabi quintessentially Muslim. Comparative religion serves the vision of religions in their Transcendent Unity not by positing a "horizontal" universalism by which the doctrines of the various revealed religions are mixed together until they lose all character, but by "triangulating," so to speak, a common point of Origin—an act which requires, geometrically, at least two entirely unique and separate points-of-view. The fact that the doctrines of all religions become more and more alike as their respective esoteric centers are approached proves that this Origin is really there, and has a real character. The fact that the doctrines of the religions, while they draw ever closer together, never actually meet this side of the Absolute, proves that this Origin is truly transcendent, and entirely beyond conception. The Word, the Divine Logos, is One; it is nonetheless the first principle of creation and division. The Paths only meet in the virginal and maternal Silence before, and out of whom, the Word is spoken.

The Transcendent Unity of Religions is not simply a doctrine, as I have said; it is also a practice. And if the practice is not kept fresh, the doctrine degenerates. I have heard traditionalist Martin Lings, in a taped lecture, floundering before an audience of religious exoterists, unable to counter the assertion that "According to the logical principle of non-contradiction, Jesus Christ cannot both be and not be the unique incarnation of God; if Christianity, based on this belief, is true, then other religions, which deny it, must be false." Lings attempted to answer this objection to the Transcendent Unity of Religions by comparing Christ to the avatars of Vishnu, like Krishna, who made the same claim to Divinity as he did. But Christ is not one among the ten avatars of Vishnu; he is, from the Christian perspective, the sole avatar, the only-begotten Son of God. Only the understanding that every view of the Absolute has a dimension of incomparability, that is it blessed by the Absolute with God's own Absoluteness, and is thus "relatively Absolute," could have answered the questioner's objection—perhaps not to his satisfaction, but nonetheless to the full satisfaction of the Truth.

The doctrine of the Transcendent Unity of Religions calls up immense social and psychological forces, which act to drive a wedge between the term "transcendent" and the term "unity." Those who unconsciously begin to err in the direction of unity as opposed to transcendence will be impelled toward a horizontal universalism; this is Schuon's analysis, in his book *Spiritual Perspectives and Human Facts*, of the fate of the Ramakrishna Order under Vivekananda and his successors. Ramakrishna, as a saint of the highest degree, was able to see and embody the unity of religions from a transcendent perspective, one which did not destroy but rather fulfilled his quintessential Hinduism. The Ramakrishna Order, on the other hand—at least according to Schuon—began to depart from Orthodox Hinduism in the direction of a shallow universalism, a charge which has been leveled, ironically, at Schuon himself in terms of Islam. At the other extreme, those who, without realizing it, begin to err in the direction of transcendence as opposed to unity will come into the field where the inexpressible and Transcendent Absolute demands a form in the relative world through which it can be expressed, and will consequently be tempted to absolutize the essentially relative aspects of their religious tradition, seeing its absoluteness through the distorting lens of its relativity rather than through the open door of its transcendence; this is the idolatrous and literalistic shadow of Schuon's doctrine of the "relatively Absolute." Thus the Transcendent Unity of Religions, given the lateness of the times as well as the simple limitations of human nature, will inevitably generate its two "guardian beasts" rising up on both sides of its temple doorway to divert the course of all who cannot really understand it: To the left, the Gog of universalism; to the right, the Magog of exclusivism, whose socio-historical expressions are modernism or post-modernism on the one hand (the principle behind political and economic globalism) and reactionary fundamentalism on the other (the principle behind the "tribalist" reactions against globalist hegemony).

To practice the Transcendent Unity of Religions is to walk a razor's edge which passes through one of the most formidable of the metaphysical "pairs-of-opposites." It is immensely demanding, psychologically, philosophically and contemplatively, because the doctrine of Transcendent Unity ultimately emanates from what is perhaps the highest intelligible level of metaphysical principle. According to Schuon, God is both Absolute and Infinite. The absoluteness of God is the source of His transcendence, and the origin of the uniqueness of each God-given religious form. The infinity of God is the source of His immanence, the origin of the underlying unity of all true religions. These are the Shiva and Shakti of His Self-revelation in the religious sphere. To hold to God's absoluteness alone and reject His infinity is to fall into religious authoritarianism; to hold to His infinity and reject His absoluteness is to drift into religious promiscuity.

In concrete terms, the practice of the Transcendent Unity of Religions comes down to six different kinds of hard work: First, to accept one of the revealed religions and remain faithful to it, both in terms of outer practice and of inner truth. Second, to view from the vantage point of one's inherited or adopted religion the vistas of Truth provided by the other religions, and intuit their intrinsic unity. Third, whenever one finds oneself strictly identifying one's religious form with God in such a way as one is actually worshipping the form instead of the Deity, to stop, and remember God. Fourth, whenever one finds oneself looking sideways at other religions, pridefully or anxiously wondering whether those forms are better or worse than one's own, to stop, and remember God. Fifth, whenever one's "monkey-mind" begins to stitch together a patchwork idol made up from fragments of many religious traditions, to stop, and remember God. Sixth, whenever one finds oneself taking spiritual pride in one's understanding of abstract metaphysical principles, looking down from this false elevation on the revealed traditions as backwaters of literal-mindedness, provincial superstition and mere humanity, to stop, and remember God.

Loyalty to a single religion, *after* one has already realized that other religions are God-given and efficacious, is like loyalty to one's spouse. My wife is my beloved, my one and only, not because she is better than all other women according to this or that set of criteria, but because she is incomparable. And I don't have to denigrate other women to prove it: "comparisons are odious." She is my "best" not because she is better than other women, but because, freely chosen, she is God's gift to me alone. If other men love their wives, should this lead me to question whether I should love my own? If she is insulted I will defend her, but I will not insult other men's wives out of some misguided sense that I am thereby doing her honor.

It is the same with religion. A person's religion is the spouse of that person's Spirit, just as someone's husband or wife is the spouse of that person's body and soul. And where true love is, comparison cannot enter. In the words of the Bengali poet Vidyapati, speaking as Radha, Krishna's beloved (from *In Praise of Krishna: Songs from the Bengali*, translated by Edward C.

Dimock and Denise Levertov),

> as wing to bird
> water to fish,
> life to the living—
> so you to me.
> But tell me,
> Madhava, beloved
> who are you?
> Who are you really?
>
> *Vidyapati says, they are one another.*

Addendum

Whatever its *academic* usefulness, the only legitimate *spiritual* use of comparative religion is to employ one's understanding of other religions to throw greater light on certain aspects of one's own—aspects which, while truly and integrally a part of that religion, have been de-emphasized due either to the vicissitudes of history or the necessity of placing greater emphasis on what, for that religion, are the central "constituting" factors. Each revealed religion has all that is necessary for salvation, if not ultimate Liberation—and yet, for example, one may have difficulty in tapping the full potential the *hadith* of the Prophet Muhammad, peace and blessings be upon him, which directs Muslims to "pray to God as if you saw Him; because even if you don't see Him, he sees you," as well as the Qur'anic passage *I will show them My signs on the horizons and in their own souls until they are satisfied that this is the Truth. Is it not enough for you that I am Witness over all things?*—not to mention St. Paul's assertion that "I live, and yet not I, but Christ lives in me"—without an understanding of the Vedantic idea of the *atman*, of God as the Indwelling Absolute Witness, Who alone—as with Yah-weh at the burning bush—has the right to say " I Am." The Vedanta knows the *atman* as "the all-seeing Eye which cannot see itself (as a separate object)," the Absolute Subject before which all else is objectified, including the body, speech and mind of you or me, to the degree that—as Frithjof Schuon points out in *Survey of Metaphysics and Esoterism* and elsewhere—what was once "me" (my entire psycho-physical being) is now "he," while what was once "He" (the Transcendent God) is now "I."

If religions are no more than "belief-systems," then the differences in emphasis and nuance between their various doctrines must be taken as paramount; human beliefs about God, not God Himself, will then be the only legitimate objects of study. But if God is Real, then He really IS (among other things) the Absolute Witness, whether or not the practitioners of a given religion, by and large, understand this truth. However, if every revealed religion is a true perspective upon God that has in fact been established by God, then somewhere within each of them, whether openly emphasized or esoterically hidden, this truth—and many others like it—must exist, waiting to be put to effective use by those whose spiritual destiny requires them to know and use it. Other religions may provide keys to deeper understanding, but the treasure chest these keys sometimes have the power to open must be legitimately our own, seeing that we have neither the ability nor the right to fully actualize any spiritual potential other than our own. "Enter houses by their doors" said the Prophet Muhammad, peace and blessings be upon him. We are not expected to act as pirates, gathering spiritual plunder wherever we may find it, but rather to recognize ourselves as potential heirs; the treasure we seek, and the only one we have the right to unearth, is buried in our own back yard.

The One and Only True Path

Timothy Scott

Seek ye wisdom, even if it be in China!

Hadīth

There are as many paths towards God as there are human souls.

Sufi adage

Hear, O Israel: the Lord our God is one Lord.

Shema

If the idea of "crossing religious frontiers" is to mean more than some kind of well-meaning but superficial "tolerance," or merely an invitation to "spiritual tourism," then we need to find a common ground on which authentic dialogue may take place. It is only at a level that transcends accidental forms or expressions that commonalities can safely be said to be more than similarities. It is just such a common ground that Frithjof Schuon had in mind when he spoke of the "transcendent unity of religion." Put simply, the various religions each refer to the one and unique Divine Object through their diverse and subjective modes of contemplation and expression. The diverse expressions and dogmas are absolutely true, not because they reduce the Absolute to a given relative aspect of the Real, but because they reveal the Absolute Truth in subjective mode. In the language of Sufism the Transcendent Unity (*al-Aḥadiyah*) is said to be beyond all distinctive knowledge; however, the Divine Unicity (*al-Wāḥidiyah*) appears in the differentiated just as principial distinctions appear in it. To talk of Unicity is to talk of the archetypal realm, wherein reside the unique realities, or essences, which universally inform the various expressions of the religions. The archetypal realm is thus the true common ground of the diverse religions. Unicity is a long way from the mere appearance of similarity between individual forms.

The "transcendent unity of religion" is also referred to as the "underlying unity of religion," a phrase that has the virtue of describing the sense in which each religion is built upon a single "ground." Meister Eckhart describes this *Grund* as "the quiet desert, into which distinction never gazed . . . a simple silence, in itself immovable, and by this immovability all things are moved, all life is received by those who in themselves have rational being".[1] Schuon's phrase has the virtue of recognizing that this unformed ground is not ontologically "inferior"[2] to the formal manifestations it gives rise to, by dint of recognizing that this unity transcends the formal domain.

The metaphysical expression of the transcendent and underlying reality which unites all religions is found in the *sophia perennis*. This "eternal wisdom" is in turn the "Wisdom of the

[1] Meister Eckhart, Sermon 48, tr. E. Colledge, O.S.A. & B. McGinn, *Meister Eckhart: The Essential Sermons, Commentaries, Treatises, and Defense* (Ramsey, NJ: Paulist Press, 1981), p. 198.

[2] In the sense that one might be tempted to say that potentially is inferior to actuality—an unsatisfactory comparison; or, to highlight this more clearly, in the sense that a plan of a building might be considered inferior to the actual building.

Eternal." The value of engaging with this wisdom may be variously recognized: for the present let us consider three points of merit.

First, and by far foremost, is the merit of seeking to know the Eternal Truth. This seeking aims at the ultimate entelechy of the human state, that is, that one should know God and in knowing God that one should love God. Let it be said that an engagement with the *Sophia Perennis* (the use of the proper noun here is deliberate) in no way requires recourse to comparative recognition of other religions, nor for that matter does it require knowledge of other religions beyond one's own. The *Sophia Perennis* is true and accessible within each authentic religion according to the internal integrity of that religion. Moreover, it is a gross confusion to think that knowledge of the *sophia perennis* gained through practice of one's unique religion equates to formal knowledge of other religions. That is to say, and this seems obvious, one may climb to the summit of one's religion without being granted information about the paths which constitute the other religions.

The second merit arises from the therapeutic effect that an encounter with truth as expressed in another tradition can have upon that seeker who has become "blind" to truth within their own tradition. This blindness can arise because of various reasons, but the sad fact is that this is most often the numbing result of mundane familiarity. The recognition of *a* truth in a "foreign" religion can awaken and revivify the dormant understanding of an element of one's own religion, which is then more efficacious (than the foreign religion) in terms of one's journey precisely because of its familiarity.

The third merit of engaging with the *sophia perennis*—one that has great immediacy in this age of the meeting of religions—is that we may recognize the Truth in different forms; that is to say, that we may recognize God in our neighbor's belief and religion, and in recognizing and knowing God in our neighbor that we should love our neighbor as our self.

*   *   *

It is not uncommon to find those who confuse the idea of the *sophia perennis* with a program of syncretic and reductionistic comparative religion; that is to say, who mistake the *sophia perennis* for the recognition of external similarities between the religions. No doubt this type of comparative religion exists; this is particularly evident within academia. This type of comparative religion is least satisfactory where it becomes little more than the cataloguing of similarities—regardless of if they are accidental or essential—which are then explained away exclusively in terms of historical "borrowings."

The other error one encounters in understandings of the *sophia perennis* is that it somehow constitutes a formal "religion" in and of itself, above and beyond the recognized world religions: that it is a meta- or uber-religion. No doubt there have been some "practitioners" who have thought to privilege themselves above the "simply religious" by declaring themselves adherents of a "religion of the *sophia perennis*." In turn, it is a not an uncommon error among academics to imagine this to be the vision espoused by the likes of Schuon and René Guénon, who are commonly associated with the *sophia perennis*.[3] However, an informed reading of the so-called

[3] Schuon is accused of this pretence, albeit in my experience those who have made this criticism have been unfamiliar with his thought in general and his writings on this issue in particular. Moreover, there seems to be a tendency to confuse criticism of a particular person's application of an idea with the idea itself, so that these critics seem to think that if a Schuon had succumbed to the pretence of a meta-religion (which is far from saying that this

"perennialist" corpus reveals the warnings against imagining the *sophia perennis* to be a new religion and the emphasis placed upon the need to fully and authentically participate in an orthodox religious tradition.

To talk of full and authentic participation in an orthodox religious tradition is not necessarily the same as saying that one may not engage in a practice of another tradition, where one is able to recognize the essential truth of the practice and where the practice does not contradict the formal and theological strictures of one's own religion. Thus, for example, a Christian may practice *salāt*—considered in a general sense[4]—with a Muslim, for there is nothing contradictory for the Christian in offering prayer to the Greatness of God through prostration. However, a Muslim would no doubt find participation in the Christian Eucharist contradictory to their fundamental conception of Jesus. Of course these comments are offered as generalizations and it is theoretically possible that a Muslim such as Ibn al-'Arabī might have been able, within himself, to accept the Eucharist insomuch as he was able to recognize Jesus as the "Word of God, the Spirit of God, and the slave of God" saying that "such a manifestation in sensible form belongs to no other".[5] But here it is probably best to say that "God knows best."[6]

* * *

It may well be asked why one would engage in a practice from a "foreign" religion if the comprehensive integrity of one's own religion deemed this superfluous? In the first place, one might participate in the religious practice of another out of due respect for that individual or even out of respect for the culture that one might perchance find oneself in. The cynic may wish to dismiss this as simply a case of "manners"—as if having manners where not worthy of praise in and of itself! However, the high regard that proper manners, and in particular the practice of hospitality to strangers,[7] had (and has) in traditional cultures worldwide is rooted in more than a simple idea of social cohesion. Rather the various practices of manners find their meaning in the charitable recognition of the divine in the other. This is precisely "charitable" in the sense of the Christian *caritas*, the love of all others held to be the ultimate perfection of the human spirit, glorifying and reflecting the nature of God. The self-sacrificial nature of *caritas* means that one may generously share in the experience of a neighbor's religious practice, and this regardless of the question of discrimination, for the higher virtue is not that one might be

was in fact the case!) that this *ipso facto* discredits the idea of the *sophia perennis* as such.

4 In a more specific sense we may find the Christian baulk at the recognition of Muhammad as "the Prophet of God"; nevertheless, Christianity *does* recognise other prophets, and there are Christians who reconcile Muhammad in this sense.

5 Ibn al-'Arabī, *Fusus*: "Chapter on Jesus," tr. R. Austin (Mahwah: Paulist Press, 1980), p. 178.

6 The cynic will no doubt see in this saying, so popular in Islam and rooted in the Qur'an (6:124; 11:33), an attempt to "avoid the question"; however, far from this I here intend precision. Let me be clear: the situation we are considering is possible, precisely because it is a spiritual possibility and in God "all things are possible"; the legitimacy of such a particular case may only be judged according to the understanding and sincerity of the individual's heart, and this only God knows (Qur'an 27:67).

7 In the Judaic tradition Abraham's entertainment of the three strangers at the Oak of Mamre is the epitome of hospitality (Genesis 8:1-8); Noah is also recognised for his charitable acts on the Ark (*Midrash Tanchuma*, Genesis 8:16); hospitality is also a key element of Arabic *adab* (etiquette). It is worth mentioning that this is an important theme in the *Odyssey*, and that Zeus was not only the head of the Greek pantheon but also the "protector of wayfarers."

able to pass judgment on one's neighbor's practice (correct or otherwise),[8] but that one may recognize God in their intention and love, and honor both one's neighbor and God in this. Thus respect and manners are elevated to the level of the knowledge of the divine Unity.[9]

A second possibility arises from the "vagaries" of the individual's natural disposition. Each religion is comprised of essential and accidental elements. The essential elements provide the means to Realization and Union with the Divine, which are the *raison d'être* of the religion; they also define the religion by excluding other formal possibilities.[10] The accidental elements act as supports, so to speak, and are contingent upon the disposition and need of the individual. Thus, to consider the Abrahamic religions: it is essential for the Jew to profess the *Shema*, the Christian to profess Jesus Christ and the Muslim to profess the *Shahadah*. It is accidental that an individual of any of these religions might find spiritual support in, for example, the poverty and silence of asceticism, or the reflective practice of meditation, or the hieratic beauty and awe of sacred art, or the symbolism and anagogic power of ritual. Thus, with respect to the individual, one may, for example, be a Christian in terms of essential belief and practice, who, according to natural disposition, is supported in one's "sense of the sacred" by the beauty of religious art and even art that is not culturally Christian.

This raises the specter of idolatry, particularly in light of the fourth commandment. However, here we must distinguish between idolatry and the intellectual and transformative participation with beauty that is rightly anagogic. As Ananda Coomaraswamy observes, "seeing that God alone is truly beautiful, and all other beauty is by participation, it is only a work of art that has been wrought, in its kind (*idea*) and its significance (*dynamis*), after an eternal model, that can be called beautiful."[11] Coomaraswamy highlights the following insight from Dionysius the Areopagite, which is fundamental in its influence on the Mediaeval theory of Beauty: "The beautiful and beauty are indivisible in their cause, which embraces All in One."[12] The Areopagite also says: "The Beautiful is therefore the same as the Good, for everything looks to the Beautiful and the Good as the cause of being, and there is nothing in the world without a share of the Beautiful and the Good."[13] Therefore, according to one's aesthetic intuition and natural disposition towards supra-formal Beauty, one may find in the art or ritual of a foreign religion support for spiritual contemplation. Here it is important to remark that this is not to be confused with profane aestheticism. As Schuon remarks, "sacred art ignores the aesthetic aim;

[8] Of course as St. Augustine says, "Charity is no substitute for justice withheld," and there is great virtue in remedying error; still, what I have in mind here is a matter of submission to right intention.

[9] Titus Burckhardt: "Charity is to recognize the eternal Word in creatures" (*Études Traditionnelles*, 1953, p. 174); Schuon: "Love of one's neighbor receives all its meaning through the love of God" (*Esoterism as Principle and Way* [Middlesex: Perrennial Books, 1981], p. 153).

[10] Schuon: "A religion is a form, and so also a limit, which 'contains' the Limitless, to speak in paradox; every form is fragmentary because of the necessary formal exclusion of other possibilities; the fact that these forms . . . each in their own way represent totality does not prevent them from being fragmentary in respect of their particularization and reciprocal exclusion" (*Understanding Islam* [London: Allen & Unwin, 1976], p. 144).

[11] A. Coomaraswamy, "A Figure of Speech, or a Figure of Thought?" in *Figures of Speech, or Figures of Thought? The Traditional View of Art*, ed. W. Wroth (Bloomington, Indiana: World Wisdom, 2007), p. 12. Coomaraswamy in turn cites Plato, *Timaeus* 28 AB. See also "The Mediaeval Theory of Art" and "Imitation, Expression, and Participation," both in this edition.

[12] *De divinis nominibus* 4.5 (701C). Colin Luibheid's translation has: "But do not make a distinction between 'beautiful' and 'beauty' as applied to the Cause which gathers all into one" (Mahwah: Paulist Press, 1987, p. 76).

[13] *De divinis nominibus* 4.5 (704B), tr. Luibheid.

its beauty arises above all from its spiritual truth and so from the exactitude of its symbolism and from its usefulness for purposes of ritual and contemplation, and only secondarily from the imponderables of personal intuition".[14] This talk of "exactitude of symbolism" and ritual "usefulness" does not necessarily entail conceptual knowledge. As Schuon said of himself, "For me visual assimilation came before conceptual assimilation."[15] The disposition towards the sacred art of "foreign" religions, which may included dress, ritual and other forms, is thus not only acceptable but may even be profitable in terms of establishing an ambience of interiorizing beauty complementary to the "imponderables of personal intuition."

A third reason why one might engage in a practice from a "foreign" religion resides in the profound recognition of the essential unity of forms. Thus, having been granted such a realization, the person engages in the various practices not for the consequence that they can bring about—which that person has already attained—but for the glory of God which resides in each form, and simultaneously as a means to praise Diversity in its totality, which is an image of the Divine Infinitude. This is to say that such a person (and we are talking of a exception to the norm) would engage wholeheartedly in the religion of their calling as a way to and a means of glorifying the Divine Unity, while concurrently declaring and participating in (where the opportunity occasioned) "foreign" religious practices as a glorification of the Absolute as Infinite.

* * *

In all this we are considering the question in the abstract; that is to say, we are considering *possibilities* that are inherent in the human condition, privileged, as it is in all traditions, by the capacity to know God both as Object and Subject. But considering "universalist" possibilities is far from advocating universalism as the norm or, for that matter, proposing universalism as a spiritual method.

From the perspective of the formal integrity of a particular religion the real issue might be summed up by the question: Are we to have orthodoxy? Undoubtedly we must. Yet this demands that we understand the meaning of "orthodoxy" beyond the mere idea of conventional or institutional "tradition." The adherent of a religion turns to orthodoxy as the arbiter of truth without necessarily questioning the criteria by which such and such a belief has been deemed orthodox.[16] Here we must recognize that institutional "orthodoxy" is proclaimed by humans, and that this allows for idiosyncrasies that are not necessarily coherent with Truth, according to the understanding and motivation of the individuals involved. Such transgressions aside, orthodoxy is founded on two essential principles which can appear contradictory but which never are: Revelation and Truth. Truth is synonymous with the *Sophia Perennis.* Again, Guénon observes that the "necessary and sufficient condition" of orthodoxy is the "concordance of a conception with the fundamental principle of the tradition".[17] This "principle" is none other

[14] F. Schuon, "Principles and Criteria of Art" in *Language of the Self* (Bloomington, Indiana: World Wisdom Books, 1999), pp. 80-81.

[15] Letter to Marco Pallis, June 8, 1982.

[16] Putting aside the question of *sola scriptura* as this pertains to certain evangelical movements, which nevertheless take scripture as orthodoxy. The issue of orthodoxy and movements such as Pentecostalism and the neocharismatics raises questions that go beyond our general considerations.

[17] Guénon, *Man and His Becoming According to the Vedanta* (New Delhi: Oriental Books Reprint, 1981), p. 15.

than the *Sophia Perennis*, as expressed by the particular Revelation.

The purpose of each orthodox revelation is the soteriological—or liberating—communication of Truth. Here Schuon remarks:

> Seeing that there is but one truth, must we not conclude that there is but one Revelation, one sole Tradition possible? To this our answer is, first of all, that Truth and Revelation are not absolutely equivalent terms, since Truth is situated beyond forms, whereas revelation, or the Tradition which derives from it, belongs to the formal order, and that indeed by definition; but to speak of form is to speak of diversity, and so of plurality; the grounds for the existence and nature of form are expression, limitation, differentiation. What enters into form thereby enters also into number, hence into repetition and diversity; the formal principle—inspired by the infinity of the divine Possibility—confers diversity on this repetition.[18]

Diversity is a metaphysical necessity of Creation; diversity of revelation is God's merciful recognition of man's remoteness, separation and isolation.

The idea of the diversity of religions can appear to be irreconcilable with the dogmatic nature of orthodoxy. For Schuon the resolution is found in understanding the purpose of dogma:

> Intrinsically "orthodox" dogmas, that is, those disposed in view of salvation, differ from one religion to another; consequently they cannot all be objectively true. However, all dogmas are symbolically true and subjectively efficacious, which is to say that their purpose is to create human attitudes that contribute in their way to the divine miracle of salvation.[19]

The diversity of religions "far from proving the falseness of all the doctrines concerning the supernatural, shows on the contrary the supra-formal character of revelation and the formal character of the ordinary human understanding: the essences of revelation—or enlightenment—is one, but human nature requires diversity."[20] Elsewhere Schuon remarks that "what determines the difference among forms of Truth is the difference among human receptacles."[21] Coomaraswamy recalls the following Indian saying, "He takes the forms that are imagined by His worshippers."[22] This recalls Abu 'l-Qasim al-Junayd's famous saying, "The color of the water is the color of the vessel containing it."[23] Ibn al-'Arabī recognizes two kinds of religion, "the religion of God and those whom God has taught His religion and those whom they have

[18] Schuon, *Gnosis: Divine Wisdom* (Middlesex: Perennial Books, 1990), p. 25. Again, Meister Eckhart: ". . . everything that falls away from the One, the First of all things, immediately falls into two and into the other numbers by means of duality" (*Commentary on Genesis*, prop. 26).

[19] Schuon, *In The Face of the Absolute* (Bloomington: World Wisdom Books, 1989), p. 110.

[20] Schuon, "No Activity Without Truth," in J. Needleman ed., *The Sword of Gnosis* (Baltimore: Penguin, 1974), p. 4.

[21] Schuon, *Gnosis: Divine Wisdom*, p. 25.

[22] As per A. Coomaraswamy, "Sri Ramakrishna and Religious Tolerance" in *Selected Papers, Vol. 2: Metaphysics*, R. Lipsey ed. (New Jersey: Princeton University Press, 1977), p. 36. [Editor's note: this article is also contained in this issue of *Studies in Comparative Religion*.]

[23] Cited in R. A. Nicholson, *Studies in Islamic Mysticism* (London: Cambridge University Press, 1921), p. 159.

taught and, second, the religion of created beings, which God acknowledges."[24] He continues to declare that "It is the servant who establishes the practice of the religion and God Who determines its nature, for submission is your action and the religion is from your act, since your being blessed may be only through that which is from you yourself. . . . All religion is for God, from you not Him, except as being your Origin."

Religion is from the human insomuch as it manifests the latent essences of the individual necessary for the miracle of salvation. At the same time Revelation precedes human diversity, insomuch as Revelation is identified with the cosmogonic Word. Hence, the diverse human collectivities manifest the principial possibility of diversity prefigured *in divinis* by the differentiation between the "Absolute as such and the Absolute relativized in view of a dimension of its Infinitude".[25] This manifestation is necessitated precisely by the Divine will to reveal Itself, which is to say, by Revelation *per se*. The apparent reversal of this relationship at the terrestrial level accords perfectly with the "law of inverse analogy."

God accepts the limitations of diverse forms as a Mercy granted to the diversity of human receptacles. Nevertheless this limitation is only contingent and God, as He is in Himself, remains unlimited. As Coomaraswamy remarks, "Very surely He is not to be thought of as confined by or fully expressed by any of these forms, Who is Himself the single form or every form, and transcendent with respect to each and every form."[26]

* * *

To speak of the "difference of human receptacles" is to recognize distinction both between individuals and between collectivities. Humanity may be seen to be divided into several fundamentally different branches, which constitute so many "complete humanities, more or less closed in on themselves".[27] This completeness is a part of the quasi-absolute character of the religions that corresponds to these "complete humanities." These human collectivities can be ordered or mapped according to temporal and geographical determinations. Even more fundamentally they may be mapped according to spiritual temperaments. A person is absolute in terms of their individuality and relative in terms of the limitations that place them in a particular human collectivity or humanity. Without such orientation the human psyche either flounders in a sea of relativism or is lost in uniformity, which, in the end, amounts to the same thing.

The diversity of human collectivities requires the diversity of revelation. Each revelation, and the tradition that arises from it, is like a different language; the Truth spoken in these languages remains one even if its expression differs. Apparent anomalies between traditions are "like differences of language or of symbol; contradictions are in human receptacles, not in God; the diversity in the world is a function of its remoteness from the diverse Principle, which amounts to saying that the Creator cannot will both that the world should be, and that it should not be the world."[28]

[24] Ibn al-'Arabī, *Fusus*: "Chapter on Jacob" (Austin, p. 113). Ibn al-'Arabī observes monasticism as something "created" by Christians, which, nevertheless, "Since the Wisdom and good apparent in it are in harmony with the divine determination respecting the purpose of revealed Scripture, it is in God's sight as that which He laid down, although *He did not prescribe it for them* [Qur'an 57:27]" (p. 114).

[25] Schuon, *In The Face of the Absolute*, p. 73.

[26] Coomaraswamy, "Sri Ramakrishna and Religious Tolerance," p. 36.

[27] Schuon, *Gnosis: Divine Wisdom*, p. 25.

[28] Schuon, *Gnosis: Divine Wisdom*, p. 26.

To speak of each tradition being "closed in on itself" is to recognize the "relative absolute"[29] nature of each of the diverse revelations. Schuon: "God, when he speaks, expresses Himself in absolute mode; but this absoluteness relates to the universal content rather than the form. . . . Revelation speaks an absolute language, because God is absolute, not because the form is; in other words, the absoluteness of the Revelation is absolute in itself, relative in its form."[30]

Man is created in the image of the Divine: transcendent and immanent, absolute and relative. The absolute inherent in the human being allows for qualitative distinction. The Infinity of the Absolute is mirrored on the ontological plane by the indefinitude of possible individuals. Relativity manifests itself in the human collectivity in terms of certain limitations applicable to humankind as a whole. The notion of limitation carries, at least in modern thought, a pejorative implication, yet to say limitation is equally to say orientation, which recognises the positive notion of "order."

Each language is specific to the psychological and spiritual needs of the collectivity to which it is directed, that is to say, it constitutes a "holy strategy," what the Buddhists call *upāya*, "skillful means." To talk of such a "strategy" is to recognise a "strategist" whose intention is precisely salvation. "One has to realize" as Schuon remarks, "that outward religion is not disinterested; it wants to save souls, no more no less, and at the cost of the truths that do not serve its holy strategy."[31] It is thanks to the efficient intention of a tradition's "strategy" that all orthodox dogmas are justified and are in the final analysis compatible despite their apparent antagonisms.

That the exotericism of a tradition is somewhat bound to "misunderstandings" concerning the validity of different traditions derives from the fact that given its mission it "has to take into account the weakness of men, and thus also, be it said without euphemism, their stupidity; like it or not, it must itself take on something of these shortcomings, or at least it must allow them some room, on pain of not being able to survive in human surroundings."[32] "[T]o speak of form" says Schuon, "is to speak of limits and at the same time therefore of the virtuality of error."[33] And this is to say that "the formal homogeneity of a religion requires not only truth but also errors—though these only in the form—just as the world requires evil and a Divinity implies the mystery of creation by virtue of its infinity."[34] As Coomaraswamy remarks, the exclusive attachment to any one dogma, however pertinent, entails the error of idolatry: "the Truth itself is inexpressible."[35] These "errors" are the illusion of Relativity, yet they are precisely illusions and suppose no integral error in either their essence or their efficient purpose.

The "sense of the absolute"—the criterion for any true religion—asserts itself on the exoteric level of a particular religion by evoking a quasi-exclusivist posture. At the esoteric heart of a tradition the "sense of the absolute" leads one to the "transcendent unity of religion." The relative truth of each of these levels acts to balance the error potential in the other: the illusion of diversity at the exoteric level is balanced by the unity in the esoteric heart; the

[29] Schuon remarks on recourse to this "unavoidably ill-sounding expression" as being one that is nevertheless, "metaphysically useful" (*In The Face of the Absolute*, p. 57).

[30] Schuon, *Gnosis: Divine Wisdom*, p. 26.

[31] Schuon, *In The Face of the Absolute*, p. 22.

[32] Schuon, *In The Face of the Absolute*, p. 26.

[33] Schuon, *Spiritual Perspectives and Human Facts* (London: Perennial Books, 1987), p. 70.

[34] Schuon, *Spiritual Perspectives and Human Facts*, p. 73.

[35] Coomaraswamy, "Sri Ramakrishna and Religious Tolerance," p. 37.

erroneous denial of the Relative in the face of the unity of the Absolute is tempered by the Divine institution of the diverse forms. The totality of a tradition demands both the esoteric and exoteric levels. Moreover, the recognition by the esotericist of the Absolute in the Relative and the moral conformity to the contingent forms of a tradition, recognized as a mode of the Absolute, means that the esotericist must submit, almost without exception, to the forms of a religion.[36]

*   *   *

The merit of the *sophia perennis*, as noted, is that it presents a cogent understanding of the diversity of truths and permits one to accept the validity of other religions. From a purely pragmatic point of view this acceptance is undoubtedly a benefit in a world savaged by the violence born of religious intolerance and fanatical fundamentalism. From a more profound point of view, this understanding opens us to see God in our neighbor and thus love our neighbor as our self. The recognition of God in one's neighbor is, in turn, the recognition of the divine Unity, which is to "know thy self."

For the spiritual traveler there is a danger in a merely peripheral awareness of the *sophia perennis* insomuch as the acceptance of the truth of each path can render the indecisive person impotent with respect to actually setting out upon a particular path. Similarly, the awareness of the relative truth of each path can lead the weak-willed to baulk at the first obstacle they encounter on a particular path, causing them to quit this path and turn to another, fancying that this will be free of obstacles. This attitude, we might add, reveals an ignorance of the spiritual value of obstacles.

Some perceive the *sophia perennis* to threaten the unique saving power of one's own religion. If we are to be unsympathetic we might say that there is something insecure or even selfish about this anxiety. A more generous reading of this attitude recognizes in this a dedication to knowing God that is most admirable. That is to say: in accepting the Unity of God the practitioner transfers this quality of uniqueness to religion *per se* so that, for them, to admit the truth of multiple religions would be tantamount to admitting multiple gods. In rejecting this, their intention and understanding—as it is—is soteriologically justified. From the point of view of the *sophia perennis* the acceptance of the Unity of God necessitates acceptance of the diversity of valid religions, insomuch as this diversity is prefigured *in divinis* by the Divine All-Possibility; moreover, the divine Unity necessitates that nothing can be other than God—"Whichever way you may turn, there is the face of God" (Qur'an 2:115)—so that each religion can be naught but an expression of God.

The advocate of the *sophia perennis* might say, as Seyyed Hossein Nasr has, that "Each revealed religion is *the* religion and *a* religion, the religion inasmuch as it contains within itself the Truth and the means of attaining the Truth, a religion since it emphasizes a particular aspect of Truth in conformity with the spiritual and psychological needs of the humanity for whom it is destined."[37]

It is *a* religion because it is one means (*upāya*) amongst others offering a saving truth. The adherent of a religion who sees in their religion the very Message of God may well object

[36] "Forms" says Huston Smith in his introduction to Schuon's *Transcendent Unity of Religions*, "are to be transcended by fathoming their depths and discerning their universal content, not by circumventing them."

[37] Nasr, *Ideals and Realities of Islam* (London: Allen & Unwin, 1966), p. 15.

to the description of their religion as simply a "means," imagining that this term somehow denigrates the glory of divine revelation. However, even if a particular religion were *the* unique manifestation of divine Mercy it would still be a mercy granted by God to guide and aid the human back to God, and insomuch it would precisely be a means.

In talking of a particular religion as *the* religion one must understand that, except in the most exceptional of cases, attainment of Realization requires the integral practice of one religion in its totality. This is more than "just" a matter of psychological expediency, although this is an important aspect of what is here at issue. At a deeper level, Realization entails identification with God or Reality, where this is the unique Unity. The divine institution of *a* religion ontologically manifests Unity; the integral participation in *a* religion existentially identifies and unites the individual with Reality.

Each religion is thus *the* "relative absolute" religion. This term may be repellent to the adherent who sees it as a mere façade used to avoid the subjective relativity of religions. However, for Schuon, this phrase refers *both* to the "theological perspective, *and the reality to which it refers*".[38] This reality is, from one perspective, Being, which gives rise to "ontological All-Possibility,"[39] which is to say, distinction and diversity. The theological perspective is that emphasis on the absolute and unique nature of God that recognizes in *a* religion the exclusive soteriological prerogative. Again let it be stressed that this is more than just a psychological expedient. The exclusivist argument is, properly understood, rooted in the reality of Unicity. The emphasis here is not on the "relative absolute" but on the Absolute in the relative. As Schuon remarks, "if the relative did not comprise something of the absolute, relativities could not be distinguished qualitatively from one another."[40] Here he is no doubt thinking of Ibn al-'Arabī who says, "Were it not that the Reality permeates all beings as form [in His qualitative form], and were it not for the intelligible realities, no [essential] determination would be made in individual beings. Thus, the dependence of the Cosmos on Reality for existence is an essential factor."[41] Yet, at the same time, the distinguishing determinations, or limits, that allow relativities to manifest as such cannot be themselves absolute. Schuon: "The Infinite is that which is absolutely without limits, but the finite cannot be that which is "absolutely limited," for there is no absolute limitation. The world is not an inverted God: God is without a second."[42]

* * *

According to a Sufi adage, "There are as many paths towards God as there are human souls." In a sense, one might say that there are as many "religions" as there are human souls, at least inasmuch as we take religion to be the language between the Divine and the human, or between the unique Object and the myriad subjects. As St. Augustine says, "God loves each of us as if

38 Schuon, *In The Face of the Absolute*, p. 57 [my italics].

39 Schuon: "The Absolute by definition contains the Infinite—the common content being Perfection or the Good—and the Infinite in its turn gives rise, at the degree of that 'lesser Absolute' that is Being, to ontological All-Possibility. Being cannot not include efficient Possibility, because it cannot prevent the Absolute from including the Infinite" (*In The Face of the Absolute*, p. 38).

40 Schuon, *Language of the Self* (Bloomington: World Wisdom Books, 1999), p. 17.

41 Ibn al-'Arabī, *Fusūs*, (Austin, p. 57).

42 Schuon, *Spiritual Perspectives and Human Facts*, p. 168.

there were only one of us"; God also saves each one of us as if we were the one and only soul.

In "crossing religious frontiers" we look into the heart of our neighbor. To the degree that we have realised God in our own heart we are able to recognise God in our neighbour's heart, for "like knows like." That which we realise is the Divine Unity. In the final analysis it is not that we know God in our neighbour, for the distinction of self and neighbour is no longer real. Rather we might say that both neighbour and self are known in God, by God. In the words of Nicholas of Cusa, "God alone knows Himself."[43] In turn, as 'Alī says, "I know God by God, and I know that which is not God by the light of God."[44]

[43] Nicholas of Cusa, *De Docta Ignorantia* 1.26, tr. Fr. G. Heron (London: Routledge & Kegan Paul, 1954).

[44] Cited in Hujwīrī, *Kashf al-Mahjūb*, tr. R. A. Nicholson (London: Luzac, 1959), p. 269.

The Metaphysics of the Feminine and its Indian Roots: Franklin Merrell-Wolff, Bede Griffiths, and Frithjof Schuon

Patrick Laude

The last decades have seen an unprecedented rise in a general interest in the feminine dimension of the divine, and the feminine in world religions and spirituality. This has been partly a result, or a concomitance, of the feminist ideas and trends permeating modern culture. These tendencies have been, by and large, an expression of the egalitarian impulse of modernity, but also the outcome of a sense of disequilibrium and loss, and the consequent aspiration toward religious dimensions of the feminine that have been presumably ignored or occulted. The Western world has been the epicenter of this newly developed interest, in conjunction with a somewhat exotic fascination for past historical periods or foreign cultural areas that may provide modern-day Western mankind with alternative models of "religious gendering;" this orientation being a response to a perceived Western one-sidedness and even atrophy. In this connection, some have been tempted to look into a distant past to unbury the vestiges of presumptive or well-attested matriarchal religions and societies, while others turned their gaze toward the East to find responses to what they deemed to be an inordinate masculinization of Western religion and civilization. The development of a manifold feminist theology has greatly contributed to the visibility and impact of such tendencies, at least in the academic arena, and it has also percolated into a number of Churches and religious communities, especially in the Anglo-Saxon world.

The very complex and highly ambiguous inspirations and aspirations characteristic of this overall context will not be the object of our critique in this current essay: our inquiry will be limited to the specifically metaphysical dimension of the feminine, as it is related to the interpretation and integration of traditional Indian concepts and practices by three Western spiritual figures of the twentieth-century. These three figures have provided expressions of the highest principles of metaphysics through Hindu spiritual idioms, and thereby converged with the deepest layers of the contemporary aspiration toward the feminine; in another sense, the profundity and objectivity of their metaphysical accounts may provide a corrective to hasty, superficial and circumstantial aspects of the contemporary quest for the feminine. Our sense is that it is on such metaphysical levels that a genuinely spiritual fertilization of Western spirituality by Hindu thought and practices may take place, while helping to separate the grain of profound meditations on the feminine from the chaff of ideological, or merely psycho-social, concerns.

As a brief introduction, it needs be stressed that the three figures about to be discussed hail from quite distinct religious and philosophical backgrounds. Franklin Merrell-Wolff (1887-1985) was an American mathematician and philosopher trained at Stanford and Harvard who reported metaphysical recognition[1] consonant with the teachings of Hindu non-dualism,

[1] Let it be clear that we do not make any claim, in this context, as to the status of this "recognition." A reader familiar with the perspective of Advaita will recognize in Merrell-Wolff's book many remarkable insights that have the ring of profound metaphysical truth, if we may say so. A discerning traditionalist will also be somewhat puzzled or disappointed by some of Merrell-Wolff's positive reading of Western philosophers or other thinkers

although without apparent outer affiliation to a living Hindu *guru*. His thoughts and the spiritual diary of his inner journey are collected into a single volume entitled *Pathways through to Space*, published by Julian Press in 1973. The hallmark of Merrell-Wolff's perspective consists in an interpretation of non-dualistic cognition, and the inner modifications that it brings about, in a conceptual language shaped by philosophical and contemporary critical training. Bede Griffiths (1906-1993), was an English Benedictine monk who lived the last thirty-eight years of his life in Southern India as a Christian renunciate. The thrust of his work, epitomized in his classic *The Marriage of East and West*, lies in an attempt at cross-fertilizing the religious and civilizational contributions of Asia and the West by bringing out their profound spiritual complementarity. His Southern Indian *ashram*, Saccitananda at Shantivanam, has shaped one of the most original collective experience in bringing together the principles of Christianity and the spiritual ambience of India. Finally, Frithjof Schuon (1907-1998) was a metaphysician of Germanic descent who lived most of his life in Switzerland and the United States, and was the main contemporary exponent of the perennial wisdom, as well as a spiritual teacher of universal scope whose function was exercised within a traditional Sufi lineage. In his considerable opus of more than twenty books, Schuon provides an extraordinarily profound and rigorous account of universal and supra-confessional metaphysics as well as a rich, nuanced and masterfully insightful study of world religions and the fundamental components of spiritual life, such as prayer, meditation and the virtues.

The common feature in these three disparate thinkers is their anchorage in the Hindu metaphysics of non-dualism. Upon the foundations of this radical non-dualism akin to the perspective of Advaita Vedānta, all three subscribe to a recognition that the Divine includes both a masculine and a feminine dimension while paradoxically lying beyond all polarities. Theirs is a metaphysical vision that sees the Supreme Self transcending all dualities while being the Substance of all that is. Within this non-dualistic outlook, India presides over their affinity with Divine Femininity. This is so both because of the Hindu recognition of the diversity of paths, and on account of the Hindu religious affinities with the Divine Mother. On the one hand, the diverse body of doctrines and practices of the Indian traditions provides an all-encompassing range of spiritual possibilities attuned to diverse human needs and vocations. The Hindu *adhikara* refers to the karmic qualification and receptivity of specific individuals. The multiplicity of "adhikaric" potentialities account for the number of ways, or *ishta*, and the diversity of perspectives on, and aspects of, the One Reality, including the masculine and the feminine. On the other hand, the emphasis on the essential unity and productive diversity of the universe explains the centrality of the Divine Mother as infinite principle and merciful energy of manifestation of Reality.

Furthermore, for all three authors, inner realization was articulated with doctrine. In fact it could be argued that the presence of the Feminine in their works is proportional to existential and spiritual "verification." This conjunction is not without correlation with the profoundly transformative nature of the Feminine. Highlighting by contrast the spiritual need for the latter,

and writers one would normally not associate with a rigorous non-dualistic perspective. Finally, the question of the validity and depth of Merrell-Wolff's insights is independent from that of the viability of a path such as his for the quasi-totality of contemporary seekers, primarily due to the absence of clear traditional guarantees and framework in the unfolding of his spiritual recognition. In studying Merrell-Wolff we will simply focus on the aspects of his thought that both confirm and complement spiritual intuitions and formulations that can be gleaned in orthodox mystical traditions.

there is also a sense that the feminine was *a priori* only latent, or perhaps even neglected, in some early phases of the unfolding of their respective vocations. The early stages of Schuon's intellectual background bore to some extent the imprint of—without being limited to it—the quasi-mathematical model of René Guénon.[2] Merrell-Wolff was a scientifically-minded intellectual clearly attuned to discriminative knowledge and the rational articulation of concepts. Bede Griffiths makes it plain, in *The New Vision of Reality*, that he had "repressed the feminine," and he attributes the sudden return of the feminine in his life to a kind of backlash.[3] In all three cases, the breakthrough of spiritual realization asserted the feminine dimension in an explicit manner. Bede Griffiths sees the irruption of the Divine Feminine in his life originating with the stroke which initiated a new phase in his spiritual path. Similarly, Merrell-Wolff's references to the "Celestial Virgin" and Schuon's emphasis on the Marian dimension coincided, at least to a significant extent, with an inner contact with the Feminine.[4]

Although hailing from the Catholic tradition, Griffiths reads the Fall in a way that seems to turn around the traditional attribution of its responsibility to the feminine: "As reason develops, and they eat of the tree of knowledge, a division grows between human beings and nature. Human beings feel themselves separate from nature; the world becomes their enemy; violence and conflict take the place of the original peace."[5] It is rationality, associated by Griffiths with male reality, that introduces alienation into creation. The tree of knowledge initiates a passing into duality and opposition. Is Eden a feminine realm of harmony, intuition and bliss? One is tempted to answer in the affirmative since the pre-lapsarian state involves a sense of unity with nature, animals and plants, a unity seen as the hallmark of the feminine. The Edenic consciousness is placed under the sign of motherly indifferentiation: it is a metaphysical womb, as it were. There is a way, therefore, in which the pre-lapsarian state, still experienced in archaic societies, refers—at least symbolically—to a stage prior to the differentiation of man and woman, while paradoxically extolling the feminine—a paradox since Eve is drawn from Adam in the Biblical account. Notwithstanding the feminine flavor of Griffiths' cosmogony—and the questions or difficulties it may raise, his works make it clear as well that the masculine bent toward rationality is a legitimate fact of existence, and that there is no way back to Eden. In the world that we know, the task is to find a delicate balance between the masculine and the feminine: this is the marriage of mankind and nature, man and woman, West and East; for the feminine is akin to India and Asia, as well as to "tribal religions." By contrast, the Renaissance led to an inordinate affirmation of masculine values, or worse to their deviation, hence its seminal function in the spread of a modern West geared toward analytical reason and technology. With it, rationality, science, discoveries, and imperial odysseys have become dangerously emancipated from the intuitive, mystical, and symbolic sense of reality, of which

2 In an unpublished journal, Schuon specifies that his love of the Holy Virgin goes back to his childhood but became somewhat latent later on during his youth when "metaphysics and the emphasis on Vedanta and Sufism came."

3 "In each person there is both masculine and feminine, and most men repress the feminine. I have done that to a very considerable extent, and I think it was the woman in me who came and hit me on the head!" (*Essential Writings*, ed. Thomas Matus [New York: Orbis, 2004], p. 76).

4 This contact is described by Merrell-Wolff in the following terms: "the exhaled breath was not simply air expelled into the outer atmosphere, but seemed to penetrate down through the whole organism like a gentle caress, leaving throughout a quiet sense of delight" (*Pathways Through to Space* [Julian Press, 1973], p. 2).

5 *Essential Writings*, ed. Thomas Matus, p. 83.

India has remained the spiritual repository. This is, in a different idiom, a critique that echoes Guénon's *Crisis of the Modern World*. By contrast with the Renaissance criticized by Griffiths and Guénon, the Middle-Ages, for all of its flaws, kept the two dimensions in balance. There was no sense of an imperial rationality, nor the need for a human conquest of nature. Even though often considered as contaminated by the Fall, Nature was also intuited as a mirror of God and a book to be deciphered, as in bestiaries in which the symbolic meaning of animals, their moral and spiritual connotations, were independent from any zoological exactitude, but grounded in the permanence of tradition and archetypes.[6] Away from this metaphysical and spiritual anchoring, Griffiths envisions the likelihood of a collapse of the current system, due to the exponential and dysfunctional growth of the masculine one-sidedness and hyperbole of modernity. However, he also sees in this forthcoming breakdown the possibility of the emergence of a new culture: "one of the characteristics of this new culture would be its feminine aspects."[7] The current civilization having reached a point of non-return in its affirmation of excessive or corrupted masculine values of conquering rationality and technocratic power, Griffiths summons the Chinese principle of alternation of *yin* and *yang* to foretell a return to feminine values of connectedness.

By contrast with the aforementioned figures of Western scientific and technological "aggressiveness," India, and to some extent the rest of the non-Western world, has highlighted modes of "development" that are radically other. This type of development gives priority to spiritual fulfillment, and culminates in the triumph of intellectual intuition and realization over mere reason, as epitomized by the *Bhagavad Gita*'s metaphysical heights. This is the main source of Griffiths' Indian tropism, and his frequent references to the *Upanishads* bear witness to it. Elsewhere however, Griffiths reveals the complexity of his position vis-à-vis Hindu metaphysics, particularly in his evaluation of Shankara. On the one hand, Griffiths acknowledges the ultimacy of the Shankarian *moksha*, or spiritual liberation.[8] However, his reticences about Shankarian non-dualism stem from the fact that the Advaitin discernment between the absolute Consciousness and the realm of *Māyā* sounds to him not fully compatible with the Christian Incarnation, nor perhaps with the feminine as Shaktic principle of cosmic manifestation. His understanding of Christ, as medium way between pure transcendent, disincarnated consciousness (that he attributes to Shankara) and pure matter (as in hedonism) indicates a descent of consciousness into matter in which the two have become one.[9] This is akin to a Shaktic apprehension of reality, and it is interesting to note that, in this context, Griffiths does not insist upon the suffering and passion that lies at the intersection of consciousness and physical embodiment, as if his Christ had been Hinduized, as it were. It goes without saying that Griffiths' reservations vis-à-vis the Shankarian perspective may be evaluated diversely. Positively, they reveal his greater affinity, apparently unacknowledged, or perhaps unconscious, with the perspective of Kashmiri Shaivism, one that stresses the dynamic radiance of absolute Consciousness over metaphysical discrimination, the Shaiva "method . . . of an ever widening

6 Cf. Louis Charbonneau-Lassay, *The Bestiary of Christ* (Penguin, 1992).

7 *A New Vision of Reality* (London: Collins, 1989), p. 294.

8 "Indeed there is a sense in which this experience (of bliss of the pure consciousness of being) is ultimate" (*Vedanta and Christian Faith* [Los Angeles, 1973], p. 74).

9 "There is a descent of the Spirit into matter and a corresponding ascent, by which matter is transformed by the indwelling power of the Spirit, and the body is transfigured" (Ibid., p. 75).

inclusion of phenomena mistakenly thought to be outside of the absolute."[10] Negatively, they may betray a failure to recognize the profoundly integrative perspective of Shankara, since discernment is ultimately less a negation of what is not (*Māyā*) than an affirmation of What is, That (*Tat*) through which everything is not without being. In other words there is no perfect transcendence without immanence, and conversely.

Griffiths' archetypical concepts of the masculine and the feminine must not be misunderstood as referring primarily to the human realities or constructs. Neither the feminine nor the masculine belongs exclusively to any individual, gender or civilization. They manifest in various proportions in all individuals, groups, and historical periods. On the highest level, which alone gives meaning to all downstream applications, Griffiths defines the Divine Mother, or Shakti, as both a receptive and a creative power. It receives, conceives and brings forth, in the image of the Christian spiritual prototype of Mary: "it is he Spirit who conceives these 'ideas' in her maternal womb and brings them forth in creation."[11] These functions clearly demonstrate a tendency toward a feminization of the Holy Spirit consonant with early and Eastern Christian interpretations. Furthermore, the conjunction of the passive and active dimensions suggests a totality of the feminine, a totality that led the Sufi Ibn 'Arabi to declare the contemplation of God in the feminine as the highest.[12]

In conformity with Merrell-Wolff's intellectual alignment with the Indian school of non-duality, his approach to metaphysics is not only doctrinal but also experiential, although Merrell-Wolff shuns from referring to it as an experience simply because experience presupposes an experiencing subject and an experienced object, therefore a dualistic outlook. Actually, the hallmark of his perspective lies in a conversion of consciousness through the interiorizing mediation of intellectual meditation. Such a recognition is concomitant of an awareness of the insubstantiality of material realities, and a transcendent cognition of absolute Consciousness as *the* Reality. In the wake of this metaphysical recognition, Reality is experienced as a Current of Bliss. Characterized by Merrell-Wolff as corresponding to the ancient concepts of Ambrosia or Nectar, the Current is an extremely subtle state of consciousness both consequent to, and independent from, human thought and action, sometimes perceived by human consciousness, sometimes not. In an important passage of his spiritual diary, Merrell-Wolff specifies that at times he can "turn to It (the Current) with the ease of a subtle movement of thought," while at other times "It breaks out spontaneously."[13] In another passage, he mentions, interestingly, that his wife Sherifa "is immediately responsive to It and recognizes Its presence, at times even before I do."[14] Therefore, it is quite clear that, while an inner predisposition to the Current of Bliss may be cultivated, it remains essentially a grace, a gift that transcends the individual's will

10 Mark S.G. Dyczkowski, *The Doctrine of Vibration. An Analysis of the Doctrines and Practices of Kashmir Shaivism* (SUNY Press, 1987), p. 38. "Consciousness is not a passive witness (*sākṣin*), but is full of the conscious activity (*citikriyāh*) through which it generates the universe and reabsorbs it into itself at the end of each cycle of creation" (Ibid., 45).

11 *The Marriage of East and West* (Springfield, Illinois, 1982), p. 191.

12 "Witnessing the Real in women is the greatest and most perfect witnessing. . . . Qaysarī mentions that the active element of man's contemplation of woman can be the fact that the reality of woman is identical with the reality of man, and thus she contains in herself both the active and passive wherein to contemplate God" (Ibn Al-'Arabī, *The Ringstones of Wisdom*, translation, introduction, and glosses by Caner K. Dagli [Chicago, 2004], p. 282).

13 *Pathways Through To Space*, p. 5.

14 Ibid., p. 6.

and even individual cognition as such. In addition, the choice of the term Current is not without suggestive value. It refers to a flow that embraces and surrounds, but also to a magnetic force that pulls individual consciousness through to a transcendent zone. It denotes transcendence, but also unity and connection. At times, Merrell-Wolff approaches this Reality through poetical or symbolic language as the least ill-fitted way to intimate the reality of Recognition. In parallel, in an important passage of his diary, Merrell-Wolff writes: "In Her Highest aspect, Woman is the Celestial Virgin, and this is none other than the Current of Bliss."[15] The essence of spiritual recognition is therefore Femininity as such. More specifically, it is the Virgin, understood here independently from any theological language, since creative and blissful consciousness remains untouched or unadulterated, as Substance, by its projections and modifications. The Current of Consciousness as creative love or bliss always remains pure because it is not only immanent but also transcendent to the forms in which it manifests Itself. In a substantial or essential sense Consciousness is always pure Consciousness, which amounts to saying that the integrity of *Atman* is never affected by superimpositions.

This emphasis on Femininity is all the more remarkable in that Merrell-Wolff's perspective is Shankarian, as acknowledged in the opening pages of his spiritual diary.[16] Everything dwells in an exclusive focus on the pure consciousness and absolute identity of *Atman*. Recognition is an a perception of pure consciousness unadulterated by the sense of an object. Merrell-Wolff refers to it as "Consciousness-without-an-object," not as negation of the manifold but as its being apprehended as projection or modification of pure Subjectivity. Consciousness-without-an-object is therefore independent of, or prior to, any polarity such as subject-object, inner-outer and the like; which means that it is also transcendently independent from the polarity masculine-feminine. However, this does not mean that the masculine and the feminine do not enter into the Reality of the Absolute, nor into its recognition.

In an important passage of his *Pathways Through to Space*, Merrell-Wolff identifies Knowledge with Fire, which separates and consumes. This is not only metaphorical. There is an essential unity between the spirituality reality of Knowledge as fire and physical combustion, the latter being actually a symbol of the former. This Fire is no different, essentially, from the Hindu *tapas*, which refers both to the psycho-spiritual energy of the ascetic, and to the discipline that induces it. In the context of metaphysical meditation, the Fire of Knowledge involves such a degree of intensity that it cannot be experienced by the physio-psychological man without danger:

> The fact is that the Fire of Knowledge is too intense a Flame for the human organism to endure if it is not sheathed in the Water of Life, the Current which is Bliss.[17]

[15] Ibid., p. 46.

[16] "I had been led to this specific program of reading through the realization that Shankara's words had peculiar power, at least in my experience. For some time I had spontaneously looked to him as to a Guru with whom I was in complete sympathetic accord. I had found him always clear and convincing, at least in all matters relative to the analysis of consciousness, while with the other Sages I either found obscurities or emphases with which I could not feel complete sympathy" (Ibid., p. 1).

[17] Ibid., p. 41.

While the active realizational principle is masculine, as exclusive isolation of pure consciousness akin to Shankarian discrimination, its integration and fulfillment pertains to the feminine. In other words, "Feminine" participation is immanent to "Masculine" concentration. Bliss is the subjacent and dynamic reality of Consciousness. Consciousness is Being and Bliss, *Saccitananda*. The Feminine is the *Shakti* of the Masculine, Shiva. Although on a lower level Shakti can be conceived as a counterpart to Shiva, She is ultimately none other than Him:

> Man is Siva, the formless Light; woman is Shakti, the Current which opposes and embodies the Light.[18]

Without the Feminine, there is therefore no integral recognition, or no integrated realization, of Consciousness as Self-Consciousness pervading the whole of reality. This metaphysical principle finds its application in our outer life, including the social realm, in that a masculine overemphasis deprived of feminine complement tends to lead to disequilibrium. This is illustrated, according to Merrell-Wolff, in the contemporary world where the "conflict" between the sexes is akin to an inordinate competition for masculine identity and values, and a foregoing of feminine qualities. Accordingly, a tendency on the part of some modern women to strive to "imitate man" amounts to "really giving to man-power and man-function a greater tribute than they deserve."[19]

Finally, Merrell-Wolff provides a fruitful comment upon his experience of the Current of Bliss: "the underlying force in religion is the same one that draws men and women together."[20] Hindus call this force *Ananda*, manifested on a lower level as *rasa*, Dante refers to it as *Amor*, while Merrell-Wolff reserves for it, at times, the words "Creative Principle." Now the level upon which this Creative Principle manifests, as well as the degree of purity of the human consciousness that serves as its vehicle, determines the quality of its spiritual outcome. There is a hierarchy in which "the higher aspects of the Creative Principle, of which there are several levels, become progressively more potent and more sacred until, at the top, we come into Recognition of the Celestial Virgin. He who fuses his consciousness with this Virgin no longer simply believes in his seeked Immortality, but Knows himself to be Immortal, nay more, He is Immortality."[21]

It can be said that Schuon's work is deeply informed by a Hindu, Advaitin, doctrinal axis while being imbued with a metaphysical sense of the feminine. On a metaphysical level, the Divine Essence is understood by Schuon as Beyond-Being, the Supreme Reality lying beyond all oppositions implied by being—*Nirguna Brahma*; and this means also beyond the polarity of genders, since It cannot be fully apprehended by the use of either. Notwithstanding the gender-free reality of Beyond-Being—the Absolute in its absoluteness—monotheistic religions envisage God as masculine, as flows from their sacred scriptures. This indicates that they do not consider *a priori* the Divine on its highest level of reality. They envisage God, rather, as Supreme Being, precisely because their spiritual economy is based upon the *relationship* between God and mankind, therefore consistent with the degree of beings. However, the monotheistic concept of God is not, in itself, exclusive of a higher degree of Reality. The "absolutely Absolute" is

[18] Ibid., p. 46.

[19] Ibid., p. 46.

[20] Ibid., p. 72.

[21] Ibid., p. 73.

thus also incidentally designated as masculine in Judaism, Christianity and Islam, as a kind of "extension" of the general idiom of the tradition. The matter becomes somewhat more complex when it comes to the domains of esoterism and mysticism. While Schuon takes note of Ibn Arabī's reference to the Absolute as *Hiya*—She, he also notes that this designation has nothing exclusive about it, for "God is indivisible, and who says 'He' says 'She.'"[22] Taking into account the fact that the Arabic word for the Divine Essence is the feminine noun *Dhāt*, and that a number of Sufis have symbolically referred to It as to a feminine reality under the poetic names of Layla or Salma, it must be added that this designation refers in fact to a situation, that of Islam precisely, in which Being *qua* masculine reality is understood as the first determination of Beyond-Being, considered, by contrast, as being feminine. The latter is then "synonymous with indetermination, illimitation, mystery. . ."[23] This Divine Femininity is none other than the Infinite dimension of the Principle, or its Potentiality. Let us quote Schuon on the ways in which this Divine Potentiality can be envisaged:

> There is . . . in the Real a principle of polarization, perfectly undifferentiated in the Absolute, but capable of being discerned and the cause of every subsequent deployment. We can represent this Principial polarity by an axis, either horizontal or vertical: if it is horizontal, it signifies that Potentiality . . . remains within the supreme Principle . . . as an intrinsic dimension of latent potency; if the axis is vertical, it signifies that Potentiality becomes Virtuality, that it radiates and communicates itself, and that consequently it gives rise to the first hypostasis, Being, the creative principle.[24]

This passage must lead us to specify that Schuon envisages dimensions, modes and degrees in the Divine Order. The question of a pre-eminence of the Masculine or the Feminine *in divinis* can be envisaged primarily in terms of dimensions, or in terms of degrees. The two main dimensions of the Divine are its absoluteness and its infinitude, that is the exclusive Reality and the all-encompassing Possibility. The former is akin to masculinity as necessity and exclusiveness, the latter pertains to femininity as liberty or potentiality, and inclusiveness. The Divine Essence is both the Absolute and the Infinite, which means that it can be conceived either as integrating the Masculine and the Feminine—while being exclusively identifiable to neither, or as being primarily Masculine or Feminine. The Infinite is the *Shakti* of the Absolute, which is why the Absolute is normally mentioned first by Schuon: the *Shakti*, as projection of Shiva, is the second of two dimensions of reality that are situated on the same metaphysical level. Accordingly, there is a kind of metaphysical "pair" or "couple" that "are horizontal when the second term is the qualitative and thus harmonious complement of the first, in other words, if it is its Shakti," while other sorts of symbolic gender configurations are "vertical when the second term tends in

[22] *Roots of the Human Condition* (World Wisdom, Bloomington, 2002), p. 40.

[23] Ibid.

[24] "Hypostatic and Cosmic Numbers" in *The Essential Frithjof Schuon*, ed. Seyyed Hossein Nasr (Bloomington, World Wisdom, 2005), pp. 351-352. In addition to the aforementioned references, our considerations on Divine Femininity are primarily based on the following passages from Schuon's works: "The Onto-Cosmological Chain" in *Survey of Metaphysics and Esoterism* (Bloomington, World Wisdom, 2000), pp. 61-62; "The Problem of Sexuality" in *The Essential Frithjof Schuon*, pp. 414-415. See also the penetrating essay by James Cutsinger, "The Virgin," in *Sophia*, vol. 6, no. 2, 2000: 115-194.

an efficient manner towards a more relative level or when it is already at such a level." Let us now consider this second type of relationship.

Along such vertical axis involving "a more relative level," Schuon considers three degrees: Beyond-Being, Being and the "existentiating Logos"; or first, the Divine Essence beyond all determinations, the apophatic Non-Being, second, the Supreme Person who relates to creation, and third, the Word by "which all things have been made." While Beyond-Being is represented by Schuon by a triangle with its basis formed by the two dimensions of absoluteness and infinitude, the passage from Beyond-Being to Being is in the form of an inverted triangle with its "upper" basis comprised of the Absolute and the Infinite and its "lower" top of Being. When the latter is envisaged as "proceeding" from the Infinite as All-Possibility, the Feminine is to be identified with Beyond-Being, and Being to the Masculine as auto-determination of Beyond-Being. In this sense, the Indeterminacy of Beyond-Being "contracts" into the Determination of Being as Principle of Relativity. The infinite space "becomes" the point from which proceeds the circles of Universal Relativity. According to such a symbolic account the "passage" from Beyond-Being to Being can be conceived more as a "concentration" than as an "unfolding" or a "development," hence its association with a vertical axis Feminine-Masculine.

Along another symbolic axis of verticality, Schuon also refers to the Masculine and the Feminine as being reflective of the relationship between *Ātmā* and *Māyā*, the Absolute and the Relative. Considering Being as part of *Māyā*, of which it is the summit, one may understand the two degrees of Beyond-Being and Being as respectively Masculine and Feminine. In fact, however, none of Schuon's work presents us with this metaphysical correspondence. Being as *Māyā* is normally envisaged by Schuon as the first *determination* of Beyond-Being, rather than as its extrinsic *projection*. Considering Beyond-Being in its Indeterminacy and Inclusiveness, it makes sense that the Feminine would be *particularly*—but not exclusively, associated to with the Divine Essence *qua* Beyond-Being when related to Being. This is no doubt why Schuon tends to emphasize the Feminine over the Masculine *in divinis*; but this theoretical emphasis also has concrete spiritual bearings.

Those are articulated in the chapters "The Veil of Isis" and "Mahashakti" included in *Roots of the Human Condition* in which Schuon approaches the Feminine from three different angles: first as Essence, as represented by Isis, who cannot be unveiled, second as productive and assisting Mother, as Divine Mercy, and thirdly as attractive and re-integrative, as Betrothed. Isis can be identified with the Divine Essence that remains forever hidden from the "sight" of relativity. She is the Virgin in the most essential sense. She can even be identified to one of the Islamic name of the Holy Virgin, *al-Bātul*, in so far as she remains withdrawn from outwardness and "devoted" to her own Inward Mystery, like woman in the Qur'ān, *hafizat li-l-ghayb bi mā hafiza Allāh*—guard of the Mystery with what God has guarded (4-34). This is the Reality that cannot be unveiled by anyone but which can "take the soul under her veil, ab intra."[25] In other words there is no way from the relative and the finite as such to the Infinite, but the latter can "extinguish" the former "within" its Essence since nothing is in fact outside of It. Secondly, as Mother, the Divine protects and nourishes. And this is no doubt the most usual sense of the Divine Mother in a Hindu context. It is also the meaning of the Arabic *Umm*, which expresses the same merciful assistance manifested in the Divine Name *ar-Rahīm*. Finally, the Betrothed, *al-'Arūs*, is the Divine Feminine is its aspect of reintegrating attractiveness, which Kashmiri

[25] Ibid., p. 22.

Shaivism would assimilate, in its own idiom, to *Spanda*, the Divine Energy. This is the beauty and immanent "perfume" of Divine Femininity that the contemplative can use as an "open door" to the Limitless, for "beauty gladdens the heart and appeases it, and perfume makes one breathe, it evokes the limitlessness and purity of air; the 'dilation of the breast,' as one would say in Sufi mysticism."[26] Thus, Schuon's feminine triad unfolds a whole cycle of the Infinite, as it were: infinitude as essential dimension of the Divine, infinitude as divine descent, and infinitude as divine ascent: Mystery, Mercy and Beauty.

In conclusion I would like to propose a few reflections pertinent to the contemporary world. First, the Divine Feminine points to an Essence which melts forms into a stream of bliss. The form can be a way of access to this Essence but it may also forbid access to it through hardening stemming from identification with matter and the ego; however, there is an aspect of inviolability of the Divine Feminine that calls for a spiritual cultivation and interiorization of form, not a rejection of them. In this sense, the form is a veil that protects against any "profanation" of the Essence, if one may say so. Negatively, this is not unconnected to the function of Kali. Secondly, the substance of Reality is mercy; rigor is but the outer edge of Reality. Religion is not a stern outer conformity, but a participation into Divine grace. However, here again, this Mercy calls for a death to egocentric illusions, and a consequent spiritual humility and childlikeness that opens itself to the maternal aspect of the Divine: the Divine Mother of India. The critique of Prometheism that suffuses the works of Griffiths and Schuon is based on a realization of this need to remain a child, spiritually. Finally, the Feminine is the grace drawing us toward the Source of all beauties; but this inner beauty requires a contemplative outlook that shuns aestheticism and hedonistic passion. The grace of Divine Beauty, and its interiorizing vibrations, can only be spiritually effective within the overall context of a life informed by inward recollection, through which the whole of existence may become, as it were, a spiritual betrothal.

[26] Ibid., p. 44.

A Note on C.S. Lewis and Ecumenism

James S. Cutsinger

In describing "an agreed, or common, or central, or "mere" Christianity," C. S. Lewis, in the preface to his book by that name, puts forward an ecumenical principle that is surprisingly perennialist in its implications. Lewis writes, "It is at her center, where her truest children dwell, that each communion is really closest to every other in spirit, if not in doctrine. And this suggests," he continues, "that at the center of each there is something, or a Someone, who against all divergences of belief, all differences of temperament, all memories of mutual persecution, speaks with the same voice."[1]

Lewis, widely regarded as the greatest Christian apologist of the twentieth century, is of course speaking here about the relationship between the various Christian churches, and not about "divergences of belief" between the world's major religions. But his words nonetheless have an important interfaith application, for *mutatis mutandis* he appears to be talking about something not unlike what Frithjof Schuon calls "esoteric ecumenism."[2] He is in any case of one mind with Schuon and other perennialists in believing that the most authentic ecumenism will be found "in spirit" among those who "in doctrine" most strongly disagree.

The great mistake of most contemporary forms of interfaith dialogue has been to think that religious believers come closest to each other along their edges, as it were, where their least distinctive—and thus least controversial—teachings lie. In order to smooth over the rough places in our relationships with those of other faiths, we are asked to ignore or forgo the central dogmas that typically lead to conflict, while concentrating instead on the Golden Rule and other platitudes. Peace is the treasured goal of such dialogue—not, however, "the peace of God, which passeth all understanding" (Phil. 4:7) but the contrived and artificial peace we have been warned "the world giveth" (John 14:27). Traditional Christians are only too familiar with this sort of thinking on the part of their modernist co-religionists, and they know how often it results in the abandonment of essential Christian truths. The English theologian John Hick provides a well-known and especially egregious example: Since Muslims and Jews are inevitably scandalized by the claim that Christ is God, Christians (as Hick sees it) are obliged out of charity to reject this claim themselves, admitting that it was based on a misunderstanding and a myth.[3]

Lewis, who would have been the last man in the world to deny Christ's divinity or compromise the integrity of the Christian tradition, clearly had in mind a very different picture. But what exactly is it? How are we to envision his topologically puzzling assertion that religious communions are must truly united, not on their surfaces where they are able to touch, but at their centers where it would seem they do not?

To get at the answer, let us imagine the world's religions as if they were geometrical figures. Exoteric believers will prefer to envision these figures as lying in parallel and therefore never-

[1] C. S. Lewis, *Mere Christianity* (New York: Macmillan, 1943), viii.

[2] See for example *Christianity/Islam: Perspectives on Esoteric Ecumenism*, ed. James S. Cutsinger (Bloomington, Indiana: World Wisdom, 2008).

[3] John Hick, *The Metaphor of God Incarnate: Christology in a Pluralistic Age* (Louisville, Kentucky: Westminster/ John Knox, 1993).

intersecting planes and as having different sizes and shapes representing various degrees of truth and comprehensiveness. And of course they will picture their own faith as the largest figure, no doubt circular in shape—the circle corresponding to perfection—while competing religions will be imagined as more or less irregular departures from this geometrical paradigm. Modernists, on the other hand, will run to the opposite extreme. Being more interested in the prospects of ecumenical unity than they are in sound doctrine, they will imagine the figures as having roughly the same human size and shape and as existing on a single plane where contact is possible. Certain of these hopeful ecumenists may picture the shapes as drifting inexorably toward one another while others may see them as already contiguous or perhaps even overlapping. The problem with all these representations, however, is that they end up depicting the relationship between the traditions in a strictly superficial or peripheral way, as if the possibility of union were a function solely of external proximity and "touch," whether between planes or between discrete figures in the same plane. But this is to understand ecumenism in merely political and planimetric categories.

Lewis offers the perennialist a very different visual model. To limit ourselves to the Semitic traditions mentioned above, he is proposing—again *mutatis mutandis*—that in envisioning Judaism, Christianity, and Islam as three distinct figures, we make them all circular and of the same size, for each of these spiritual economies is the expression or manifestation of God's perfect grace and saving will for mankind. Moreover these circles are not to be constructed and deployed in just any fashion; since there is a common "something or a Someone" at their centers, the best representation will be one in which they actually share the same center and are thus inscribed as great circles inside a single sphere. Of course their exoteric differences must not be forgotten, and it is therefore important that they not coincide; their "dogmatic" planes must be positioned at least a few degrees apart from each other if not at right angles. The reader who has followed this rather elaborate construction will see that the defining point of all three figures is the center of the sphere; any two circles will share their diameters,[4] but the center alone—God Himself—is common to all.

Needless to say, the majority of serious Semitic believers will be less than pleased with this picture, and true perennialists will be the first to sympathize with them. A man who is struggling to love God with his entire heart, soul, and mind—who is intent upon moving within his own circle along the shortest path to the center—does not wish to be bothered by other paths than his own. Ecumenists, esoteric and otherwise, may have the leisure to ask themselves what it would mean theologically to rotate two or more circles around the axes of their diameters until their circumferences coincide, or similar recondite questions. But when it comes to actually living the spiritual life, spherical modeling can easily become a distraction. From a practical or operative standpoint we must all be "flat-earthers," and we need to be careful that our busyness around the *oikoumenē*—the ecumenical household—does not divert us, like Martha, from the "one thing needful" (Luke 10:42). Like her sister, Mary, we should on the contrary be constantly mindful of the One in whom alone we are one.

How can we realize the truest and most transformative unanimity among the traditions? Not by merely gazing at their scriptural surfaces or debating the lengths of their ethical circumferences, but instead by prayerfully moving toward their esoteric and mystical centers—which are nothing finally but the Center itself.

[4] I have tried to work out what such a diameter might represent in "Disagreeing to Agree: A Christian Response to *A Common Word*" (http://www.cutsinger.net/pdf/disagreeing_to_agree.pdf; forthcoming in *Christian-Muslim Understanding: Theory and Application of* A Common Word (New York: Palgrave Macmillan, 2010).

The Depth-Dimension of Religious Dialogue

Swami Abhishiktananda (Fr. Henri le Saux)

Man is Communion

Man is a social being, Already ontologically he is communion, relationship, fellowship with others. *Koinonia* is an intrinsic dimension of the *person.* There is no "person" apart from communion with others. Man discovers himself, realizes himself, only in meeting with others. And the deeper the meeting, the more man finds himself and blossoms into a "person."

Christian revelation puts a new stress on the dignity and nature of man as a being of relation and communion. The ultimate secret of God's life, as shared with us by Jesus, the Son by nature, is the Trinitarian mystery of the Godhead. In its very source, being is relationship. It therefore had to be that man, the apex of God's creation, should reflect in himself the "being-one-together" of the divine Persons. Christ himself is a "corporate" being. What theologians call his "Mystical Body" is no less real and no less his than is his individual self. Each believer in Christ, nay more, each man, is, with Jesus, in Jesus, a kind of corporate being; each lives in a most intimate and ontological relationship with the whole of the Mystical Body, and with the whole of mankind.

History shows that man develops only in relation with others. In isolation, man would shrink from his own humanity; life in solitude is only possible for man after a long preparation in human fellowship, and provided also he has discovered in himself that center where no human being, indeed no other creature, is distant from him. The growth of humankind, the advance of cultures and civilizations has sprung from the combination of individual talents and abilities. Even the rising of the great civilizations came generally from a mutual fecundation between already existing cultures.

Inter-relationship between men becomes dialogue when it reaches the level of the person—that is of the consciousness and the mind. Dialogue has its principle in relationship with others, when this relationship is accepted and integrated into the person itself. It is the person freely accepting its condition of being a relation, of being a *thou* to others; that is, accepting to live with them on the level of exchange, of *symbiosis* of giving and receiving.

Accepting to be a *thou* for the other is accepting him as an *I*, with all the characteristics of "I-ness" which I experience in my own person. That means recognizing the other, no longer as an object to which I have at least a potential right, but as a subject like myself a source, an absolute, a universal center. The other becomes someone with whom I relate at the very level of my self-awareness, to whom, paradoxically, my own self-awareness is open. My meeting him as subject far surpasses all bodily and mental expression, situated as it is at the very center—or source—of my own being.

True dialogue between men is indeed at that very level. It is meeting, exchange, mutual donation. Not donation of anything one has, for the meeting is at the level not of *having* but of *being.* It implies the mutual donation of what is the most essential to both.

Two persons cannot meet without each giving himself to the other, at least in some way. Initially, perhaps, they will give part of their attention, of their consciousness, of their own life. But a true meeting takes place only in the depth; and a meeting which is not in the depth is not a meeting with my brother. The priest and the Levite went past the wounded man on the Jericho road; the Samaritan alone *met* him. And is not the most pressing message of the Gospel that I am called to *meet* God, to *meet* Christ in everyone of my fellowmen? God is met only in the depth.

There are meetings on the surface, no doubt, in all human lives, like those of ships abandoned on the high seas, which drift alongside for a while and then separate as they are carried by the waves. But we speak here only of meetings at the level of man as man, nothing short of which is included in true dialogue. To meet my brother in the depth does not, however, necessarily mean that I have to open to him my most intimate thoughts and feelings. The gift of myself, the oblation I make of myself to God in my brother, passes through the most common acts of exchange in human life. However, there is a *difference* when a man lives in the depth. In him, one can feel that each act, each, word, each gesture, even the most ordinary one, comes from the deepest and the most intimate center of his soul.

Religious Dialogue

Coming to the domain of religion, we must say that religion in itself is already a dialogue. It is first a dialogue with God, as is magnificently stressed in the Bible, and exemplified above all in Jesus, whose life was an incessant face to face dialogue with God his Father. It is also a dialogue among men. It is by exchanging their personal experiences of God that men have progressed and still progress in their knowledge and understanding of the divine mystery.

Even religious instruction, as all true education, is in the form of dialogue. It is not simply giving on one side and receiving on the other, as, alas, it is too often thought to be. Religious truths and formulations do not reach the mind of the listener as if it were simply blank, a *tabula rasa*. They meet in his mind something which is already there, even if only latent. They aim at awakening the mind, at helping it to bring into view intuitions which so far may have remained at the archetypal level. In the case of a divine revelation, the mind is enabled to go, in faith, beyond previous intuitions and formulations, these being at once "redeemed" and fulfilled through the grace of the Holy Spirit. If it were not so, revealed truths would remain forever, as too often happens, extrinsic to man; they would not take root in him; they would not become integrated into his own personal and deepest experience; they would never become in him something vital. Truly, divine revelation aims at awakening and bringing to completion what had already been placed by God in seed form in man through the very process of creation—the first step in God's call to man to participate in the divine life.

Man is ceaselessly in dialogue with others. He seems less and less capable of silence. He is in dialogue at all sorts of levels. There are the levels of external activities, of techniques, of mental exchange and sharing; but above all these, there is religious dialogue which reaches in man a depth of interiority and personal commitment beyond the reach of any other dialogue. Religious dialogue is indeed immediately directed to that fundamental experience of *I* and *Thou* to which we already referred.

Obviously, we are not concerned here with a religious dialogue that remains on the plane of religious formulations or social contacts. True religious dialogue originates in the depth of man's mind and spirit. It reaches levels to which no mere philosophical dialogue (at least in the Western sense) can attain. It aims at the ultimate concern of man, the point where man is related to the *beyond*—whatever name may be given to it. It is not, however, to a *beyond* turned into an object of speculative contemplation and brought into discussion, but the *beyond* which is the existential concern of man in regard to his own personal and "eternal" destiny. Dialogue at the philosophical or theological level takes its worth precisely from being rooted there; otherwise, it is purely academic discussion or even an egoistic search for self-affirmation.

Religious dialogue is concerned with that depth of human experience. It aims at awakening it and at deepening it. Such experience exists in every man, at least in an initial or latent stage. It is not the preserve of so-called mystics. We do not, however, refer here to feelings and mental impressions, even less to parapsychic phenomena which are but the outgrowth of the subliminal self. We precisely refer to that fundamental experience which each man possesses and which is the mark of his being man, namely that *he is* goes beyond anything he may perceive or think of himself, being something deeper and more primary than the consciousness of which he is aware on the phenomenal level.

That self-awareness has been reached, in a unique way in the philosophical and religious history of mankind, by the Hindu tradition. We may say that the Hindu *sadhana* is entirely directed to discovering existentially the coincidence between man's conscious phenomenal awareness and the ultimate experience of the self in its absolute purity. It is the oversight of this fact that has brought to a deadlock most of the attempts at a dialogue between Christians on one side and Hindus—and also Buddhists—on the other.

As long as religion remains for a man—at least principally and concretely—on the level of rites, practices, formulae, structures, ethics and the like, it cannot but appear as something superimposed on what is his fundamental concern. True religion and true faith are necessarily rooted in self-awareness. Faith and revelation are precisely meant to release in man that level of self-awareness and to lead it at the level of the mind to a formulation and at the level of life to an expression which will do full justice to it. Religion could rightly be described as the relation of man with the depth of himself because it is only in the depth of his being that man reaches the depth of being itself and shares in the very mystery of the Godhead.

The main reason for the present outcry against organized religions is that they are cut off from life. And this, indeed, is often true, not only in the sense that man is cut off from the ordinary life by which he comes into contact with other men and with the world, but even more from that fundamental source of life in him which is his own experience of self-awareness.

The salvation of religions, even of cultures, in these critical times will depend on the renewal of man's awareness of that fundamental depth. Religious dialogue, properly understood, will be an invaluable help for all religious-minded people to discover and awaken in them the primary experience.

Religious Pluralism

Pluralism is a mark of human society, precisely because man is a being in community. Communion implies likeness but not identity. Identity suppresses communion and is the death of all relationships. Pluralism is a gift of God; it is part of the gift God makes to men in their human nature. The recognition and welcome given to it in our days by a growing number of people is certainly a sign of the times which no believer should disregard.

Pluralism is cultural and religious as well. Becoming conscious of it means for Christians a great change of outlook, and their theologians find it hard to interpret and formulate the consequences of that awareness. For many centuries, in fact, they had remained happily confined behind the high walls with which they had surrounded themselves, prepared to condemn to hell anyone who refused or even was ignorant of the Christian faith, or any Christian who did not belong to their own denomination or did not accept their own interpretation of Christ's message. Until quite recently they fought with utmost zeal against religious pluralism, trying to suppress it by converting all others to their own convictions.

The fact has at long last dawned on their consciousness that the other great religions of the world are very much alive. If these are threatened by the growing "humanism" of today, the same threat exists within Christianity itself. It is true that Christianity is now increasingly drawing to itself the followers of primitive religions; but this is mainly due to the incapacity of those religions to stand the impact of the modern world, and their members flock to Islam or communism in even greater numbers than to the Church. Within the compass of Christianity itself, pluralism fares well enough and crossing over from one group to another seems in practice equally balanced. Christians are wondering more and more whether the different historical forms of Christianity do not have sufficient roots in the New Testament itself for them to be accepted as valid expressions of the Christian experience, and whether the unity for which Christians are longing has not to be defined in a quite different way than was supposed up to now.

Not all religious people, however, look upon pluralism, even today, with this positive approach. Many still keep to the old fundamentalism which condemns indiscriminately all others; or, as is the case with Buddhism and Hinduism, they hope that in some future birth the "others" will have the chance to enter into the right path to salvation. Another attitude, steadily on the increase, and brought about precisely by the narrowness and intolerance of too many self-proclaimed believers, is a sort of estrangement from all religious forms and structures, with resort to merely personal sincerity and commitment or, especially in the East, to personal spiritual experience. Such an attitude should not, however, discourage the Christian endeavor to engage in dialogue any more than should the negative attitude still prevalent among most humanists. It is in their own faith and in their inner experience of the universal presence of the Spirit that Christians will find the way to bring others, not necessarily to their own doctrine and institution, but at least to the joyful acceptance of the multiplicity of forms through which the divine Spirit brings men to the Father.

Christians are now realizing with wonder—as did the Jews who accompanied Peter to Cornelius' house in Caesarea—that in his boundless freedom God has spoken mysteriously to humankind and is still doing so in many diverse ways—last but not least among which is the call for social justice, though this at first was heard more clearly by non-believers. Standing on the most secure biblical ground, Christians cannot but recognize the Presence of the Lord across the boundaries of their internal divisions as well as beyond the frontier of the visible Christian fold. Is it not a biblical truth that God wants all men to be saved, and therefore provides them with the proper means for it, even in their actual historical and individual setting? Did not Christ say that trees are recognized from their fruits? And who can honestly deny the presence of the fruits of the Spirit in many men who were never incorporated into the Church through water baptism? Is it not also an accepted truth for Christians, already found in Isaiah and later on in the whole New Testament, that all things have been made for Christ, and therefore that all the spiritual riches of mankind are destined in the plan of God to adorn the Church, the Bride of Christ, and thus to contribute to the growing unto its fullness of his Mystical Body?

Interreligious dialogue is the immediate consequence deriving from the acknowledgment and acceptance of religious pluralism. It is the concrete way to raise that pluralism to a personal and human level. It is through dialogue that spiritual riches will be mutually shared, in complete disinterestedness on the part of the giver and humility on the part of the receiver, whose roles are likely to alternate continuously in the process. Spiritual riches, even more than material riches, belong to all. They are the common property of all the children of God, and no one ever enjoys them more truly than when sharing them with his brothers.

Meeting Point

But religious dialogue, as already pointed at, cannot be any kind of dialogue. Dialogue of Christians with people of other religious persuasions can only take place at the very center of themselves. At the superficial, if not pragmatic, level of structures and formulations, dialogue is always limping, whether it be conducted between Christians or with any men, believers or humanists, concerned with the ultimate reality.

The only real meeting-point between men concerned with the ultimate is in the center of the self, in "the cave of the heart," as the Upanishads put it. Here is the very center of the human being, the principle of its unity. The same Upanishads call it now the *atman* then the *purusha*; we need not enter here into these distinctions. The fact is that man finds in himself, in his ultimate depths, the very center of the universe. There, beyond all symbols and concepts, he experiences his unity, his being together with all, despite or rather by means of differences on the bodily, mental and sociological planes. On those external levels, if taken in isolation, the unity of humankind and its harmony are always threatened: egoism emerges at all points, rivalry and competition set in, and with them strife. Religious matters have, in fact, perhaps been the most potent cause of dissension and hatred among men throughout history. Any unity eventually reached on those levels would forever remain precarious, because it is based on what is essentially changeable. The only unity and harmony which has a chance of enduring and of standing up to the ever-recurring assaults against it is the one which is founded on the sharing of our common experience in depth. Because it is rooted in such solid ground, that unity, and that alone, can make room, without thereby being shaken, for the mutual otherness of all men, their cultures and civilizations. It recognizes that all are one in their origin and principle, diverse and complementary in their manifestations. The unity and understanding aimed at by interreligious dialogue is no easy and shallow syncretism, but the courageous acceptance of both the unity and diversity of God's creation. Should not both be readily acceptable to one who has contemplated the mystery of the indivisible Trinity, where otherness of Persons and identity in nature combine together, leaving infinitely behind them any concept of otherness and unity man can formulate?

So long as anyone has not first penetrated within himself, he can hardly discover the possible meeting-point for dialogue, either between Christians or between Christians and other believers or humanists. The ideal preparation for dialogue would be that all partners have realized that depth. At least the one who initiates the dialogue must have discovered it; otherwise the danger is great that the dialogue will quickly come to an end or remain indefinitely at the level of superficial social relations. If one partner lives at the level of the Spirit, he will automatically give to the dialogue its proper dimension and depth; he will prevent it from staying on the plane of mere thoughts and feelings, and so from being at the mercy of the egoism and self-seeking always latent in the heart of man.

The real meeting-point between all religious-minded people can only be the place within themselves where they are on the watch for the Spirit, where their own spirit is so intimately joined with the Holy Spirit that there no longer is any movement within them that does not originate from the mysterious action of the Holy Spirit himself (cf. Romans 8:141).

The Present Kairos

Interreligious dialogue is coming to the fore in a crucial moment of human history and of the evolution of cultures, civilizations and religions, when all previous values are being shaken and arc no longer recognized, and when no one really knows what will tomorrow take the place of what is disappearing today.

In this crisis of religions, dialogue between believers should not, however, take the form of a crusade against atheism and humanism. It must not be prompted by a reflex of self-defense or self-protection. Not all the values of the past are worth retaining, at least in their present form. Times of crisis are provided by divine Providence to free man from unnecessary tics or crutches. These may once have been necessary, but man never ceases to develop, and is still far from having realized the newness of the Gospel and the message of total liberation which it has brought to the earth.

The object of interreligious dialogue is not, at least in the first place, the promotion of the temporal or spiritual welfare of any one of the groups which share in it. It aims first at the spiritual (and where necessary, the temporal) well-being of the whole of mankind, indeed of every member of the human family, in his actual situation and environment. Religions will learn from it how better to serve the common good, how to help realistically towards the salvific process which is developing in the heart of each man, whether or not each will have in his lifetime the opportunity to come to the "true" religion.

Far from considering their mutual dialogue as the first step of a universal crusade against atheism or humanism, the religions should rather welcome in their dialogue representatives of those groups. It is together with them that they will search for the means of saving the soul of mankind in the present rush to gratify the senses and satisfy the mind.

The solution for the crisis of the world must be found in common by all people of goodwill, by all men devoted to truth, in whatever way the truth may have manifested itself in the depth of their hearts. Their dialogue will be a searchlight which will probe the present societies of men, but will first scan the heart of those taking part in it. It will be the test of their allegiance to truth alone in their respective religious or humanist commitments.

Not only Christians, nor only believers, but every man who ever appeared on this earth is consecrated to truth as his birthright. Does not the light of the Logos shine in each heart as St. John says in the prologue of his Gospel? Society, together with each of the concentric circles with which man is surrounded—his family, those with whom he lives and works, his nation, his religion, etc.—is for him a means to realize that consecration, to discover more and more its exigencies. Christ proclaimed himself the Truth. He came to earth as the supreme witness to Truth; he reminded us that God desires to be worshipped in truth. And one of the favorite teachings of his beloved disciple was the need to walk in truth, to remain in the truth and to "do the truth."

Dialogue originates from a sincere and insatiable desire to know the truth more and more, to be more and more alive to the truth in our depth, to make our thoughts, desires and actions more and more expressive of the unique truth. For we know that in us truth is always mixed up with much that is untrue, like the gold, silver, wood, hay and straw which Paul mentions to his disciples at Corinth (I Corinthians 3:12). Is not, in fact, that mixture—unconscious but persistent even in people of good will—the main cause of the present moral crisis?

Dialogue also comes from the desire to share with others what we hold most precious, not, for sure, to impose it on them, but to help them to discover its source in their own hearts and to lead them to become more and more attentive and docile to the voice of the Spirit, who mysteriously reveals himself to them both inwardly and outwardly, in the depth of their soul as well as in the whole universe and history of man.

The remedy for the sickness of the world must be sought in common. It requires realistic assessments, starting from the inner demands of truth. But the demands of truth will only be discovered by men whose hearts are, unreservedly given to truth itself.

Rethinking Theology

The only principle of interreligious dialogue is truth; the only way for it to succeed is love. Dialogue docs not aim at shaking the convictions of others, but only at confronting each of the participants more vividly with the truth. The sincerity of each and his commitment to the Spirit will then act automatically.

Real dialogue will never end in minimalism or an easy syncretism. No one sharing in it will be inclined to part with his own true convictions. The result will be something quite new and unconceivable beforehand. It will be a purification of each one's own faith, not indeed in its essence, which is pure gold, but of the alloy with which it is always mixed. It will be a discovery of unity in diversity and diversity in unity.

From the depth at which it takes place, it will bring to light the mutual convergence of all religions: it will free groups and individuals from all negative attitudes. It will make them sensitive to common values and open to each other.

Only a man who has penetrated into his own depth is able to discover and meet the depth of another. Indeed, to penetrate into one's own depth is to penetrate into the depth of all. Only such a man has understood the depth and the very essence of his own religion. Religion is no longer for him a conventional pattern of thought and behavior received from his tradition, but a living experience of the Presence of God in himself and in the whole universe with the necessary commitments that flow from it.

This does not amount to saying that formulations, structures and rituals have to be discarded. They are necessary signs at the level of mental perception and of life in society; casting them aside, except perhaps in some extreme situations—this precisely is the intuition underlying the Hindu *sannyasa*—would result in depriving oneself of the normal ways of making manifest in actual life one's deep intuition of the mystery of God and man. But, in order to be true and to remain alive, those external elements must always be related in a living manner to that deep experience of which they are the sign. The danger is great, indeed, chiefly for minds formed on "Greek" lines to take the *eidos* for the reality itself and to move in the world of signs, formulae, rites and structures, as if they had value in themselves.

A theology which does not put dialogue with other theologies and that necessarily includes other religions as well—at the very center of its outlook on the things of God or of its interpretation of the Word—is a limping theology, a one-legged Brahman, as Yajnavalkya used to tell king Janaka. A theology in which dialogue—between Christians, men of various religious traditions, and finally with all people of good will concerned with the ultimate—is only an appendix without any bearing on the substance, and therefore something unessential, not an integral theology. The ecumenical or trans-ecumenical dialogue which goes along with such a theology runs the risk of remaining at the level of kindly attitudes—a smile we are prepared to give to our "other" friends when per chance we meet them, but which we soon forget when we are back safely home. Such is the danger of any dialogue which remains on the social or intellectual plane. Only dialogue in depth avoids being "added," "superimposed," for it is founded on the very emergence of theological thought in the mind of the partners. Dialogue on the intellectual level, on the contrary, deals with only a compartment of our theological or religious thought, without reaching to our deep religious convictions which remain unaffected; it has no existential value.

Dialogue cannot be something extrinsically added to life, to thought, to prayer. If it is not an integral part of the man, of his thought and his prayer, it is not real. It is not an optional part of spirituality or theology, but an intrinsic component. If it is real, it springs from the depths of the soul.

The fate of practically all Christian theologies so far has been that, while starting from the Gospel, they have speculated on it at leisure with the help of successive philosophical systems, especially Greek essentialism, down to the present existentialism. They have determined in a rigorous manner the divine plan of salvation and have given ample intellectual foundation to the structures at work in the Church, thus deciding here below all matters concerning the other world. All went well as long as the human mind accepted, without raising questions, that the *others* are practically excluded from the economy of salvation—even if in fact these *others* included the majority of God's children. Then the realization came slowly that such an attitude is not only inhuman but unchristian, and it became impossible to follow Augustine's idea of the *massa damnata*. Theologians then tried to work out a plan of salvation which would somehow include the *others*, but without altering the brilliant construction and synthesis they had already made. No accepted theology has yet tackled the problem adequately; dialogue in depth, however, is bound to call for a revision of the system, and it may be anticipated that the shock will be great.

Vatican II has given us useful directions in the matter. Yet it must be said that even the best chapters of the Constitutions on the Church and on the Church in the Modern World do not draw the ultimate conclusions deriving from their generous admittance of the possibility of salvation outside the Church. They do not satisfactorily integrate the others into the plan of salvation. Even in those excellent documents it still seems that the salvation of others is an act of condescension on the part of God, something happening outside the normal dispensation. Yet theological reflection in its very starting point should give as much importance to the consideration of the *others* as it does to the "special" situation of the "children of the promise." This does not lead to an easy syncretism, but merely to recognizing that the plan of God extends far beyond the limits which our little minds are only too ready to impose on it.

Theology should never be a mere intellectual exercise. Being a *word* about God, word of God (*theologia*), it cannot but be based on the experience of the Spirit. No one can say "Jesus is Lord" except in the Spirit (1 Corinthians 12:3). A theology of dialogue and ecumenism must be based on true spirituality. But this, again, does not mean that spirituality or theology need to be in some way adapted to answer the needs of ecumenism and dialogue; rather, the high demands of dialogue and ecumenism precisely oblige us to deepen our theology and spirituality to the point when they become automatically integrated into it. Dialogue and ecumenism are graces offered to us that we may become Christian in a deeper and richer manner.

Only a contemplative spirituality can be the proper foundation for a pluralistic theology. As long as God is known only through formulae and meditated upon through a mere operation of the mind, as long also as our love for him is confined to feelings and sentiments, it remains impossible for us to realize the limitations of our own approach to the divine mystery. Only the experience of the divine Presence beyond all concepts and feelings will make it possible for us to accept the mystery of the multiform grace and love of the Lord. God is the Absolute. No one of his manifestations can express him completely: yet God is fully present in such manifestations. At the same time, only such a contemplative attitude removes from dialogue the danger of syncretism. The center of the soul is not the intellect, as a theology too dependent on Plato and Aristotle is inclined to believe. It is the real center—the *atman* of the Vedantic tradition—that man must discover in himself, beyond all manifestations. From that center only can man transcend himself, his thoughts, his senses, as well as the whole universe, beyond all man-made distinctions. At the level of the soul's self-consciousness, man recognizes both the presence of God, the Absolute, in each of his manifestations, and the impossibility for any of those manifestations to express the mystery of the Absolute in a fully integral manner. Here is the very foundation for a pluralistic, not syncretistic, theology. And this is in fact what the apophatic tradition always stood for in the Church.

East and West

Only people who have at least some experience of the depth are able to come together or a real and fruitful dialogue. Mere thinkers will forever remain unable to understand the real faith and commitment to truth of others.

The dialogue between Hinduism and Christianity, for instance, will remain in a blind alley as long as people are content with confronting Shankara with, say, Aquinas or Barth. At that level of theology, technical philosophical reflections and formulations have already petrified the primordial intuitions. We are, for the main part, on the plane of *eidos*; and *eidos*, proud of its worth, is generally reluctant to allow itself to be referred to its source, to the intuition, that is, the fundamental, supra-mental, experience and perception as it emerges in the mind. *Eidos* is undoubtedly of extreme value; but its value is that of a sign, always pointing beyond itself.

It is the intuitions themselves which arise at the horizon of the mind, that need to be compared and confronted with each other if we wish really to discover their mutual connections, to test the possible osmosis between them. In view of this, each partner in dialogue must try to make his own, as far as possible, the intuition and experience of the other, to personalize it in his own depth, beyond his own ideas and even beyond those through which the other attempts to express and communicate them with the help of the signs available in his tradition. For a fruitful dialogue it is necessary that I reach, as it were, in the very depth of myself to the experience of my brother, freeing my own experience from all accretions, so that my brother can recognize in me his own experience of his own depth.

The detachment and the freedom required by such dialogue is no doubt enormous; yet at no lesser cost is real fellowship and communion possible between men. Interreligious dialogue is something too important to be taken lightly. If it does not bring me to the center of my heart, to the very source of my life and faith, it is a lie.

Communion in depth is especially necessary if Christians wish to engage in dialogue with the religions of the East, namely Buddhism and Hinduism. Even more than Christianity and Islam, these are primarily religions of inner experience. Christianity, and Judaism and Islam as well, spring from the inner experience of their founders and tend to develop in their adherents the same inner experience of the mystery of God. Yet all of them are historical religions, rooted in Abraham's experience—shared by the subsequent prophets—that God spoke to him in a particular place and at a definite time of world history. The same God was not content to unveil his presence in the spirit of the patriarch; he gave him a special revelation, imposed on him a particular *dharma*, made with him and his progeny a definite covenant. The religions which came in the wake of Abrahamic revelation could not but be strongly marked by a sense of history, attributing great value to the mental and sociological signs that embodied the Abrahamic covenant.

For Hinduism and Buddhism, all dharmas, formulae, rituals and institutions, however useful and necessary they may be at the growing stage of religious consciousness, remain forever provisional and have no other value except that of leading man to the direct awareness of his depth. The day comes for each believer—even if only after a thousand births—when all externals, even the Scriptures, have to be discarded lest, when the final experience begins to dawn in the depth of the soul, they become an impediment to liberation and salvation.

We do not want to enlarge here on the fundamental problem raised for Christianity by Hinduism and Buddhism. But we must stress that to discard a priori the standpoint of Hinduism–Buddhism because it does not seem to fit into the fundamental affirmations of the Christian faith would not be an honest, or even intelligent, attitude. The Christian should instead become aware that the Abrahamic, and later on the Mosaic and evangelical revelations, took place in a milieu—the semitico-mediterranean one—strongly marked by a practical dualism: in that cultural context the idea that God and man encounter each other face to face raised no problem. On the other hand, the fundamental religious attitude of the East, consciously lived and expressed since the earliest Upanishads, is that man, when he comes to the experience of the divine Presence, is absolutely unable to situate himself apart, and, as it were, in face of that *Other*, overwhelmed as he is by the all-pervading and unencompassed Glory. This attitude too is valid. It is true that God's special revelation to man took place by divine choice within the Mediterranean religious and cultural area. Yet, the catholicity of Christianity is precisely put to the most severe test when it comes into contact with those Eastern religions. The integration of their fundamental intuition is vital for Christianity, if it wishes to survive and develop organically in the East, however remote that integration may seem to be at present.

However, before comparing and relating the two approaches to the divine mystery, the Christian must first try to understand, to plumb the depth of the Eastern religious experience. As long, for instance, as Vedanta is for him a mere concept, unrelated to his own spiritual life and experience of God's presence, he is absolutely incompetent to make any judgment of compatibility or incompatibility between the Christian and the Vedantic experiences. The self-awareness of advaitic experience is the highest human experience. It must therefore be capable of being taken up, redeemed and transformed by the Holy Spirit, into the very experience of divine sonship which was the foundation of Jesus' personal self-awareness and which he imparted to all those who give their faith to him. No dialogue, therefore, is possible between Christians and Hindus or Buddhists which does not take into account that experience of self-awareness and the advaitic expression given to it by those who have made it.

The Christian, however, who accepts such a deepening of his own consciousness will not fail to be wonderfully rewarded. Penetrating deeper and deeper into his own soul and nearer and nearer to the Spirit who dwells in it, he will share in a living manner in the experience of Jesus himself of being both one with the Father and from the Father. He will understand in a new and marvelous light what Jesus says in the Gospel of his relation with the Father and men, his brothers.

In Full Freedom

Only if it takes place in the depth can interreligious dialogue be marked with full freedom, integrity and unshakable dedication to truth—all essential conditions without which it is not serious. We cannot deny that many people are genuinely afraid of dialogue. They well realize—even when they shrink from admitting it—that dialogue may bring about changes in their mind, in their attitude and approach to reality.

Men are always ready to teach others, in order to "convert" them to their own view of the Real. They are willing to argue, on their own basis, determined not to yield an inch of ground to their "adversary," but wanting by all means to defeat and confound him. Such "dialogue" is in fact no dialogue at all; it does not involve any commitment. It remains entirely on the level of feelings and concepts, and has nothing to do with truth. It is but self-assertion. Real dialogue aims at truth, whatever the price. Is not truth the pearl spoken of by Jesus, to acquire which, man goes and sells everything he possesses? Dialogue is possible only if people accept to put themselves entirely at the service of truth and no longer to act as if truth was their possession. This implies that, deeply and unshakably attached to his own religious convictions as he may be, man nevertheless admits that the expression of truth, as it is formulated by his own religious group and translated, more or less consciously, in his own pattern of thought, can never claim full coincidence with Truth itself.

People do not mind superficial dialogue, that namely which by tacit agreement or by the will of one of the persons involved, remains at a level where no one feels personally concerned. In this kind of platonic discussion, the interlocutors are only interested in playing logic and asserting themselves. Mutual acceptance, on the academic level, even of contradicting ideas has nothing to do with the acceptance of pluralism, referred to above, where the most personal plane in man is involved.

But people are really afraid of any dialogue which would lead to exposing the deepest recesses of their minds, the true reasons for their strongest attachments and convictions; often at work in these are reactions, outgrowths of a poorly integrated subconscious, dregs of past experiences, compensations. On the other hand, each man is anxious to give himself and others the most lofty reasons for action, decisions, conversion.

Real dialogue is bound to operate as a kind of searchlight, no less disturbing to our false securities than is a course of psychoanalysis. Only men of full sincerity and complete interior freedom will open themselves to it without misgivings.

We can very well see why individuals and groups—believers and atheists alike—are afraid to expose themselves to such light. A protective attitude, a desire for security is common to all closed groups. Yet why be so much afraid? When the house is built on the rock, there is no fear of torrents or cyclones. . . . Why then be afraid of books or people who do not fit into our own thought-patterns? Does not, in fact, such fear lead to the suspicion that our convictions are not as unassailable as we pretend they are?

We are afraid of being shown up and shaken out of our complacency, we are afraid of losing something of our identity, or rather of the identity we are building for ourselves day after day, along the line, most often, of what we approve of in ourselves. Yet is not rather such an identity an alienation which prevents us from realizing our inner and real self? Is not dialogue in depth the best means to free us from false identities and personal alienations, to discover our true self and to base our faith and religious convictions and practices on the solid and unshakable rock of self-awareness?

Freedom and total dedication to truth are possible only when a man's conscious identity coincides with his true depth. Until then, man is not free. He remains the slave of a mass of complexes, always afraid to lose himself. He identifies himself with superficial—even if deep-rooted—knots of his psyche. He is at the mercy of his impulses: what he takes for truth is what is more conformable to his own ego. The man who is really free has nothing to hide. Certainly, he will not spontaneously exhibit himself, but neither will he be ashamed or nervous to be exposed in full light.

Fear, moreover, is not Christian. There is no room for fear in the mind and heart of a man who has been redeemed by Christ, except the fear of being separated from God. Christ has delivered man from all fears. This is the message of the Bible, especially of Paul and John: "Fear is driven out by perfect love" (1 John 4:18); "With God on our side who can be against us? . . . Who shall separate us from the love of Christ?" (Romans 8:31ff).

Man is liable to fear as long as he looks for stability at a level established by him. Once he has discovered in himself that deeper level of himself which is the Spirit, he becomes as unshakable as God himself.

This stability is both a grace and a personal psychological achievement. But it may not be confused with the stubbornness of the unintelligent or the ego-exaltation of the Stoics and of many hatha yogis. Self-integration and deep stability is in man the highest point of his psychological development. Western methods of psychoanalysis help in the process, chiefly by treating malformations standing in the way; Eastern methods of *sadhana* aim directly at realizing it. But the Christian, more than anyone else, knows that integration and realization is, first of all, a grace, the supreme gift of the indwelling Spirit.

The pity is that religion, and, in our case, Christ as well, have too often been put at the service of our own identity, whereas we should have built it on, or rather discovered it in, him—not in any idea of him. We have made use of Christ and of truth; they have been for us a means to develop our personality; we have acted as if Christ belonged to us.

We do not deny that religion is a powerful means of self-integration, the most powerful indeed, even in the present age of mankind. Religious archetypes help more than anything else to express on the phenomenal level our real and hidden life. Yet, the real lies beyond all archetypes. Formulations are necessary aids, but they are not the central core of faith.

Fear is absent when faith is fixed on the center of our being. Danger is present only when faith is built on some ex-centric knots, like guilt-complexes, compensations, and the like. Such faith does not save. Real faith is beyond all formulations. The faith which is shaken when some formulations are threatened is not real faith.

Dialogue supposes in all partners the total freedom of the children of God. Man has really nothing to lose in it: what can be lost is not worth retaining. True dialogue will not compromise with truth; it will put those engaged in it unreservedly at the service of truth.

All development of man—at the individual or social level—aims at making him realize his true identity. It all aims at his self-awareness in the depth of his spirit where he shares in the *Aham asmi*, the *I am*, of the One-Who-Is, and thereby fulfills his own destiny.

Dialogue helps man to free himself from all structures superimposed on him by his culture, language, and the like—including the so-called worldwide civilization of today, no less oppressive than anyone in the past—as well as from all the defenses and false securities he has built around himself. It leads him to recognize truth in *itself* and in *himself*. It leads to worship *in spirit and truth*.

At the Level of the Spirit

Dialogue begins with the acceptance of oneself before God in full freedom and in the freedom from fear which characterizes the children of God. It naturally springs from a soul which, in its depth, is constantly on the watch for and at the disposal of the Holy Spirit. Man cannot stand the searchlight of interreligious dialogue—either as an individual or in the name of the group of believers to which he belongs—unless he has first accepted to be searched within, down to the remotest and darkest corners of himself, by the Light of the Word of God (cf. Hebrews 4:12).

Openness to others in dialogue depends on openness to the Spirit in oneself. Openness to others is, indeed, openness to the Spirit who is present everywhere, in the core of every being and event, and more still in the heart of every man and in all outward manifestations of his heart. Jesus never ceased to contemplate his Father while he looked at the fields and the lake, and even less while he looked at men, his brothers.

The most effective and fruitful dialogue will, therefore, be the one which is conducted at the level of the Spirit. Ideas are conveyed and transmitted by means of words; words are exchanged through the medium of sound waves. All those external channels of communication are true in proportion only as they are signs of internal communication.

The Spirit is the proper milieu of communication of those who participate in him. On the external level of words and ideas, men never attain to their true unity. There they are at the mercy of their feelings and of their own concept of truth: their mind and will are carried away in the ever moving "flow of becoming" in which the whole universe is engulfed. Only at the level of the Spirit is there stability, underlying the flow of the surface. And only those who are attuned to the Spirit in themselves can attune themselves to the Spirit in others.

This attuning goes far beyond sharing in formal prayer as may or may not be done at the beginning and end of a meeting. It means the kind of "looking inwards," the *antar-mukha* of the Hindu tradition, which in the man who has made the experience of the Spirit underlies all activity.

True dialogue originates in the silence of the Spirit, and ends in the same silence. Words and ideas, exchanged in the interval, arc penetrated and enriched by this silence. A religious meeting which does not spontaneously lead, at least at the end, to moments of deep and felt silence is suspect of having altogether missed the point. This is why ecumenical or interreligious dialogue through formal meetings and discussions is not in fact the most effective. That stage must by all means be reached one day, but such exchanges of words and ideas need first to be prepared by a long fellowship in life and service.

Communion in the depth is already present when "separated" Christians or Christians and non-Christians live together the full commitment of their inner convictions. They may be silent on the subject of interreligious dialogue, while working together for justice and charity among men; they may even be simply silent and engage in no special activity whatsoever, simply sharing together, without trying to analyze it, a life of prayer, silence and humble service.

If all are living in their own depth, as intimately aware as they can of the Spirit present in them—no matter under which name or form he makes himself known—there takes place between them, beyond words, a wonderful communication at the level of the Spirit through the *milieu* that is the Spirit. This happens between Christians and other believers, and it happens as well between believers and non-believers. It is from such a communion of life and discovery of the Spirit in each other that the ecumenical movement derives its power, and those pioneering it the boldness to forge ahead with prophetic initiatives.

Man at times mistakes his own spirit for *the* Spirit, and Christians need to remain on their guard to avoid this danger. Yet, the Spirit cannot be stilled (cf. 1 Thessalonians 5:19). It is indeed by becoming increasingly free in themselves and from themselves that men can be made into true instruments of the Spirit within them, and give to both the Church and the world the prophets for whom there is a crying need today.

The salvation of the world and the overcoming by the Church of its present crisis will depend on all people of goodwill coming together in truth and in the Spirit; all men, that is, who within themselves have heard the voice of the Spirit and have not been afraid to listen to it and to abide by it.

III
ENCOUNTERS

In the Cave of the Heart: A Meeting of *Sanatana Dharma* and *Sophia Perennis*[1]

Barry McDonald

In this life there are moments which are written in the heart; they leave one permanently changed because they participate in a realm outside of time. Such was our audience with Swami Avimukteshwarananda at the Shankara monastery in Banaras. Reminiscent of gatherings—which I had the privilege to attend—where Frithjof Schuon, the great Spiritual Master and exponent of *Sophia Perennis*, and Thomas Yellowtail, Crow Medicine Man and Sun Dance Chief, spoke and interacted with each other, our meeting at the Shankara monastery near Kedar temple on the banks of the Ganges was a universal affirmation, across time and space, of the essential identity of *Sanatana Dharma* and *Sophia Perennis.* Unlike the meetings, however, between Schuon and Yellowtail, which rarely touched upon metaphysical doctrine, but served more as lessons in character and virtue, reflecting the beauty of Yellowtail's spiritual being and what one might call the "ontological" pole of the Red Indian spirit, our audience with the saintly young *Jnanin* underscored in a vivid manner the profound relationship between certain metaphysical teachings of Adi Shankara and how they are mirrored in the doctrinal perspective of Frithjof Schuon.

The anchoring Shiva temple has an imposing position on the Ganges; it presides over the southernmost section of the city and it is one of the most important temples in Banaras because in its *sanctum sanctorum* is a "self-manifest" *linga.* As Diana Eck notes in her book on Banaras the priestly tradition teaches that this *linga* was a jewel in the Golden Age; in the Silver Age it turned to gold; in the Bronze Age it turned to silver; and in the current Iron Age—or *Kali-Yuga*—it turned to stone. The Banaras temple is affiliated with Kedarnath, high in the Himalayas, considered one of India's twelve *lingas* of light. Near the Kedarnath temple is the *mahasamadhi* of the spiritual giant Adi Shankara, the great eighth century exponent of *Advaita Vedanta.* Like Banaras, this temple is considered a *tirtha,* an earthly place charged with purity and power; a doorway between Heaven and earth.

Near Kedara temple in Banaras is a Shankara monastery, affiliated with Kedarnath in the Himalayas, where we arrived in the afternoon for an audience in the small cell of Swami Avimukteshwarananda Saraswati, a young saint who received *sannyasa* directly from H.H. Jagadguru Shankaracharya Swami Swarupananda Sarasvati, the current Jagadguru who is, exceptionally, the Shankaracharya of both Dwarka and Jyotirmath; two of the four *Vidyapithas*, or monastic centers of spiritual wisdom, founded by Adi Shankara. We were informed prior to our meeting that Swami Avimukteshwarananda will most likely be the next Jagadguru of Jyotirmath. Along with the young sage, who understood English well but spoke very little, was his translator Sri Sadashiva Ashrama, a highly articulate *sannyasin* who studied at Oxford and Harvard before renouncing. Also present were the weaver Rebecca McDonald, the artist and musician Susanna Marin, and the author and publisher of Indica books in Banaras, Alvaro Enterria, who had kindly arranged for our meeting and made the introductions. After formally greeting, I received the impression that the young Swami, who manifested great kindness and

[1] From a journal entry dated March 11, 2006 in Banaras.

attention to our every word, was like a man surrounded by silence of *Jnana*. In contrast, Swami Sadashiva was animated and articulate; he translated freely, and gave the impression of being like a flowing river of light. In the presence of these sages one immediately felt spiritually drawn to them, and felt as if one were in the presence of living exponents of the still-flowering tree of the primordial Indian tradition. We told these two saintly figures that we were very happy to be in this holy monastery in the spiritual heart of India and that we wished to offer the greetings of our *Guru*, Frithjof Schuon, who having left the body some eight years ago still lives in our hearts; and also the greetings of his many disciples throughout the world. We told them of his meeting with Swami Ramdas many years ago in London where Mr. Schuon, known by many as the *Sufi Shaykh Isa Nur ad-Din*, said that "At heart we are like Hindus—Hindus in the *Sufi* form." We further explained that Mr. Schuon's spiritual teachings mirrored those of the *Vedanta* and that it could be summarized as follows: discernment between the real and the illusory (*Vedanta*); concentration upon the Real (*Japa*) and conformation of soul to the Real (*Dharma*). The Swamis expressed a lively interest in this three-fold message. We explained that Mr. Schuon's outlook was that of the *Sophia Perennis*, which expresses the permanent and universal Truth at the heart of every Revelation, Swami Sadashiva noted that the word "perennial" was a close translation of the Sanskrit word "*sanatana*." Additionally, we continued that like the *Vedanta*, which expounds the nature of Reality over and above the theologies as such, the *Sophia Perennis* points to the absolute Oneness of the Real and that all of the religious traditions stream like rays from this single Sun. At this point, Swami Sadashiva said: "Sir, this is true *Vedanta*. For people like you there is no place but India; you have the mind of an Indian and you belong to us." Swami Avimukteshwarananda nodded in agreement and added: "Unlike the ordinary Muslim, the *Sufis* find *satguna* in all things." Swami Sadashiva said: "This teaching is the cream of *Sufism*." He also commented that the disciples of a spiritual man are "a blessing for the entire world."

Following these comments a discussion began concerning the ultimate relationship between the *Shahadah*, which is the root of Islam: "*La ilaha illa 'Llah; Muhammadun Rasulu 'Llah*": "There is no God but God; and Muhammad is the Messenger of God" and the famous dictum of Adi Shankara, which is the quintessence of *Advaita Vedanta*: "*Brahma satyam jagan-mithya; jivo brahmaiva naparah:* "*Brahman* is Real; the world is not Real; the individual soul is non-different from *Brahman*." We explained to the Swamis that our Master provided an esoteric interpretation of the *Shahadah*: "There is no *Atma* but *Atma*, and *Maya* is the Messenger of *Atma*," or "There is no Principle but the Principle and Manifestation is the Messenger of the Principle." They indicated that they understood perfectly well how the first part of the *Shahadah* correlated with *Vedanta*; however, there was some lack of clarity in the second part. Also, Swami Avimukteshwara noted that unlike the dictum of Shankara, for Muslims the *Shahadah* is a commandment. Without denying the truth of his statement in terms of Islamic theology, we would clarify by explaining, like the *Vedantic* formulation, the *Shahadah* is an expression of universal Truth, over and above the fact that it is also the testimony of faith; the second part of the *Shahadah* relates—according to Schuon's teaching—"to the manifested Principle (*Muhammad*), the manifesting Principle (*Rasul*) and the Principle in itself (*Allah*)." According to this teaching, one must understand *Maya* not exclusively as that which veils the One, but as the infinite power of its Self-Disclosure, its Unity underlying the diversity of creation and allowing for the sage to understand the interconnectedness of all things. There followed some comments regarding what the Sufis term the "*haqiqah Muhammadiyah*," the essential Reality of the Prophet (upon whom be blessings and peace) which may be understood in a parallel sense to the *Vedantic* "*jivo brahmaivah naparah.*"

As a side note, for the interested reader who may wish to further pursue this line of thought, Schuon writes in his chapter "The Quintessential Esoterism of Islam" in *Sufism: Veil and Quintessence*: ". . . *Muhammadun Rasulu 'Llah* refers to Unity, not exclusive this time, but inclusive; it enunciates, not distinction, but identity; not discernment, but union; not transcendence, but immanence; not the objective and macrocosmic discontinuity of the degrees of Reality, but the subjective and microcosmic continuity of the one Consciousness. The second Testimony is not static and separative like the first, but dynamic and unitive." To highlight this profound connection with *Vedanta*, Schuon has written that the *Shahadah* is both *Mantra* and *Upanishad*.

Returning to the narrative, the question of disagreement between the religions arose. This audience took place only a few days after the bombing at the Sankat Mochan temple, less than one kilometer from our hotel. We said that Mr. Schuon taught that a fundamental problem with the religions is that in their exoteric forms they are entirely enclosed within *Maya*. By this Schuon meant that each religion is a kind of "saving mirage" with its own "confessional face" and though of the utmost importance to believers, the personal God as understood by the vast majority of religious people must be at the level of the "relative absolute," not the pure Absolute, as such, which is beyond all name and form. Swami Avimukteshwara, laughed lightly and it was commented upon that trying to understand *Maya* is like examining darkness with a torch. This allowed us to mention again the idea of the transcendent unity of the religions, which must be understood in the light of the essential and universal metaphysics of the pure Absolute, and again Swami Sadashiva affirmed that this idea is pure *Vedanta*. As the audience unfolded and the subject of *Jihad* arose, and we were able to explain that the greater *Jihad* pertains to overcoming the *tamas* within the soul; to transcending oneself in view of God. The fundamentalists who betray Islam have perverted this idea to serve a political end, and they will be judged by God. Swami Sadashiva then spoke these unforgettable words: "Our spiritual warfare is keeping a calm mind in the turmoil of the world." When we showed the Swamis a photograph of Mr. Schuon, they viewed it for some time before commenting. Swami Sadashiva then spoke, and said that it is the face of an *Avatara*.

Swami Avimukteshwara asked how we found Banaras and I told him that it was like a struck tuning fork; vibrating at a very high spiritual frequency. Both Swamis liked this image and Swami Sadashiva said that in Banaras one need not do anything except enter the frequency of this vibration; God will do the rest. This observation reminded us of an occasion when our Master remarked that we need not make an extraordinary effort to be intelligent; rather, we should simply stop being stupid. This recollection caused both Swamis to openly laugh in agreement. We went on to say that we believed in the truth of the tradition that Banaras is *Atman* in the form of a city, and that *Ganga Ma* is the stream of *Jnana*. The young saint was radiant at hearing these words, and Swami Sadashiva added that "this consciousness must continually flow." According the tradition of *Kashi Moksha Nirmaya*, "Here sleep is yoga, and going about town is sacrifice. O Goddess, eating whatever one pleases is the great sanctified food-offering to the gods. One's play, O Goddess, is a holy act of charity. Everyday conversation is the repetition of God's Name. And lying on one's bed is prostration." To our great delight, we were invited to return to the monastery the next morning for another meeting, this time alone with Swami Sadashiva, who would give us a traditional commentary on *The Morning Hymn* of Shankara, a discussion of the life of Sadashivendra Sarasvati, a seventeenth century Tamil saint, his namesake, and one of the favorite saints of the *Jagadguru* of *Sringeri*, from whom he learned

Vedanta, and a reading from the *Bhagavad-Gita*. Our afternoon audience concluded with his chanting from memory of the entire seventh chapter of the *Gita*.

It has been said that sages like Adi Shankara and Frithjof Schuon appear once every thousand years, but spiritual men and women everywhere and in all traditions may be grateful to Heaven that from the headwaters in the mountain ranges of the highest metaphysical Truth there flows through time a stream from which all seekers may drink. The words of Krishna to Arjuna in the seventh chapter of that great hymn of the Lord, once referred to by Schuon as the "bible of esoterism," and with which Swami Sadashiva concluded our second day at the monastery, will ever resonate in the mind:

All these are indeed noble,
But the man of wisdom is thought to
be my very Self.
He, indeed, whose mind is steadfast,
Abides in Me, the supreme goal.

Muhammad Pickthall and the Twilight of Classical Islam

Rodney Blackhirst

The reputation of Muhammad Marmaduke Pickthall (1875-1936) in contemporary Islam is strangely ambiguous. He is, on the one hand, well known as a foremost British convert to the Muslim faith and is even better known, or even famed, as a translator of the Holy Koran into English. On the other hand, he is a character from another era, one that has passed, and so contemporary Muslims, including today's converts to Islam, have some difficulty appreciating his life and work. He is always mentioned among renowned Western converts, yet such mentions rarely extend far beyond his name; his story is not related because it does not resonate with Islam in our times. Pickthall's Koran, although rightly celebrated as a great achievement, is written in an English that is now archaic and difficult for contemporary readers. His life is the same. His journey, his struggle and his point of view is not relevant to our times. Today's Muslims—especially British Muslims—are happy to claim him as one of their own, and they know that he was a significant figure in his own era, but it is hard to place him within the landscape of contemporary Islamic ideas, and so reception of his legacy is muted. He was once the pre-eminent convert to Islam from the English speaking world; in today's Islam that title goes to Cat Stevens, a pop star, (or perhaps Cassius Clay, a pugilist?)—Marmaduke Pickthall is an old-fashioned name from the past.

It is, however, the fact that Pickthall does *not* fit neatly into the contemporary Islamic milieu that makes him a useful subject of study. The fact that things about which he was passionate, such as the Ottoman Empire and the Nizamate of Hyderabad are now causes long lost and quite irrelevant to our times, can still serve to remind us of the extent to which the world, and Islam, have changed. Pickthall does not belong in modern Islam; he saw and belonged to the twilight of what we might call "classical" Islam, and a study of his life and works alerts us to how remarkably different the Islam of today is to the Islam that he loved and eventually embraced. The purpose of the present article is simply to draw attention to the most obvious of these differences and to give a sketch of the "classical" (or traditional) Islam to which Pickthall belonged.

The son of an Anglican minister, Pickthall was raised in an atmosphere of comfortable middle-class English piety and attended good schools, but as a young man he developed a deep interest in the so-called "Orientalist" scholarship of his day and then began traveling to the Middle East with a view to learning the "oriental" languages. He had been sickly, suffering from chronic bronchitis, from an early age, and the warmer climate of the east suited him far better than did England. And so, from his early twenties onwards, he became of lover of the Levant and of Turkish and Arabic culture. In England he became a leading member of the Anglo-Ottoman Friendship Society and began to promote tolerance for and understanding of the oriental "Other." His travels were supported by his mother and by his writings. He was the author of over thirty novels, most set in the "Orient," and of travel books, journals and essays.

His interest in Islam, as a spiritual home and as an alternative to the Christianity into which he was born, seems to have developed early, but his official conversion to the Muslim creed did not occur until much later, either because of his own hesitations or, as some supposed, because he was waiting until after his mother died. By his own account, the matters that galvanized him and set him firmly on the road to conversion were a reflection of the political climate in English society and a hardening of public opinion against the Turks. The British had once seen the Ottoman Empire as a friend against Russian Czardom. It was felt that the Turks were benign, civil—indeed noble—and maintained peace and good governance in the east. Consequently there was a considerable foundation of cross-cultural relations and good will with Turkish civilization. For their part, the Ottomans were looking to closer relations with European powers. This was mainly because their once-great Empire had, in fact, grown complacent and corrupt, had been out-stripped industrially, technologically and militarily and so was weakened and increasingly vulnerable to external aggression. Its hold over its territories and over the ethnic groups under its administration was slipping. It had gone into terminal decline, but it maintained a kind of faded glory and the pretence of a sumptuous greatness which Europe remembered and admired.

Then, late in the nineteenth century, British interests began to shift, and from about the prime ministership of Gladstone onwards, antagonism grew between the Turkish and British Empires. Public thinking soured and to "turn Turk" became synonymous with treason and treachery. Pickthall relates an occasion where he was attending Sunday service at an Anglican Church and being shocked and upset by prayers and psalms dedicated to the Ottoman's demise. He reached a point, he says, where he could no longer participate in Christian worship—then it was only a matter of time before he would accept Islam. When he finally announced his conversion publicly, it was a dramatic event. He was a well-known figure, and his conversion was taken as a statement of protest and defiance.

Contemporary Muslims can appreciate the rising tide of anti-Islamic sentiment against which Pickthall made a stand, but his political context was almost the reverse of our own. Pickthall was a Tory, a social and political conservative, a lover and defender of religious tradition and indeed of the British Empire and the Crown. He was very far from being a radical left wing activist. In his time the British upper classes and aristocracy tended to be sympathetic to the Ottomans and there were a surprising number of converts in those circles. In terms of British politics it was Labor that led the frenzy against the "evil Turk." In our own time it is not a generalization to say that the conservative wing of political life is, on the whole, averse to Islam, while the more "multi-cultural" and internationalist left tends to a more sympathetic perspective. The right tends to view Islam as a threat to "Western values" and to Western cultural integrity, while it is leftists who are less inclined to view Muslims as the enemy in a "Clash of Civilizations" scenario and who are opposed to such "Western supremacist" and interventionist misadventures as "regime change" in Iraq. Today's politics are quite different to those of Pickthall's time. For this reason alone, Pickthall is hard to situate within contemporary Islam. A right-wing conservative convert to Islam? The Muslim communities now living in the West, including Great Britain, are working class immigrants and the new generation of converts is largely drawn from disaffected and unemployed urban youth. Pickthall's politics makes little sense to them. The political axis has shifted fundamentally in this regard.

It is Pickthall's lifelong endorsement of *empire*—both the Ottoman and the British, and as a mode of government in general—that especially places him in a by-gone political milieu. Our post-colonial world can only imagine empire as an evil, as a device of oppression. For Pickthall it was a precondition of freedom. He writes of the Levant that greeted him as a young man as a world of extraordinary freedom. In our age we associate freedom with the nationalist liberation struggles of peoples clamoring to rid themselves of imperial rule. In their strategic moves against the Ottomans the British gave support to Arab nationalist aspirations. When first the Ottoman and then the British empires dissolved, they were replaced with a patchwork of local nation states. Pickthall saw this as an approaching danger. He warned against the rise of petty nation states and valued the stability and commerce that empires allowed. In his view the Ottoman Empire in the east, and also British rule in India, enabled religious and ethnic tolerance and a broad and diverse pan-Islamism to prevail. Pickthall warned that if these empires crumbled their territories would become arenas for civil war, tyranny and ethnic cleansing, with Muslim at war with Muslim. And worse, it would bring to the east a new insidious institution: the intrusive modern state.

The freedom that Pickthall found in the east was a libertarian freedom from the state. He describes how, in Palestine, local life continued under Ottoman rule exactly as it had done for centuries. Most people, he says, would never see a policeman in their entire life. Instead, life was regulated by the organic patterns of Islamic law and culture. People knew that they were ruled by the Caliph in Istanbul, and they respected him and mentioned him in their daily prayers, but they also had nothing to do with him and they expected that he would stay out of their daily affairs. Pickthall found rich pockets of traditional, local Islamic life in the Levant sheltering under the umbrella of Ottoman rule. He feared what would happen if the Ottoman lands were broken up. His views on this were surely prescient: the monster of nationalism—Jewish and Arab—has since torn Palestine apart. His views on what constitutes "freedom" were prescient too. He witnessed communities living in the bosom of a benign *nomocracy* free of an over-bearing state. Since his time we have seen the ugly reality of the modern "Islamic nation state" and what happens when traditional codes of law are perverted by centralized and technological bureaucracies intent on "micro-managing" their citizenry. Pickthall knew an Islam from before the nation-building ideologies, nationalist revolutions and reconfigurations of modern Islam.

The demise of the Caliphate is the most obvious difference between the Islam of Pickthall's era and that of our own. An Islam without the Caliph was once as inconceivable as Catholicism without the Pope, but twentieth century Islam has had to adapt to the final dissolution of the Caliphate after the collapse of the Ottoman elite in Turkey. Modern Islam is a post-Caliphate Islam, and, as well, the medieval geographical reality called the "House of Peace" (a distinct Islamic world) over which the Caliphate ruled came to an end. It was chopped up by national boundaries and then by migrations. In Pickthall's era it was impossible to imagine that by the end of the twentieth century many *millions* of Muslims would be living in northern Europe. Today, remarkably, there are more Muslims in Germany than in Lebanon. The idea of a distinct geographical entity, the "House of Peace," is today as unreal as the concept of "Christendom."

The more important change in modern Islam, though, was a direct result of the British endorsement of Arab nationalist struggles against the Turks—namely the elevation of the Wahabi sect into power and prominence. The British stirred the Arabs against the Turks. This necessarily entailed supporting the Arab's style of Islam. The Arabs had long been under Turkish domination. Turkish Islam was moderate (of the Hanafi school) with strong mystical, Sufi elements. In the eighteenth century a reactionary reform movement—later called "Wahabism" by its opponents—had begun among the Arabs, purporting to return Islam to its pristine roots in response to the supposed pollution of the faith by foreign (Persian, Turk and Indian) innovations.

Based in strict Habalite law, and viciously anti-Sufi, Wahabism sought to rid Islam of all its medieval abuses. This meant stripping the religion of medieval developments and promoting a puritanist form of the faith. The Wahabis, and the British, supported the warlord chieftain Ibn

Saud and legitimized the Saudi dynasty and its struggle against the Ottomans. In the periods when Wahabis took control of the Holy Places in Arabia from the Turks (with British support) they proceeded to destroy 1500 years of Muslim heritage, including the desecration of the tombs of the wives and companions of the Holy Prophet. In due course they established themselves as a modern kingdom and, subsequently, blessed with massive oil reserves, have used their central place and their wealth to promote Wahabism as a normative Islam. We forget that the Wahabi sect had little or no influence upon the Muslim *ummah* before the 1930s. Today, Wahabi thought (and money) has left a mark on every corner of Islam right across the globe. By this factor alone, the entire religion has changed. Reading Pickthall reminds us of what Islam was like before the Wahabi ascendancy. It was an Islam tempered by the earthy wisdom of an old civilization rather than an Islam inflamed with the zeal of puritan reform. In many ways the Islam to which Pickthall converted has completely disappeared and been replaced by an entirely different entity, largely formed by Wahabi control of the Hajj and radiating out from that centre. Pickthall warned that puritans and fanatics would move into the void if the moderate codes of Ottoman Islam were recklessly overturned in the Muslim heartland; he saw that Turkish control of the pilgrimage had a moderating effect upon the entire body of world Muslims and feared the alternative.

A key feature of Wahabism is a rejection of the traditional Sunni schools of law. It regards the medieval legal infrastructure of such schools to be unnecessary innovations (*bida*) that detract from the plain teaching of the Koran and the Hadith literature. Wahabism is characterized by a stark literalism in contrast to the complex and nuanced methodologies of the four schools. In Pickthall's works—both his fiction and his travel writings—we encounter the tapestry of traditional life created and sustained by the Ottoman legal codes under the auspices of Hanafi law as a living edifice. As Pickthall observed, the patterns of traditional law yielded a rich, profound culture, at once pious and tolerant, and "moderate" by today's standards. When modern revivalists clamor for the re-institution of *shariah* law it is the ossified, literalist law of Wahabism they mean, enforced by a modern state. This is not Islamic law as Pickthall saw it. Again, for him the traditional ways of life—patterns built around the five daily prayers and an understanding of domestic life as a prolongation of the mosque, for example—was a vehicle of *freedom*. In modern Islamic states such as the Wahabi-inspired Taliban state established in Afghanistan, *shariah* becomes a tool of terror and oppression, caustic revolution and social purging. A modern reader can hardly appreciate Pickthall's altogether benign and felicitous descriptions of life under Islamic law at the close of the nineteenth century.

Several features of Pickthall's celebrated Koran underline the extent to which his views and approaches anticipated and worked against modern "fundamentalist" ideas. For example, he deliberately chose to not translate the word *islam* to mean the religion "Islam" but instead translated it and its derivatives as "peace" and its synonyms. He reasoned that there was no such religion as "Islam" in the Koran, and certainly not in the partisan sense of Islam as one religion amongst others. This should be contrasted with the new "official" English translations being promoted worldwide by the Saudi Arabian religious authorities who in fact interpolate the word "Islam" or "Islamic monotheism" (as against the nefarious Jews and Christians) in the most aggressively partisan sense at every turn. Pickthall's translation is a masterpiece of careful, judicious and moderate language; the extent to which it is shaped to counter pernicious trends then emerging in modern Islam is among its less appreciated qualities. For the contemporary Wahabis, the mere fact that Pickthall was not a native Arab speaker disqualifies his translation from all consideration regardless of its qualities. One of the most famous episodes in Pickthall's life was his heroic attempt to have his translation accepted by the ulama at Al-Azar University in Cairo, then the unquestioned intellectual centre of Sunni Islam. He debated toe-to-toe with the Muslim scholars in Arabic (a feat, he said, that turned his hair grey overnight), responding and meeting their objections and discussing the very nature of the Koranic revelation and its language. In the end the body of scholars remained unconvinced, but Pickthall was urged to proceed with the publication of his rendering all the same. This was the first time that a rendering of the Koran into a European language had received the imprimatur of the leading scholars of the Muslim world. After Wahabism gripped modern Islam Pickthall's translation was shunned in favor of that of Yusuf Ali, purely on the grounds that Yusuf Ali was a born Arab Muslim and not a convert.

After the calamities that led to the dismantling of the Ottoman Empire Pickthall turned his attention to British India and spent the second half of his life as an educator working for the Nizam of Hyderabad. The Nizamate consisted of a Muslim state extending throughout central India; it was, in many ways, a surviving prolongation of Moghul Islam. The Nizam was great friend of the British and developed intimate links with British aristocracy. He well understood that the survival of the Hyderabadi Muslim state depended upon the shelter of the British Empire—without that, Muslim and Hindu would be at each other's throats and the Nizamate would be over-run. Pickthall did not live long enough to see exactly this occur, but he must surely have known that the old Nizamate that he saw was, like Ottoman Turkey, a vestige of a passing world. After the Second World War, even though the Nizam had supported the British War effort with a generous number of troops, the British gave up on the Nizamate and it was engulfed by the new state of modern India. For a brief period the Nizam declared his independence, but the British would not endorse him, and the last stronghold of classical Islam in the Indian sub-continent disappeared.

The present author visited the old city of Hyderabad in mid 2009 and spent time exploring the world that Pickthall knew there. The Nizam's palace complex, like the old city in general, is quite dilapidated, although one palace has been restored and so offers a contrast to the remainder. The many halls of photographs and records show a world in which the automobile was still a rarity and in which simple pre-industrial men and women went about their crafts and trades in the shadow of the vast Makka Masjid and the Charminar. Little of that era remains. The streets are clogged with cars and rickshaws and motorcycles. The air is polluted. Whole families depend upon selling cheap wristwatches made in Asia from a market stall. Only a small congregation responded to the Call to Prayer at the main mosque, and on local television were graphic scenes of bearded Wahabi fanatics smashing the shrine of a Sufi saint with mallets and axes. Only two signs of Muhammad Pickthall were to be seen; his photograph in one of the Nizam's displays and a ten-page pamphlet about his life and work in a dusty bookshop in Laad Bazaar. On the far side of the city is new Hyderabad and a hi-tech "cyber-city" for the booming IT industry. As for the current Nizam himself, he long ago purchased a sheep station in Western Australia and moved there.

* * *

Contemporary Muslims are far more comfortable claiming a convert such as Leopold Weiss (Muhammad Asad) as their own. Weiss converted several decades later than Pickthall and his "Road to Makka" involved him in the establishment of the Saudi regime, nationalist struggles against European colonialism and the founding of the state of Pakistan, ostensibly as a model of what a modern Islamic state should be. His translation of the Koran is an ambitious re-interpretation serving to accommodate science and evolution. For these reasons Weiss is accessible to Muslims today, but not so Marmaduke Pickthall. To reclaim Muhammad Pickthall as a leading light among those Westerners who have followed the Call to Prayer and embraced the Muslim faith it is necessary to appreciate the extent to which the world and Islam have changed and to extend our view back into another milieu. For Muslims this means acknowledging the fact that the faith as we find it now is a modern *construction* that deviates from the traditional patterns. Traditional, or classical Islam—with direct continuity with medieval Islam—was finally shattered in the early twentieth century and has been replaced by a form of the religion characterized by many of the things Pickthall foresaw and feared. It is tempting to dismiss Pickthall's Islam as merely "romantic," as if it were unreal. It was certainly an Islam in decline, and it is certainly not a reality today, but that is no reason why we should ignore or diminish the witness of Pickthall to an Islam that was richer and deeper than the brash, simplistic and sentimental forms that tend to prevail today.

Ito's Cave

Titus Burckhardt

I was once a guest in the cave village of the Aït Tserrūsh ("the sons of the jackal"), a Berber tribe of the Middle Atlas. When I woke up in the morning, I did not at first understand why I was surrounded by uneven patches of semi-darkness. But when I turned over on my sheepskin I saw, through the narrow cave mouth, the brilliant light of day. A soft whimpering had awakened me: in one of the large niches that opened out from all around the inside wall of the cave, there lay a small Berber child who was wriggling under some earth-colored blankets. All of a sudden, in the section of sky cut out by the cave mouth, I could see Ito, the child's mother, who had appeared in response to his cry. She put down a jug of water, picked up the child, and laid him on her lap in order to suckle him. Once more in the cave all was silent; one could barely hear, in the distance, the sounds of the day: the cry of an animal or the clattering of hooves. The Berber woman sat in the half-light, motionless as a rock.

When the infant was satisfied, she let it slide to the ground, sat down in front of a mortar, and began to grind wheat. She sieved the flour, mixed it with water in a wooden bowl, and then kneaded the dough with powerful and regular movements. Finally, she divided the dough into six equal-sized balls, which she carefully flattened into circular pieces of bread, having first kept behind in the bowl a piece of dough about the size of an apple, which would be used to leaven the next day's batch.

Ito was too powerful and too solid to be truly beautiful. But her broad face, with its wide-open eyes, looked as if it had been carved out of some bright stone, and shone with a proud and powerful femininity. She carried her dignity with an innocent awareness. Tattoo marks on her forehead and chin both decorated and protected her.

The air in the cave smelled slightly of stone. At this depth one is protected both from the heat of the day and the cold of the night. The world above seemed no longer to be of any concern, and the cave enveloped one maternally; one felt a reluctance to climb up to the hot ground above, rather as if one struggled not to be born.

Once more someone filled the small piece of sky. The child's father, Mohaudris, made his way down. He was a young Berber with regular features and an impenetrable expression, as if he bore on his countenance the reflection of the vast and rocky steppe. He was dressed in a wide, white shirt, and had a narrow turban round his head. Over his shoulders hung a *selham* or burnous (a simple cloak of rough wool), on the back of which a long cross was embroidered—perhaps the sign of the remote Christian origin of his tribe. His name, Mohaudris, is the Berber abbreviation of the double name Mohammed Idrīs.

"Peace be upon thee," came his greeting, "blessed be the morning, may no harm befall thee!" He had brought with him the head of a young goat, and set about preparing it for my breakfast.

I asked him about the life of the community in which I was a guest. A part of the population had gone into the mountains with their tents to pasture their sheep and goats. Those remaining behind attended to the fields of maize which lay further down in the valley.

My horse was tethered in a neighboring cave. When I led him a few yards up into the daylight, he shied at first, as if blinded by the sun. On the surface of the ground, all one could see of the village were the cave openings protected by thorn bushes and a defensive wall that surrounded everything. Looking towards the north, over the edge of the plateau, one could just make out the large yellow hollow in which Fez lay. To the south extended the undulating steppe, a vast plateau where, in the spring, exquisite flowers appear amongst the boulders; but now, in summer, the bare ground was decorated only by tough bushes such as broom and juniper.

On a hill nearby a new mosque had been built. This was the tribes' answer to a French edict promising the Berbers their own legislation independent of that of the Koran. "Why does the Rumi (the European) covet my stony valley?" asks a Berber song, "he who possesses everything that a man can desire? Does he reach out his hand to snatch the faith from my heart?"

The mosque was built of gigantic cedar trunks from the mountains in the south. The outside walls and the flat roof were covered with sun-dried mud. In the inside, trunks with their bark removed stood in rows like high, reddish pillars. The archaic impression made by this building, in its powerful simplicity, was increased even further by the earnest faces of the Berbers, who stood or sat between the cedar pillars. In the faces of several of the older men there was a profound concentration and resignation.

From one end of the village could be heard the haunting sounds of a flute, accompanied by a dull, steady drumbeat. It was the music of a Sufi brotherhood that had its roots amongst the people of the region. The musicians were standing in front of a cave entrance and a Berber woman gyrated in an ecstatic dance. Her hair, held together by a woven ribbon, became undone because of her rapid movements, and swirled through the air like a large black bird.

In the center of the village, beautiful children were playing. And heavily laden beasts of burden entered the village through the gate.

On the horizon of the great plain, down to which I was now riding, there were still some fine strips of morning cloud, light pink in color. The light of dawn sparkled on the dark metallic-looking leaves of the dwarf palms which covered the slopes. Gradually the brown earth flattened out, and seemed to stretch endlessly ahead of me. The caravan track was covered with a network of cracks, and left and right stood desiccated thistles, which looked as if they were made out of blue glass. Further away were low black tents, and half-wild dogs barked at me as I passed.

The Moroccan earth, which from June onwards is almost bare, is everywhere near to man. The Bedouin sleeps on it and rests on it, and his cloak, however often he may wash it, always has in it something of the earth on which he lives. Nothing separates man from the immense and austere body of the earth, which nowhere has an end. But the sunlight filling the sky, the sunlight unobscured by any mist, relieves the earth of its heaviness and unites all things, without suppressing their proper forms, in its infinite crystal.

Towards midday I reached the first wheat fields, already mown, and then the villages of the *fellāhīn* whose white houses of sun-dried mud rested like sarcophagi on the vast plain. A stallion tethered in front of one of the houses raised its head, and neighed loudly. While the flocks crouched down together on top of their own shadows—the sun being now almost vertically above them—I rested awhile beside a well, under an acacia tree. Then I rode on in the direction of Fez, and the nearer I came to the city, the more I overtook small caravans of mules and donkeys making their way there with loads of cedar logs, animal skins, or goatskin bottles full of olive oil. Many had come from afar, having trotted for days over the rocky plateau.

The sun was already sinking before I could see, in the distance, the hills surrounding Fez, with their bright, ocher-colored ridges and silvery green clumps of olive trees. No sooner had the sun set than the scene was transformed into a world of antique gold, jade, and opal, beneath a sky of turquoise.

Slowly the colors were extinguished like a dying brazier. The earth retreated and the sky opened up, a measureless ocean with silvery islands and shimmering shores. Underneath, the caravans, as if drunk with sleep, followed their drovers' song.

Dweller on the Threshold: Simone Weil, Universalism, and the Perennial Philosophy

Mark Stone

> So far from its being his person, what is sacred in a human being is the impersonal in him.
>
> *Simone Weil*[1]

> From a scientific point of view, we can make no distinction between a man who eats little and sees heaven and the man who drinks much and sees snakes.
>
> *Bertrand Russell*[2]

In his iconoclastic essay "Sainte Simone—Simone Weil," George Steiner attempts to shatter her popular image as a "secular saint", while at the same time incidentally highlighting many of the problems surrounding the critical discussion of mysticism in the modern context. The most striking feature of Steiner's essay is the conspicuous degree to which he ignores Simone Weil's mystical experience, instead largely reducing her work to the level of the pathological, the psychological, and the racial.[3] When he does address Weil's mysticism, he does so skeptically. Referring to her desire to imitate the suffering of Christ, he says: "However concordant it may be with a mystical tradition of holy maceration, such a sentiment lies at the shadow-line of the pathological."[4] It seems Weil's mystical transformation is barely worth mentioning, let alone taking seriously. For Steiner, Weil is clearly mentally ill: ". . . the pathology (perhaps, indeed, the "madness") is there—and why are Simone Weil's acolytes so unwilling to acknowledge the facts? . . ."[5] As evidence for this claim, he cites the testimony of Weil's brother, and more curiously, that of General Charles de Gaulle.[6]

> With characteristic reserve her brother Andre Weil the great algebraic topologist concluded that his sister's "sensibility had gone beyond the limits of the normal."

[1] Simone Weil, *Simone Weil: An Anthology* (New York: Grove Press, 1986), p. 54.

[2] Bertrand Russell, *Religion and Science* (London: Oxford University Press, 1935), p. 188. Cited in Brian Davies, *An Introduction to the Philosophy of Religion* (London: Oxford University Press: 1993), p. 125.

[3] Steiner makes much of Simone Weil's Jewish heritage, seeing in her asceticism symptoms of racial self-loathing. "In Weil's detestation of her own ethnic identity . . . the traits of a classical Jewish self-loathing are carried to fever pitch" (George Steiner, *No Passion Spent* [New York: Yale University Press, p. 177]). Yet—and Steiner fails to mention this important fact—Weil's eccentric personality traits began in early childhood, long before she ever discovered her Jewish ancestry.

[4] George Steiner, *No Passion Spent*, p. 177.

[5] Ibid., p. 171.

[6] Steiner's use of this anecdote is somewhat misleading: de Gaulle's comment referred specifically to the wild impracticality of Weil's idea of establishing a front-line nursing corps (see Thomas Merton's essay, *The Answer of Minerva: Pacifism and Resistance in Simone Weil*, in the anthology, *The Literary Essays of Thomas Merton* [New York: New Directions Books, 1981], p. 139). It therefore does not seem to have been a simple attempt at amateur psychology on the part of the French general.

> More brusquely, de Gaulle, a masterly judge of human beings, declared that "the woman was mad."[7]

In spite of what is, at times, an openly hostile and tendentious approach, Steiner does highlight an important point: writers gushing over Weil's "saintliness" teach us little or nothing meaningful about her life or thought. We might add the qualification that such writers do, at least, reveal our desperate desire to find saints in our midst, to guide us through the hell of the modern world. This desire is understandable, and is in itself not to be ridiculed. Yet if we wish to know anything about Weil, her life, her thought, Steiner argues, we must look deeper than the stereotypical and the clichéd.

At the same time—and this is the great difficulty— we must equally not commit Steiner's error, and neglect that Simone Weil was, in fact, a mystic. She did undergo an experience which left her transformed forever, which indeed went far "beyond the limits of the normal," and which gave her insights of a demonstrably universal order, insights which transcended the shallow thought which so often in modern times passes for philosophy. The Truths of suffering and redemption through love, which form the heart of her universality, have not become a dead-letter for us; when read today, her writings still, in Steiner's words, retain the power to "make one's blood stop."[8] Can we say this about the writings of Jean-Paul Sartre, or Heidegger, or Foucault, or Bertrand Russell? When Steiner compares Weil the philosopher unfavorably with the likes of Schopenhauer and Heidegger, he fails to recognize that Weil was not a philosopher in the way those writers were, nor did she pretend to be: Weil was first and foremost a mystic, and all the power, authority and universality in her writing proceed from this fact. But both mystical experience, and the authority that is its prerogative, belong to a different category to that of purely discursive thought, and a modern western critic such as Steiner—the quintessential twentieth century "man of letters" if there ever was one—is unlikely to show any great sensitivity on this subject. No, for such sensitivity, we would need to turn to a Frithjof Schuon, or any of the other writers of the *Philosophia Perennis*, with whom Weil actually shares certain affinities. Both Weil and the Perennialist writers addressed the precipitous collapse of religious belief in the modern world not by reference to science, rationalism, materialism, or the pernicious ideology of progress, but instead, by an appeal to transcendent Principles of universal validity, and their realization in *gnosis*. What we propose therefore is a reassessment of Weil's legacy—particularly as it relates to her universalism—in the light of the Perennial Philosophy. Through this comparison, Weil's particular form of mysticism, and consequently her universalism, can be seen not merely as a form of sentimental humanism, but rather, as largely informed by traditional metaphysical doctrines, and above all, by her own mystical experience. We do not propose that Weil should be regarded as an exponent of the *Philosophia Perennis*, but rather, that she cannot be understood without reference to those eternal Truths which inform both her own thought, and that of the Perennialists. Moreover, the intellectual framework which Perennialism provides makes it possible to identify Weil's mystical thought in light of the tradition to which she belongs, rather than isolating her in the constricted discourses of modernity. From this perspective, it becomes clear that Weil was not "mad," but rather, that she was an authentic mystic in utterly unfavorable and desperate times; or rather, if indeed she

[7] George Steiner, *No Passion Spent*, p. 171.

[8] Ibid., p. 178.

really were "mad," it is equally true that in the context of the mid-twentieth century, madness is a relative and difficult matter to judge. Could there be a mystic from any period in history, who, in the modern era, would not be regarded as mad? Would a Ramakrishna not be locked up if found wandering the streets of Paris or London in Weil's time, let alone today? And what would George Steiner have to say about a Rabbia of Basra, a Ramana Maharshi? Surely many of the worst madmen of the twentieth century have been those who at the time appeared most sane.

Philosophy and Mysticism

Before proceeding to an examination of Weil's mysticism and universalism, it is necessary to make certain preparatory observations on the subject of mysticism itself.[9] In academic discussions of the philosophy of religion, mysticism perhaps receives the least serious attention. This is understandable, as unlike the various rational arguments for and against religious belief, the inner experience of the mystic is essentially impossible to communicate to others and, it must be admitted, is therefore difficult to discuss. Yet without such experience, religion is greatly impoverished. Take an example: the flourishing of Christian mysticism in the medieval period of European history coincided with a highpoint in the spiritual life of the West, artistically, intellectually, philosophically, and this was in no way accidental. In medieval Christianity, as in all intact traditions, the great mystics were able to transcend local forms by realizing their meaning to the highest degree, and their presence was both a proof of the inner spiritual vitality of that religion, and equally, in its turn, vitalized the outer religious forms. While inversely, wherever the legalism and literalism of a religion becomes excessive, mysticism provides a means for the realization of otherwise unmanifested spiritual possibilities. In the terminology of the *Philosophia Perennis*, this function of mysticism represents the anagogical movement inward, from the exoteric outer shell of religious forms to the esoteric kernel which those forms enclose. As Schuon has written:

> Mysticism results from the tendency towards inwardness, towards inner experience; it is "supernaturally natural" to man, which is to say that it corresponds to an innate need and is found wherever there is a religion, the legalism of which being unable to satisfy all aspirations. Thus, mysticism cannot not be; the knowledge of its levels, its degrees, its lines of demarcation is another matter altogether.[10]

The last point in Schuon's quote we will return to later. But for the present, suffice to say that the mystics, by their living example, are able both to embody a religious tradition in themselves, and, through differing levels and degrees, are ultimately able to transcend its specific forms through *gnosis*. Moreover, when mysticism, in the broadest possible sense, is entirely absent from a tradition, the religious forms in question are also likely to be found in a hardened and moribund condition.

[9] Throughout this essay, the term "mysticism" will be used in its broadest possible sense to mean that aspect of the religious and spiritual life concerned with a direct experience of metaphysical realities. While acknowledging the validity and importance of the more restricted technical definition given by René Guénon, we believe the danger of "hair-splitting" and arguing over precise technical definitions of a word like "mysticism" can at times unnecessarily confuse what is an absolutely crucial subject.

[10] Frithjof Schuon, *Survey of Metaphysics and Esoterism* (Bloomington: World Wisdom, 2000), p. 165.

Indeed, one could argue that the greatest and most cogent argument for the existence of a universal Truth, informing and at the same time transcending all religious forms, is not the explication of metaphysical doctrine—crucial and indispensible though that is—but rather, the presence of saints. In the saints, we are presented with a kind of immediate, irrefutable proof, higher than any written doctrine. Without these sacred presences in the world, the danger always exists of religion being reduced to the level of exoteric belief and ritual alone. One can argue against belief *ad infinitum*, but one cannot argue with the spiritual presence of a Ramana Maharshi. One need not subject the *ana l-Haqq* of the Sufi mystic Al-Hallaj to a logical or empirical "verification principle." That "peace of God, which passeth all understanding" mentioned by Saint Paul is a peace beyond creed, race, or any local and formal distinction whatever. In such a presence all philosophical arguments fall silent.

Simone Weil was not, perhaps, a saint of the kind with which we are familiar, a Ramana Maharshi, a Rumi, a St. Francis. Perhaps she was not strictly speaking a saint at all. Yet Simone Weil was undoubtedly a mystic, which is to say, she experienced the Divine as a living reality, and was transformed permanently by that experience. In this sense, she differs fundamentally from almost all other modern "philosophers" whose work concerns itself with dialectical thought alone. If we are to take Simone Weil seriously as a thinker, we must therefore approach her thought not from the point of view of empirical or logical "verification," but rather, from one such as that of the Perennialists, where the possibility of *gnosis* is acknowledged on the basis of traditional doctrine. Only in this way can we make any sense whatever of Weil's ideas. The following quote offers a useful starting point:

> The word "mystic" denotes anything that refers in one way or another to a suprarational communication with Divinity; since this word is European it must of necessity coincide with the mode of spirituality known in the West, which is a way of love.[11]

For Weil, the proper end of human life was the realization of impersonal Truth within the heart, through affliction and love. In her own words:

> Every man who has once touched the level of the impersonal is charged with a responsibility towards all human beings; to safeguard, not their persons, but whatever frail potentialities are hidden within them for passing over to the impersonal."[12]

This end was, for her, the heart of Christianity. Moreover, because this Truth was impersonal, it was necessarily universal, and therefore in no way exclusively the possession of the Christian religion.

In this very broad sense at least, Weil is at one with the writers of the *Philosophia Perennis*. In parallel with the writings of René Guénon, Ananda Coomaraswamy, Frithjof Schuon and others, she turned the philosophy of religion away from a narrow theological parochialism, or a redundant and superficial obsession with rationalist argumentation, towards the mystical, the

[11] Frithjof Schuon, *Spiritual Perspectives and Human Facts* (Middlesex: Perennial Books, 1987), p. 89 (fn. 44).

[12] Simone Weil, *Simone Weil: An Anthology*, pp. 57-58.

metaphysical, and the experiential dimensions of religion. This in turn led, as we shall see, to Weil's identification of a universal Truth informing all religions, a Truth not socially or politically conditioned, but of transcendent origin. Equally, Weil, like the Perennialists, was a perceptive and relentless critic of the evils of the mechanized and destructive aspects of modernity, which she had personally experienced as a laborer in factories, and as a non-combative participant in the International Brigade in the Spanish Civil War. Her critique of modern science and art was no less trenchant and intellectually rigorous than that of the Perennialists, even if comparatively elliptical in expression, and informed by mystical terseness.[13] Where Weil differs significantly from the Perennialists in her thought, however, is in her emphasis upon volitive mysticism and love, rather than upon pure metaphysics as such; especially, in her negative attitude to collectives of all kinds, religious or otherwise. In both these respects, the parallels between Weil and the Perennialists are more problematic.

Mysticism, Universalism and Tradition

An important question, one generally poorly understood, and with crucial implications for her universalism, is that of the precise nature of Weil's mysticism. Weil was born in Paris in 1909, and died in Kent in 1943, after a self-imposed fast which she undertook out of empathy with the privations of soldiers on the front lines in World War II. Her childhood was decidedly secular, affluent, and marked by intellectual precocity (she was already an accomplished scholar of Greek at the age of twelve). Classical literature and philosophy, especially that of Plato, formed the basis of her thought. After a period of Marxist activism, Weil—according to her own testimony—underwent a mystical experience without precedent in her life, one which fundamentally contradicted her previous assumptions. The following excerpt from one of Weil's letters gives a powerful description of this experience, which subsequently changed her life forever:

> . . . the word God had no place at all in my thoughts. It never had until the day—about three and a half years ago—when I could no longer keep it out. At a moment of intense physical pain, while I was making the effort to love, although believing I had no right to give any name to the love, I felt, while completely unprepared for it (I had never read the mystics), a presence more personal, more certain and more real than that of a human being; it was inaccessible both to sense and to imagination, and it resembled the love that irradiates the tenderest smile of somebody one loves. Since that moment, the name of God and the name of Christ have been more and more irresistibly mingled with my thoughts.[14]

How are we to understand the nature and significance of this experience? Reading this passage, one feels at one and the same time both its urgent veracity and its essential incommunicability. Weil resorts to the simplest analogy—that of a smile—and leaves almost everything unsaid. How then can we discuss such an experience when verification is out of the question?

One way is to attempt to identify the experience by comparison with those of other mystics. Weil's case is in some ways parallel to an experience like that of the Hindu saint Ramana

[13] For Weil's perspective on modern science and art, see *Simone Weil: An Anthology*, pp. 54-57.

[14] Simone Weil, *Simone Weil: An Anthology*, p. 262.

Maharshi. In both cases, an unexpected spiritual experience profoundly transformed a human life, without any previous religious practice—even, in Weil's case, explicitly contradicting her previous commitment to Marxism. And in both cases they subsequently sought explanations of their spiritually transformative experience through the forms and doctrines of religion. Ramana's experience, although not preceded by a religious vocation of any kind, nevertheless occurred within the context of a living primordial tradition, and when the saint was suddenly called forth from the boy, Arunachala was already there awaiting his arrival. In Weil's case, her spiritual vocation was played out in the context of a profane western world being ravaged by mass-industrialization, revolution, fascism, violent class-conflict, racism, "total war," and the disastrous collapse of religious belief. Even if indeed Weil were really a saint—and, in order to accept her mysticism, we need not necessarily suppose that she was, as not all mystics are saints as such—she could not help but be one of a different kind to those familiar to us from tradition. If Weil's very "modernity," so close to our own, makes such comparisons seem fanciful, we might turn to traditional doctrine for guidance. Once again, the Perennialist thinkers are enlightening. The following passage by Frithjof Schuon is highly significant for the light it sheds on this difficult matter:

> Voluntaristic mysticism is a path of love which—in contrast with Hindu bhakti—is characterized by the fact that no intellectual element intervenes in an active fashion in its method; thus the qualifications it demands are almost exclusively moral: at most it demands a general predisposition which, together with moral factors and on contact with grace, becomes a "vocation." It is true that this mysticism thrives on dogmatic symbols and theological concepts, but not on intellections: it is entirely centered on love—on the will with its emotive concomitances—and not on gnosis. In a certain sense, passional mysticism is "negative," since its method—apart from sacramental graces—consists above all in the negation of the natural appetites, whence the cult of suffering, and the importance of trials and consolations; the activity is purely moral and ascetic, as the following opinion of Saint John of the Cross shows well: "By its nature, this [our mind] is limited to natural science; but God has nevertheless endowed it with an obediential power in regard to the supernatural, so that it can obey whenever it pleases Our Lord to make it act supernaturally. Strictly speaking, no knowledge is accessible to the mind except by natural means; therefore all knowledge must pass through the senses" (*The Ascent of Mount Carmel*, I, 2). This is the negation of the intellect, the reduction of the intelligence to reason alone.[15]

In many ways, Weil's mysticism superficially resembles the "voluntaristic" form here outlined by Schuon. A general predisposition towards the moral, the contact with grace becoming a "vocation"—what could better describe Simone Weil's life and work? The problem arises, however, when we consider the intellectual aspects of Weil's spiritual method. Weil's Platonism is entirely opposed to what Schuon describes as the "negation of the intellect": on the contrary, Weil is in this sense actually closer in some ways to a Hindu *bhakta* than she is to the extreme emphasis on faith, over and above the intelligence, which we find in much Christian mysticism,

[15] Frithjof Schuon, "Characteristics of Voluntaristic Mysticism," in Mateus Soares de Azevado (ed.), *Ye Shall Know the Truth: Christianity and the Perennial Philosophy* (Bloomington: World Wisdom, 2005), p. 1.

as in the above quote from Saint John of the Cross, with whom Weil has often been compared. Weil's spiritual application of "contemplative mathematics" alone puts her in another class of mysticism to those who would deny the intellectual path in favor of pure faith. But what is this class precisely? According to Schuon:

> Gnosis coincides with "esoterism," with the difference that the latter includes a dimension of volitive and emotional mysticism of the type of Hindu *bhakti*. Only the highest degree of that dimension, the way of gnosis, represents a virtually absolute esoterism; the way of love is a relative and conditional esoterism—as far as method is concerned, for love itself is also a dimension of knowledge like beauty.[16]

Again, the Perennialist conceptions of the exoteric and esoteric aspects of religion are highly pertinent. Weil clearly belongs to the former, properly gnostic degree of "volitive and emotional mysticism," rather than the latter form of "relative and conditional esoterism" as defined in Schuon's quote.[17] Her path is indeed a path of *gnosis*, but one travelled not by means of pure metaphysics, but instead, by the complementary interplay of the intellect and love; moreover, and crucially, a love not envisaged as sentiment, but rather, as a "dimension of knowledge."[18] For Weil, even the solution of a geometrical problem was a devotional act with implications of a properly metaphysical and not simply a rational order. This understanding of love and beauty—as dimensions of an esoteric knowledge—is fundamental to Weil's thought. It is not surprising, then, that Weil took such an interest in the *Bhagavad Gita*, that most "Christian" of Hindu scriptures, in which we see the reciprocal interplay of *jnana* and *bhakti* most perfectly articulated. Weil's mysticism represents a harmony of the Christian mysticism of love, on the one hand, and Platonic intellectuality on the other; a "virtually absolute," yet nonetheless properly gnostic esoterism, and by no means a rejection of Divine Knowledge. To depict Weil as a passive ecstatic hostile to rigorous intellectuality would be a grievous wrong. It is this properly esoteric depth to her thought which makes of her universalism something more than an expression of mere sentiment.[19]

Moreover, regarding Weil's universalism, there is a crucial distinction to be made between, on the one hand, the transcending of discrete religious forms, by following them through to their ultimate realization in mysticism, sainthood and enlightenment, and, on the other hand, the simple disregarding of those forms altogether in favor of a privileged, essentially personal

16 Frithjof Schuon, *Logic and Transcendence* (Bloomington: World Wisdom, 2009), p. 1.

17 Here, by "gnostic", we refer to the path of Divine Knowledge, not to the heterodox sects often grouped under that title.

18 In this connection, it is worth remembering that traditionally the *locus* of the Intellect is in the heart.

19 This notwithstanding, the question of whether a workable spiritual universalism can ever be founded upon a primarily devotional mysticism is highly problematic. We see the difficulties most clearly illustrated in the life of Ramakrishna and the 'universalism' of his disciple Vivekananda. Where Ramakrishna's intensely mystical and devotional transcending of religious forms, his embrace of multiple religious paths, his extraordinary capacity for synthetic intuition, were utterly compelling in the inimitable example of his sainthood, they subsequently became, through the activities of Vivekananda, a charismatic but shallow spiritual 'globalism', ultimately a betrayal of his teacher's legacy to the world. To attempt to transform mystical insight into a universally applicable doctrine is perhaps unworkable when it is not based primarily upon pure metaphysics, such as we see in the thought of the Perennialists.

experience. Superficially, Weil's life may seem to resemble the later, except that Weil never in her mature post-Marxist work attempts to undermine the validity of, or adherence to, a religious tradition. Her decision to remain upon the threshold of formal religious affiliation was inseparable from her sense of her own spiritual vocation, not a rejection of religion as such. Far from being opposed to following one specific religious path, Weil believed, with Frithjof Schuon and the Perennialist thinkers, that real inter-religious understanding comes only from the fullest immersion in and devotion to one's own particular religious tradition. Weil's universalism was therefore in no sense relativism or a wishy-washy "religiosity." To quote Weil on this important point:

> There are others again who think they are capable of impartiality because they have only a vague religiosity which they can turn indifferently in any direction, whereas, on the contrary, we must have given all our attention, all our faith, all our love to a particular religion in order to think of any other religion with the high degree of attention, faith, and love that is proper to it.[20]

We see here that Weil demanded from religious devotion the same degree of intense, uncompromising presence of mind as she applied to the solving of a mathematical problem. Nor was her mystical experience "personal"; on the contrary, Weil wrote polemics against the modern tendency towards improperly exalting the personal over the impersonal Truth.[21] Obedience to God was her overwhelming priority, to realize the state of perfect "slavehood." In her own words:

> To be perfectly obedient is to be perfect as our Father in heaven is perfect.
>
> Among men, a slave does not become like his master by obeying him. On the contrary, the more he obeys the greater is the distance between them.
>
> It is otherwise between man and God. If a reasonable creature is absolutely obedient, he becomes a perfect image of the Almighty as far as this is possible for him.[22]

Notwithstanding this, Weil claimed for herself the inner freedom which is necessarily the privilege of the mystic. For her, the forms of religion were to be respected, but not blindly accepted where they contradicted the universalizing insight of her own mystical experience. For Weil, as for Guénon, Schuon and others, the discrete forms of a religion or mythology are relative perspectives upon an ultimate Reality which expresses itself in many local adaptations, and therefore no one religion is inherently more "right" or "wrong" in relation to the others.

> A good starting point is to think, as Wittgenstein did—and Simone Weil would have agreed with him—that "all religions are wonderful." Not that some are right and others are wrong, but that all spiritual traditions are worthy of respect and have something to teach us. We mistakenly compare religions with scientific truths, but

[20] Simone Weil, *Waiting for God*, p. 119.

[21] For Weil's critique of the "personal" in modernity, see Simone Weil, *Simone Weil: An Anthology*, pp 56-59.

[22] Ibid., p. 115.

> they are more like ways of life, which need not, and should not, exclude each other.[23]

As Leslie Fiedler has written of Weil's universalism:

> To those who consider themselves on the safe side of belief, she teaches the uncomfortable truth that the unbelief of many atheists is closer to a true love of God and a true sense of his nature, than the kind of easy faith which, having never experienced God, hangs a label bearing his name on some childish fantasy or projection of the ego. Like Kierkegaard, she preached the paradox of its being easier for a non-Christian to become a Christian, than for a "Christian" to become one. To those who believe in a single revelation, and enjoy the warm sensation of being saved... she expounded the doctrine of a gospel spread in many "languages," of a Divine Word shared among rival myths, in each of which certain important truths, implicit elsewhere, are made explicit.[24]

This raises the central question of what Weil understood by the word "religion." Weil's conception of what constitutes religion proceeds from the essential character of her mysticism, rather than from any social, anthropological or humanistic basis, something truly extraordinary for a former Marxist philosopher, and evidence of the profundity of the change which Weil's mystical experience had worked in her soul—a true *Metanoia.* In this light, the following quote is crucial to an understanding of Weil's religious metaphysics and therefore also of her universalism:

> The love of institutional religion normally has as its object the prevailing religion of the country or circle in which a man is brought up. As the result of an inborn habit, everyone thinks first of that each time he thinks of a religious service.
>
> The whole virtue of religious practices can be conceived of from the Buddhist tradition concerning the recitation of the name of the Lord. It is said that Buddha made a vow to raise to himself, in the Land of Purity, all those who pronounced his name with the desire of being saved by him; and that because of this vow the recitation of the name of the Lord really has the power of transforming the soul.
>
> Religion is nothing else but this promise of God. Every religious practice, every rite, all liturgy is a form of the recitation of the name of the Lord and in principle should have a real virtue, the virtue of saving whoever devotes himself to performing it with desire.[25]

We see from this quote that for Weil all religion is *Dhikr Allah*, *anamnesis*, *Aum*, remembrance of the Divine Name. No more and no less. And this, too, is another expression of her devotional mysticism; the repetition of the Divine Name as a spiritual method is characteristic of the path of the *bhakta*, specifically in Hindu terms, that of *Japa Yoga.* Again, Schuon:

[23] Henry Finch, *Simone Weil and the Intellect of Grace* (New York: Continuum, 1999), p. 104.

[24] Simone Weil, *Waiting For God*, pp. 8-9.

[25] Ibid., pp. 117-118.

> The Name, in the Christian form—as in the Buddhist form and in certain branches of the Hindu tradition—is a name of the manifested Word, in this case the Name of Jesus, which, like every revealed Divine Name when ritually pronounced, is mysteriously identified with the Divinity. It is in the Divine Name that there takes place the mysterious meeting of the created and the Uncreate, the contingent and the Absolute, the finite and the Infinite. The Divine Name is thus a manifestation of the Supreme Principle, or to speak still more plainly, it is the Supreme Principle manifesting Itself; it is not therefore in the first place a manifestation, but the Principle Itself.[26]

In light of these considerations, Weil would no doubt have liked the *hadith* of the Prophet Muhammad, where, when asked, if a man were unable to fulfil all the daily rigors of the faith, what the most essential obligation for a Muslim was, he answered: "Keep your tongue moist with the remembrance of Allah."

Weil, along with the Perennialists, understood religion not as a construct of culture but rather as originating in a divine source, and therefore, although in a sense each religious form is relative in respect of the Truth, nonetheless it is qualitatively distinct from all other worldly forms by virtue of its being anchored in the transcendent perfection of God:

> Religious things are special tangible things, existing here below and yet perfectly pure. This is not on account of their own particular character. The church may be ugly, the singing out of tune, the priest corrupt, and the faithful inattentive. In a sense that is of no importance. It is as with a geometrician who draws a figure to illustrate a proof. If the lines are not straight and the circles are not round it is of no importance . . . the convention by which religious things are pure is ratified by God himself. . . . This purity is unconditioned and perfect, and at the same time real.[27]

This quote is interesting, as it clearly distinguishes between, on the one hand, the worldly imperfections of religious institutions and particularized forms, and on the other hand, the spiritual Realities to which they refer. In light of this recognition, Weil's dismissal of all collectives, even religious ones, seems surprising, and therefore needs to be more closely examined.

Anathema Sit: Institutional Religion and the Problem of Force

Another problem of great importance in understanding Simone Weil's universalism, especially in light of the *Philosophia Perennis*, is her reluctance to enter formally into a religious tradition. Where the Perennialists all place great emphasis upon participation in a particular tradition, Weil's universalism actually seems to have prevented her from becoming baptized as a Catholic. Her vocation as a perpetual "dweller on the threshold," her conception of human life as something to be lived as an equilibrium between opposites, meant that for her, entry into the Catholic Church would have been in a sense redundant. And she objected to the formal

[26] Frithjof Schuon, *The Transcendent Unity of Religions* (Illinois: Quest Books, 1993), p. 145.

[27] Simone Weil, *Waiting for God*, p. 121.

exclusivism required by the Church, which meant the damnation of a large part of the human race not baptized, and those who had been deliberately excluded by excommunication. Yet for Weil, this was in no sense an act of disobedience or rebellion, but rather, an intellectual and moral position. In the following quote, following her master Plato, Weil distinguishes the negative and positive aspects of the social collective:

> The first is the "the Great Beast" of Plato and the second as the repository of cultural values that symbolizes respect for the past and aspiration for the future. Each collectivity is unique. There is an obligation to preserve its roots in the past to the extent that it provides sustenance for a certain number of people. But if the collectivities themselves are not nourishing, if instead they devour souls, there is no such obligation.[28]

Here, Weil refers not specifically to religions, but to society generally ("the repository of cultural values"), although these views, with due modification, would presumably apply to collectives of all kinds, including religious ones. In this respect, there is much to be said for Simone Weil as a kind of urban Sufi or renunciate, born into a modernized Christianity which provided her with no appropriate esoteric path for one so gifted as she clearly was; like the Sufis, her life represents an uneasy and even antagonistic relationship with the forms and institutional structures of exoteric religion, politics, economics. At times her denunciation of all forms of collective human activity becomes extreme:

> The far more dangerous screen of the collective must be broken by abolishing every part of our institutions and customs which harbors the party spirit in any form whatsoever. Neither a personality nor a party is ever responsible either to truth or to affliction.[29]

This rather rhetorical, one might even say "revolutionary" statement, needs to be understood as that of a deeply sincere person with a profound mystical vocation, whose own institutional religion, the Roman Catholic Church, required exclusive belief, and which had an appalling record of the infliction of force upon non-Christians and Christians alike. Further, as a Jew by race, Weil regarded Jewish history as one characterized by the misapplication of collective force.[30] This crucial problem of the power of the collective over and against the individual was one of the great themes of Weil's career. This could not have but been so: she was a Jew living in Europe during the rise of Nazism, and during the war was banned from working in her profession as a teacher. She experienced racism; she knew of the atrocities being committed, not only by the Nazis, but also by her former comrades of the left, all in the name of the Utopian aspirations of "the collective." She witnessed the dehumanizing effects of force of all kinds: upon factory laborers, upon the bodies of men and women in war. Of modernity she wrote:

> . . . for every person there should be enough room, enough freedom to plan the use of one's time, the opportunity to use one's time to reach even higher levels of

[28] Simone Weil, *Simone Weil: An Anthology*, p. 39.

[29] Ibid., p. 68.

[30] Henry Finch, *Simone Weil and the Intellect of Grace*, p. 106.

> attention, some solitude, some silence. At the same time a person needs warmth, lest it be driven by distress to submerge itself in the collective.
>
> If this is the good, then modern societies, even democratic ones, seem to go about as far as it is possible to go in the direction of evil. In particular, a modern factory reaches perhaps almost the limit of horror. Everybody in it is constantly harassed and kept on edge by the interference of extraneous wills while the soul is left in cold and desolate misery. What man needs is silence and warmth; what he is given is icy pandemonium.[31]

Weil also saw that the Church itself, rather than protecting people from such abuse of force, had actually been culpable itself of the same kind of abuse. The specific example most unacceptable to her was that of *anathema sit*, or the power of the Roman Catholic Church to formally exclude a believer from the sacrament and therefore from salvation, as well as from the community of believing Christians. This judgment could be imposed on any person believed to hold views in contradiction to those held infallible by the Church. This was not merely, then, a matter of the necessary defense of dogma—to which Weil did not object—but a means by which the Church could inflict collective force upon the individual. For Weil this was therefore something abhorrent, on its own a bar to her formal entry into the Church:

> I should like to draw your attention to one point. It is that there is an absolutely insurmountable barrier to the Incarnation of Christianity. It is the use of the two little words *anathema sit.* It is not their existence, but the way they have been employed up till now. It is that also which prevents me from crossing the threshold of the Church. I remain beside all those things that cannot enter the Church, the universal repository, on account of those two little words.[32]

Here we see that what Weil objected to was not the possibility of excommunication as such, but what she saw as the corrupt way the Church had employed this possibility. We see, moreover, her absolute rejection of religious exclusivism in any form:

> Christianity should contain all vocations without exception since it is Catholic. In consequence the Church should also. But in my eyes Christianity is Catholic by right but not in fact. So many things are outside it, so many things that I love and do not want to give up, so many things that God loves, otherwise they would not be in existence. All the immense stretches of past centuries, except the last twenty, are among them.[33]

As a corrective to all of this, one might perhaps recall here the observation of Frithjof Schuon: "It is illogical to prefer an evil that involves some benefits to a good that involves some evils."[34] What is important to note, however, is that Weil was in no sense advocating

[31] Simone Weil, *Simone Weil: An Anthology*, p. 59.

[32] Simone Weil, *Waiting for God*, p. 33.

[33] Ibid., p. 32.

[34] Frithjof Schuon, *Light on the Ancient Worlds* (Bloomington: World Wisdom, 2006), p. 42.

secularism. On the contrary, she understood this position on the threshold of formal religion as the fulfillment of her particular *dharma*, so to speak. And in this, she was serene:

> I have never once had, even for a moment, the feeling that God wants me to be in the Church. I have never even once had a feeling of uncertainty. I think that at the present time we can finally conclude that he does not want me in the Church.[35]

We should also note that for the spiritually realized person, the forms of religion are in any case relative. Weil did not need to be baptized by the Church, because providence had already baptized her in the spirit. In this, her life was "the exception that proves the rule." This also explains why Weil never advocated remaining outside the Church for anyone else. Quite the opposite:

> If one is born into a religion which is not too unsuitable for pronouncing the name of the Lord, if one loves this native religion with a well directed and pure love, it is difficult to imagine a legitimate motive for giving it up.[36]

We see here implicit recognition of the Perennialist teaching that each religious revelation is precisely adapted to the character of the particular human collectivity to whom it is addressed. As Weil wrote elsewhere, converting to a foreign religion is like learning to write in a second language: the results tend to be mediocre. On the other hand, while religion always involves the transmission of an essential Wisdom, faith does not necessarily involve the unconditional acceptance of all collective religious manifestations. Clearly, there are aspects of religion—particularly those associated with religious exclusivism— which have historically involved the application or the sanctioning of collective force. For Weil, this was true of collectives of all kinds, and always an evil. In her view, then, the path to the transpersonal was solitary, something impossible for a collective. As she wrote: "A group of human beings cannot even add two and two. Working out a sum takes place in a mind temporarily oblivious of the existence of any other minds."[37] This is Plato's path out of the cave through mathematics: it is an escape from the collective through pure contemplation, pure inward attention, into the realm of the transpersonal, *gnosis.* The following passage reads strikingly like Meister Eckhart:

> The human being can only escape from the collective by raising himself above the personal and entering into the impersonal. The moment he does this, there is something in him, a small portion of his soul, upon which nothing of the collective can get a hold.[38]

Indeed at times Weil comes very close to the philosophy of non-duality which she would have known from the *Bhagavad Gita* and the *Upanishads,* both of which she had read and cherished in Sanskrit: "As a child, for a joke, hides behind an armchair from his mother, God plays at

[35] *Waiting for God,* p. 12.

[36] Ibid., p. 120.

[37] *Simone Weil: An Anthology,* p. 56.

[38] Ibid., p. 57.

separating himself from God through creation. We are this joke of God's."[39] This is the ultimate perspective of esoterism, one which goes far beyond the frontiers of an exoteric religious faith, and links Weil's thought directly to the *Philosophia Perennis*.

* * *

Simone Weil was, as we have seen, very far indeed from being "mad." She was a genuine mystic whose insights were in accord with those of diverse religious and esoteric traditions. Rather than resorting to vulgar racial clichés, or a facile psychology, we can, in the light of the *Philosophia Perennis*, identify a plethora of traditional doctrines in her thought—not the least being her universalism—which are all the more remarkable considering the volatile and difficult circumstances in which she lived and wrote. Although her work cannot be assimilated to the *Philosophia Perennis*, it forms, along with that philosophy, a parallel response to the series of escalating crises which constitute the modern world.

In Weil's life it was as if so many antinomies and tensions in modernity—those external and visible, and those internal and felt only secretly in the hearts of men and women—were focused upon her in a concentrated way; moreover the struggles of her life were the struggles of a noble human soul in a world almost entirely hostile to the kind of person she was. In the Middle Ages she might have been a saint. In the modern world she was an unflinching witness to Truth in what was spiritually the darkest epoch of human history. Simone Weil believed that, in our troubled times, "universalism must be made explicit."[40] No doubt the writers of the *Philosophia Perennis* would agree. Her example provides us with an impetus towards that end, and demands of us the respect and understanding due to authentic mysticism. For, as she wrote in reference to *gnosis*: "He who knows the secrets of all hearts alone knows the secrets of the different forms of faith."[41]

39 Ibid., p. 34.

40 Simone Weil, *Waiting for God*, p. 11.

41 Ibid., p. 120.

The Writings of Swami Abhishiktananda (Fr Henri Le Saux)

Harry Oldmeadow

> I have only one message, the message of the Absolute. It is the same message that Jesus and all the seers have taught.
>
> *Abhishiktananda*[1]

> Truth does not deny forms from the outside but transcends them from within.
>
> *Frithjof Schuon*[2]

Henri Le Saux was born in Brittany in 1910 and entered a Benedictine monastery in 1929. In 1948 he travelled to India to join Father Jules Monchanin in a radical monastic venture, the establishment of Shantivanam, a Christian ashram. He was never to leave the shores of his adopted country. After a visit to Ramana Maharshi at Arunachala he spent several extended periods as an ascetic in the caves of the holy mountain, and later became a disciple of Sri Gnanananda Giri of Tiruykoyilur, taking on the name Abhishiktananda. For the rest of his life he immersed himself in the spiritual practices of Advaita Vedanta without ever relinquishing his Christian affiliation. He gradually loosened his connections with Shantivanam and spent much of his time in his later years as a wandering *sanyassi* in northern India. He formalized his Indian citizenship in 1960 and founded a small hermitage on the banks of the Ganges, on the outskirts of Uttarkashi in the Himalayas. Most of his books were written here, near the source of the Ganges. He also often participated in retreats, conferences and inter-faith gatherings, and was closely involved in the "indigenization" of the Indian Church. He crossed to the further shore in 1973.

Abhishiktananda was one of the spiritual luminaries of the last century. Through his many years in the land of the Vedic *rishis* he undertook an intrepid journey of spiritual exploration. His quest for "the secret of Arunachala" attained its goal in the last years of his life when, in the deepest recesses of the "cave of the heart," he experienced fully that inner awakening to the mystery of the Self which the Upanishadic sages had extolled millennia before. In his last years he found, too, the resolution of the acute existential tensions arising out of the "dual presence" in his heart of the Christian Gospel and the *Upanishads.*

This humble monk confronted many of the challenges which face the spiritual wayfarer in our own crepuscular era, in particular the problem of religious pluralism and the inter-relations of the world's integral traditions. He was immediately concerned with the encounter of Christianity and Hinduism, but his experiences and his ever-deepening reflections on this subject illuminate a range of more far-reaching issues. His vocation was realized primarily in his commitment to the interior life and to *sannyasa.* Certainly Abhishiktananda would not

[1] D 25.7.71, 332. See List of Sources at the end of this article for abbreviations used in this article and full bibliographical details.

[2] F. Schuon, *Spiritual Perspectives and Human Facts* (London: Perennial Books, 1967), 112.

have countenanced the thought that his spiritual practice had as one of its ends the production of books! Nonetheless, having attained various insights, especially through the medium of traditional Indian forms, he felt moved to share these with his fellow-Christians of European background.

In this article we will take a conspectus of Abhishiktananda's *oeuvre*. Our discussion does not track the chronological appearance of these works but rather presents them thematically. The dates provided signal the publication of the first English language edition, sometimes lagging behind the French editions at a distance of some years. Readers should also bear in mind that some works were written many years before their first publication date: for example, most of *The Secret of Arunachala*, one of the author's most captivating books, was written in the mid-50s, soon after the experiences it recounts, but was not published until 1979.[3] But in all cases it as well to bear in mind the admonition of his friend Odette Baumer-Despeigne: "To grasp the precise significance of the thought of Henri Le Saux, it is important never to separate his writings from his personality and from the very special circumstances in which his life unfolded."[4] Of his own books Abhishiktananda had this to say:

> All is biographical—and nothing is! Everything comes from the experience of this tension [between Vedanta and Christianity], but everything has been rethought by the mind, in the halo of a double culture. The "I" naturally is literary. Who has the right to say "I," when he speaks of advaita?[5]

A. Major Works

Prayer (1967)

Prayer was first published in India in 1967 but only made an impact in the West when issued by SPCK in 1972. It probably remains Abhishiktananda's most widely known work. There is much in this slender but concentrated volume which might be found in any number of works by other Christian contemplatives—Thomas Merton, Henri Nouwen, Metropolitan Anthony of Sourzah come to mind. There is also much that is reminiscent of Simone Weil's writings on prayer. The Christian sources on which Abhishiktananda draws will surprise no one: apart from the Scriptures (with which the author is obviously intimately familiar, the Johannine and Pauline works being amongst his favorites), Ignatius of Antioch, St John Climacus, Gregory Palamas, Augustine, Aquinas, St John of the Cross, the *Philokalia*, *The Way of the Pilgrim*. The book's originality consists in the way in which Abhishiktananda gently assimilates Hindu insights and techniques into his discussion of prayer. Like many of his books it is, in the first place, directed towards Christian readers; the whole orientation of the book is uncompromisingly Christian whilst being at the same time deeply informed by the East. Abhishiktananda wrote of it, "though it is very elementary, to those who understand it conveys many things."[6] Yes indeed!

Abhishiktananda's keynote is evident from the opening pages:

[3] Those interested in the publication history of various works are directed to James Stuart's bibliography in *Swami Abhishiktananda: His Life told through His Letters* (Delhi: ISPCK, 2000).

[4] O. Baumer-Despeigne, "The Spiritual Journey of Henri Le Saux-Abhishiktananda," *Cistercian Studies*, 18, 1983, 310.

[5] L 23.1.69, 209.

[6] L 8.3.68, 198.

> To live in constant prayer, to lead a contemplative life, is nothing else than to live in the actual presence of God. . . . To live in the presence of God should be as natural for a Christian as to breathe the air which surrounds him. Furthermore, to live consciously and worthily in this presence should never have for him even the appearance of a duty which he is bound to perform... No, for him to live in the presence of the Almighty is a birthright; it is the deepest aspiration of his nature.[7]

The author goes on to consider prayer from various angles: its relation to reason and faith, to "works," to various other activities of the Christian life, and its place in the "universal theophany." He considers various forms of prayer—what in Christian circles is often called "meditation" (focusing the mind on God/Christ, his existence, his attributes, his love, and so on), the prayer of the affections (devotional prayer) and of petition ("the outpourings of the soul confiding all her needs to the Lord").[8] Each has its place—after all, as Frithjof Schuon remarks, "[One] of man's endowments is reasonable thought and speech; this dimension must therefore be actualized during that encounter with God which is prayer."[9] But Abhishiktananda repeatedly stresses that prayer, in its highest form, is neither an intellectual nor an emotional undertaking, these easily lapsing into mere mental activity/verbiage and sentimentalism respectively, but a *state of being* in which, through the stilling of the mind, we are most fully open to the workings of the Spirit. Ultimately we find God in silence, in the "cave of the heart":

> Man is made not merely to work with his hands and to think with his mind, but also to adore in the deep silence of his heart. Even more than to *adore* he is called to plunge into silence and to lose himself there, unable to utter any word, not even a word of adoration or praise; for no word can express the mystery of God. . . . There the mind cannot even think or conceive a thought, for it is overwhelmed, silenced, blinded by this light.[10]

The influence of Abhishiktananda's Indian experiences is most apparent in several of his formulations; for instance, "Truly speaking, there is no outside and no inside, no without and no within, in the mystery of God and in the divine Presence," or "God has no form. He is beyond every form. Precisely for that reason he can reveal and manifest himself under any form."[11]

Abhishiktananda often refers to the relationship between faith and prayer, although at times they seem to be barely distinguishable—and this for good reason. From the way the word is used we can be confident that the author would accept the notion that faith is "the participation of the will in the intelligence." Therefore, "faith takes seriously the promises of God and the almost incredible revelation that we have been raised to the dignity of being children of God."[12] Schuon makes the same point even more dramatically:

[7] Pr 2.

[8] Pr 37.

[9] F. Schuon, *Prayer Fashions Man*, ed. J. Cutsinger (Bloomington: World Wisdom, 2005), 1.

[10] Pr 28-29.

[11] Pr 14, 22.

[12] Pr 44.

> One can spend a whole lifetime speculating on the suprasensorial and the transcendent, but all that matters is "the leap into the void" which is the fixation of spirit and soul in an unthinkable dimension of the Real. . . . This "leap into the void" we can call . . . "faith".[13]

How well that phrase, "the fixation of spirit and soul in an unthinkable dimension of the Real," captures the very vocation of Abhishiktananda! Prayer and faith can also be defined as "internal realities" and as "the simple acknowledgement of the presence of the Spirit in everything, everywhere and at every moment."[14] Thus,

> To look with eyes enlightened by faith at trees and plants, at fruits and flowers, at birds and animals—all of them created by the Father to help and serve us and to be used by us in our ascent towards him—is also nothing less than prayer and contemplation.[15]

In this context, the boundary between "faith" and "knowledge" becomes somewhat fluid. Indeed, in another work Abhishiktananda refers to *jñāna* as "a *mysterium fidei*, a mystery of faith."[16]

Abhishiktananda surveys the history of the contemplative Christian orders, particularly the Carthusian and Carmelite, and regrets the fact that in recent times the Church has marginalized the vocation of the solitary contemplative. Here he sees an extraordinary role for the Indian Church:

> It is to be hoped that the Church of India will in the end bring to the universal Church an authentically Christian *sannyāsī* as the crowning of monastic life. Thus the Church will recover after centuries the purest traditions of the Desert and of the Hesychast movement, and at the same time drink deep at the inexhaustible sources of the Hindu ideal of renunciation in a life devoted to God alone. The Church is in the Spirit awaiting that ultimate inwardness of her life, in which she will discover the true depth of her own mystery. . . . In our day more than ever before the Church needs to hear the testimony that God is beyond all things, beyond all attempts to define him in thought or word or to reach him by activity. The Church has need of an inner silence . . . so that she may reach the fullness of the sacramental sign which she herself is.[17]

This was a plea which Abhishiktananda was to make over and over in his remaining years.

The last four chapters of *Prayer* deal with yoga and prayer (particularly yogic techniques for quietening the mind), *lectio divina* and liturgical prayer, the Prayer of the Name (*nama-japa* in Hinduism, the Jesus Prayer in the Orthodox tradition), and with "OM" and "Abba"

[13] F. Schuon, *Logic and Transcendence* (London: Perennial Books, 1984), 202.

[14] Pr 11.

[15] Pr 18.

[16] EL 29.

[17] Pr 33.

as mantras *par excellence*. All these subjects are handled with the quiet assurance of spiritual maturity. *Prayer* is quite free of both the strident exhortations and the sentimental excesses which sometimes mar writings on this subject.

The Secret of Arunachala (1979)

The Secret of Arunachala recalls Abhishiktananda's formative experiences at Tiruvannamalai in the years between 1949 and 1955, and his decisive encounter with Ramana Maharshi, the sacred mountain and the great Temple of Siva—one which inaugurated his vocation as a Hindu-Christian *sannyāsī* and changed the trajectory of his life. During these years Abhishiktananda's many sojourns at Arunachala covered periods ranging from a few days to several months, his most extended stays coming in 1952 and 1953.The book defies easy generic categorization, blending elements of memoir, journal, biography, travelogue, spiritual manual, mystical love-song. In this respect it is somewhat reminiscent of such classics as Marco Pallis' *Peaks and Lamas*, Anagarika Govinda's *Way of the White Clouds* and *In the Paradise of Krishna* by Klaus Klostermaier. It might well be described as a rhapsodic paean to the three "channels of grace" which left such a profound impression on Abhishiktananda: the sage, the mountain, the temple. Certainly it is one of Abhishiktananda's most lyrical works and, perhaps better than any other, captures his abiding love of eternal India. The accounts of Ramana, the "flame-crowned mountain" and the Temple of Annamalaiyar are the cardinal points around which the book is organized, but there is much else besides. Deftly sketched portraits of some of Ramana's disciples, exemplary and often amusing anecdotes about the many ascetics living in the mountain's network of caves, and descriptions of time-honored Saivite rituals and ceremonies all texture a narrative which never sags. It is free of the pompous solemnities which so often mar Western accounts of Vedanta, and of the gush which churns through much of the hagiographical literature on Ramana; Abhishiktananda's portrait of the sage is thereby all the more compelling.

Although it is little more than a vignette, Abhishiktananda's portrayal of the sage must rank as one of the most illuminating of the many written by Westerners who experienced something of his extraordinary *darsan*.[18] One might mention such figures as F.F. Humphreys, S.S. Cohen, Lanzo del Vasto, Somerset Maugham, Paul Brunton, Jean Herbert and Arthur Osborne. Whilst leaving no doubt whatsoever about the status of Ramana, Abhishiktananda reminds us that he is only one amongst the many—albeit "the greatest belonging to our own time"—"who in the course of ages have quenched their thirst at this fountain which never ceases to flow, and in the shelter of the Mountain have discovered in the depth of their own heart the living mystery of Arunachala."[19]

After an initial tour of Arunachala—"something like Cassian's pilgrimage to the Egyptian desert of Scete"—Abhishiktananda is invited to take up occupation of one the mountain's many caves wherein he can practice austerities, living in silence and solitude. His description of this encounter with the mountain explicitly recalls Ramana's own *Marital Garland* and gives us a fair sample of Abhishiktananda's poetic style of writing:

> That was how the call of the Mountain came to me, the first of Arunachala's spell-binding wiles—the call and the wiles of a lover. . . . It is all up with anyone who

[18] Another, more detailed account of the sage can be found in SAC, Ch 2.

[19] SA 23.

> has paused, even for a moment, to attend to the gentle whisper of Arunachala. Arunachala has already taken him captive, and will play with him without mercy until the bitter end. Darkness after light, desertion after embraces, he will never let him go until he has emptied him of everything in himself that is not the one and only Arunachala and that persists in giving him a name, as one names another—until he has been finally swallowed up, having disappeared for ever in the shining of his Dawn-light, *Āruna*.[20]

Although Abhishiktananda discusses some weighty subjects the book is written with a light touch. Its considerable charm derives, in part, from Abhishiktananda's gentle irony, sometimes self-deprecatory, and from his clear-eyed but loving renditions of people and places. Amongst those making cameo appearances are several remarkable disciples—or, more precisely, followers[21]—of Ramana: Harilal W.L. Poonja, Punjabi Brahmin, ex-army officer and industrialist; Sundarammal, daughter of a wealthy Madras family who came to Tiruvannamalai in melodramatic circumstances, never thereafter leaving the precinct for the remaining fifteen years of Ramana's life; two women who lived for many years in silence, Lakshmi Devi and Radhabai Ammeyar, the "Ammal of Valadur." Other well-known figures who appear in the narrative include Ananda Mayi ("the Mother"), the scholar and biographer of Ramana, Dr T.M.P. Mahadevan, and the "Bengal tiger," A. Bose. Then too there is a larger cast of those humble and pious folk who showed Abhishiktananda himself such solicitude and hospitality during his several visits to the mountain. The author makes very little of the physical and psychological tribulations which his austerities must have entailed, and is generous in his accounts of the many colorful characters he meets on the mountain and its environs. At the same time, he is by no means oblivious to the hypocrisies and complacencies which can be found in any religious community, and sometimes unleashes a sharp and well-aimed shaft:

> There are indeed crowds of people in India who talk learnedly about *advaita*, especially in the south and in ashram circles; but they are generally the first to run to the temples to offer *pūjās* for the success of their ventures on the stock exchange or to obtain some promotion; not to mention the terrible ego-centeredness which so often accompanies the intellectual profession of the Vedanta.[22]

But such barbs are reserved for certain types rather than directed at particular individuals.

The discussion of such subjects as the Vedic hymns and myths, the doctrine of non-duality, the nature of the Self, the nature of symbolism and sacred geography, traditional architecture and iconography, is informed by Abhishiktananda's awareness that such matters cannot be *reduced* and *abstracted* to the level of *ideas* but must be *experienced* as *living realities*. Here, for example, is a characteristic passage, this one about the Vedic Revelation:

> These Vedic hymns, even when their outward meaning escapes one, have a uniquely penetrating power, at least for anyone who allows himself to be inwardly

20 SA 23.

21 Strictly speaking Ramana had no disciples as such; nor did he ever refer to himself as anyone's guru. On this matter see GD 84-85.

22 SA 83.

> open to their spell-binding influence. We could say that, as they issue from the archetypal sources of being, so they irresistibly draw those who chant them, and equally those who hear them, into the same most secret sources of being. The mind thus finds itself carried off as if to an unknown world, a world in which however it has a marvelous sense of belonging, a world which is revealed in its very source, and yet which seems to disappear as soon as one attempts to define it in rational terms or to grasp it in concepts.[23]

Recalling his congenial philosophical discussions with a Brahmin follower of Ramana, Abhishiktananda observes,

> But now, as I look back, I cannot help smiling gently at such attempts to define in intellectual terms that which by its very nature excludes the possibility of being reduced to ideas. But even so, we have to recognize that this has to be a starting-point for some—at least for those impenitent "Greeks" which most westerners are![24]

A scholar of comparative religion has acutely observed that,

> Religions do not all inhabit the same world, but actually posit, structure, and dwell within a universe that is their own. They can be understood not just as so many attempts to explain some common, objectively available order of things that is "out there," but as traditions that create and occupy their own universe.[25]

More than most Western pilgrims, Abhishiktananda was able to enter into the world of South Indian spirituality, to experience it directly, to live it. His descriptions of such practices as *pūjā* (worship), *japa* (invocation), *tapas* (austerities) and *pradaksina* (circumambulation), and their place in Saivite spirituality, are those of a participant rather than a detached scholar or "spiritual tourist." The book closes with a vivid account of the Festival of Light, the Thibam of Kartikki.

Certainly there are moments when Abhishiktananda's European background and habits of mind pose some sort of obstacle or land him in difficulties—but these are rare. More remarkable is Abhishiktananda's ability to understand the spiritual ambience of southern India in its own terms. Whilst he makes some discreet references to his own religious tradition he does not view Hindu spirituality through a distorting Christian lens.

> India only reveals herself to those who are prepared to be still and over a long period to listen humbly at close quarters to the beating of her heart; only to those who have already entered sufficiently far into themselves, into their own depths, to be able to hear in the inner chamber of the heart that secret which India is ceaselessly whispering to them by means of a silence that transcends words. For silence is above all the language through which India reveals herself . . . and imparts her essential message, the message of interiority, of that which is Within.[26]

[23] SA 7-8. Readers may be interested to compare this with Bede Griffiths' equally eloquent account of "The Vedic Revelation" in *The Marriage of East and West* (London: Collins, 1982), 46-58.

[24] SA 13.

[25] W. Paden, *Religious Worlds* (Boston: Beacon, 1988), 51.

[26] From the original Introduction to *Guru and Disciple*, quoted in Odette Baumer-Despeigne's Introduction to *The Secret of Arunachala*, viii.

Guru and Disciple (1974)

Guru and Disciple hinges on Abhishiktananda's transformative encounter with Gnanananda, and much of the book is given over to a sketch of the swami and his teachings ("a perfect echo of the teachings of Sri Ramana"[27]), and their immediate impact on the author. But, as with *The Secret of Arunachala*, there is also a generous admixture of anecdote and of keen observation of the life of the ashram and the surrounding village. The book is cast in the form of a narrative about "Vanya" who clearly is none other than Abhishiktananda himself. This device allows Abhishiktananda to depict his experiences with a certain detachment.

Although Gnanananda attracted a great many followers and was widely revered as an authentic teacher of the wisdom of the *Upanishads*, he was little known in the West until the publication of *Guru and Disciple*. Even today, outside south India he remains much less recognized than many of his less imposing contemporaries. It goes without saying that he himself was quite indifferent to any kind of "fame." A wealth of material about the *jñānī* has been gathered together by some of his followers in *Sadguru Gnanananda: His Life, Personality and Teachings* (1979)—a book also, we note with interest, dedicated to Abhishiktananda himself, with these words from the editors:

> We have drawn a deep inspiration from . . . *Guru and Disciple* and we are sure that the haunting beauty and power of his exposition would capture readers' hearts as it has ours. To the hallowed memory of Swami Abhishiktananda, who could recapture the transcendent beauty of the spirit, and hold aloft the radiance of self-realization to light up the path of spiritual seekers, this book is dedicated with a profound gratitude and reverence.[28]

Such a passage serves to remind us not only of the significance of *Guru and Disciple* but of the spiritual affinity of Gnanananda and Abhishiktananda, and of the esteem in which the French monk was held by the community at Tapovanam.

Gnanananda emerges from Abhishiktananda's pages as the "genuine article"—a fully-fledged *jñānī*, in the tradition initiated by Sankara and crowned in modern times by Ramana himself. His teachings, on Abhishiktananda's account, are as orthodox as one could wish. His "personality" is suggested by his perpetual smile, an infinite patience evinced in the gentle solicitude with which he always dealt with the simple village folk by whom he was forever being importuned, his boundless kindness, especially to children, his indifference to his own material welfare. Also a man of tireless energy and vitality, quite unpredictable in his doings (often frustratingly so for his assistants!), radiating love and good humor but capable of sharp words to lazy or pretentious followers, involved in every aspect of the life of the several ashrams over which he presided. But above all a *jñānī* dedicated to the eternal message of the *Upanishads* and to the tradition of Vedanta in which those teachings were ever being actualized by those who had walked "the royal road of *dhyāna*." Like all authentic spiritual masters, Gnanananda exemplified and transmitted those qualities encapsulated in the Vedantic ternary of *sat-cit-ānanda*: a reality of Being, of intelligence and awareness, and of love-bliss-union.[29]

27 GD 36.

28 C. Indra et al., *Sadguru Gnanananda: His Life, Personality, and Teachings* (Bombay: Bharatiya Vidya Bhavan, 1979), vii.

29 On this subject see F. Schuon, *Logic and Transcendence*, 217.

Guru and Disciple leaves the reader in no doubt not only about Gnanananda's status as a spiritual master but about his impact on Abhishiktananda:

> He [Vanya] was absolutely convinced that here indeed was the guru he had so long dreamed of, the one who would enable him to leap over the crest, if only he were to agree to abandon himself to him in complete trust. . . . The guru's words rang bells within him in a way no one else's had ever done. It was as if, deep in his own heart, profound secret mysteries were coming to light which up till then had been buried in unfathomable depths. What the guru said vibrated through his whole being and the harmonies thus evoked were incomparable.[30]

In a letter from the interval between his first and second visits to Tapovanam Abhishiktananda had written, "How mysterious that Christ can take for a Christian the form of a Saivite guru!"[31] Later, in *Guru and Disciple*, he describes how his encounter with Gnanananda was "like a burn which marks one for life and leaves a permanent scar. Or like a fire which continues to burn as long as something remains to be devoured."[32]

Abhishiktananda is at pains to emphasize that his illuminations at Tapovanam had nothing to do with new *ideas* or *concepts* transmitted by the guru: he was already thoroughly versed in the traditional Upanishadic teachings. In any case he was no longer one of those "impenitent intellectuals," addicted to endless speculations and ratiocinations. At the level of the mind "he already knew everything that had been said to him here. He had read about it, heard tell of it, meditated deeply upon it."[33] In Abhishiktananda's case Gnanananda himself was ruthlessly insistent on the one thing needful—*dhyāna*:

> These discussions on wisdom and the so-called science of the Brahman are so much hot air. *Dhyāna* alone leads to the *ātman* who is *Brahman*. All the rest is just fun and games![34]

And yet, now, through the words of the guru, "an ineffable communication had been established between the master and himself in the depths of the one as of the other."[35] What Abhishiktananda *realized* at Tapovanam, more powerfully than ever before and under the influence of Gnanananda, was the reality of the Self "beyond all possible verbalization or experimentation," "an experience of totality which . . . wells up from the depths of one's being." As Abhishiktananda observes, "When this experience has hit a man one can say that he is "done for," at least with regard to all the ways in which he has so far sought to express himself and be aware of himself." His ego is "consumed by this implacable devouring flame."[36] In short, at Tapovanam Abhishiktananda experienced a transfiguring alchemy of the soul, triggered by

30 GD 107.

31 L 20.1.56, 89.

32 GD 27.

33 GD 26.

34 Quoted in GD 106.

35 GD 26.

36 GD 11.

his surrender to Gnanananda—one for which his long and arduous apprenticeship had prepared him. As the master was fond of saying, one can't make a fire with green wood!

This brief account of *Guru and Disciple* leaves much out of the reckoning; there is much else of considerable interest in the book—one might mention Abhishiktananda's resonant meditation on the primordial sound-syllable OM, his night-long vigil in the temple and his ruminations on the symbolism of the Siva *linga*, the delicate evocation of the rituals with which the Saivite devotees greet the dawning of each new day, the pen-portraits of such figures as the faithful temple priest Kailasandar who continues to discharge his duties though unpaid for a full year, or the impish children who scuttle about temple and ashram. Though there are many such delights, *Guru and Disciple* never achieves quite the vibrancy and charm of *The Secret of Arunachala*, perhaps because of the third-person narration. But its significance in the corpus at large can hardly be doubted, this being the book in which we are made witness to a pivotal moment in Abhishiktananda's life. As Abhishiktananda remarked,

> The meeting with the guru is the essential meeting, the decisive turning point in the life a man. But it is a meeting that can only take place when one has gone beyond the level of sense and intellect. It happens in the beyond, in the fine point of the soul as the mystics say.[37]

More generally the book made both Indian and Western readers aware of Sri Gnanananda—that alone would ensure the book an honored place. Interestingly, Abhishiktananda himself regarded *Guru and Disciple* as his most durable and significant work, writing in the last year of his life that of all his books, it "is almost the only thing that remains afloat. All the rest consists of *nama-rupa* amusing itself with "the theology of fulfillment.""[38] We need not share this harsh judgment of his other work while saluting *Guru and Disciple* as a very fine book indeed.

Saccidananda (1974)

By the early 60s Abhishiktananda was spending more and more time at Gyansu. In his modest hermitage he plunged ever deeper into his reading of the *Upanishads* and into his meditations on Hindu-Christian themes. It was also in these years that he participated in a series of retreats and seminars, organized with Dr J.A. Cuttat, which addressed the ways in which Christianity and Vedanta might be mutually illuminating. Two books grew directly out of these experiences: *Hindu-Christian Meeting Point* and *Saccidananda. Saccidananda* is much the more satisfactory of the two. Both books are somewhat weakened by the theology of fulfillment to which Abhishiktananda still subscribed at that time. He also concedes that the treatment of the Trinity is still circumscribed by "the formulation of the dogma . . . which was originally worked out in terms of Greek thought."[39] The revised English language smoothed out some of the excesses of fulfillment theology though, as the author readily concedes, the book still bears its imprint. He eventually became somewhat frustrated with his attempts at "the patching up of an old wall"[40]

37 GD 29.

38 L 4.2.73, 286.

39 SAC xv.

40 L 18.10.72, 278.

and spoke of the difficulty of revising "a book whose thesis one no longer accepts."[41] Starting his revisions for the English edition of *Saccidananda* (first published in French as *Sagesse hindoue mystique chrétienne*), he wrote in his journal:

> *Sagesse* is an attempt, "begging for help," "agonized," to recover one's footing when the waves—the ground-swell of *advaita* that seizes and bears all away—are carrying one off to the open sea. Why then desire at all cost to regain one's footing? The waves—just like the air—surely provide as safe a support as the sand of the shallows.[42]

Later he would write, "My whole thesis in *Sagesse* has collapsed, and in this total collapse is the awakening."[43] From Abhishiktananda's own point of view, then, *Saccidananda* is overtaken by his later writings.

Notwithstanding these skeptical qualifications on Abhishiktananda's part, for many Christian theologians it constitutes Abhishiktananda's most significant work—perhaps because it is the work in which we find his most mature Christian theology and his most considered reflections on the theme signaled by the book's subtitle, "A Christian Approach to Advaitic Experience." Fr Emmanuel Vattakuzhy calls *Saccidananda* "his most important work, containing his most mature theological thinking," while Judson Trapnell considers it "his most sustained theological work."[44] But, to deploy one of Abhishiktananda's own favorite images, the book overflows many of the limits that such a term implies.

For the moment let us attend primarily to the Introduction for the English version, written in 1971. It offers one of the author's most succinct statements about the urgent imperative of Hindu-Christian dialogue in the fullest sense of the term. Abhishiktananda opens his Introduction with some remarks about the changes which have taken place in the Church and in the world at large since the book's composition in the early 60s. As is well-known, the Second Vatican Council was a watershed in the ways in which the Church perceived its relations with other traditions. Abhishiktananda is now able to write,

> The Vatican Council took it for granted that salvation is open to any sincere man, whatever religious convictions he may or may not have, and thereby recognized the fact that only a minority of men will work out their eternal destiny with any reference to Christ's incarnation. Not only is it necessary to grant the actual existence of religious pluralism here and now, but it is also impossible to foresee a time in the historical future when Christianity might become for mankind as a whole even the predominant—let alone the only—way of realizing their transcendent vocation.[45]

[41] L 4.2.73, 286.

[42] D 25.8.70, 317.

[43] L 2.2.73, 369.

[44] E. Vattakuzhy, *Indian Christian Sannyasa and Swami Abhishiktananda* (Bangalore: Theological Publications in India, 1981), 83; J. Trapnell, "Gandhi, Abhishiktananda, and the Challenge of Perceiving the Religious 'Other'," Infinity Foundation website.

[45] SAC xi.

This momentous development really sounded the long over-due death-knell of both "crisis theology" (all outside the Biblical revelation is "darkness and sin") and "fulfillment theology" (all religions will find their ultimate "fulfillment" in Christ).

Abhishiktananda is happy to leave theologians to wrestle with the *theoretical* problems posed for the Church by these new developments, but in this changing environment the need for "more and more intimate contacts at various levels between men of different faiths and cultures" is making itself ever more urgently felt.[46] Furthermore, real inter-religious dialogue must go well beyond "relations of mutual sympathy" and beyond debate about doctrinal matters, and aim at

> a kind of inner communion at the level of the spirit, so that, even when a difference of opinion cannot be bridged at the conceptual level, both parties instinctively look for a higher and deeper insight to which their opposing ways of expressing themselves are only partial approximations.[47]

It is in this context and in this spirit that Abhishiktananda hopes the book will now be read.

Finally, in this Introduction, Abhishiktananda stresses that *Saccidananda* is not a work of systematic theology but rather,

> Its form is that of a continuous meditation, starting again and again and continually returning on itself, concerning the fundamental themes of the [Hindu-Christian] encounter. It is the meditation of one who is rooted in the spiritual and intellectual traditions of the Church, but has now come into direct contact with the intuitions of the *Upanishads* and the living experience of the sages. One cannot believe that such intuitions will not evoke wonderful echoes in the Christian soul.[48]

Some of the subjects and themes which *Saccidananda* unfolds: the mystery of the Absolute, "beyond all names," as it is prefigured in both the Biblical revelation and the *Upanishads*; the significance of Ramana Maharshi as a living embodiment of the wisdom of the *Upanishads*; the interior quest for the Self and the challenge posed to the monotheistic faiths by *advaita*; the Cosmic Covenant and *Sanatana dharma* (perennial or eternal wisdom); the experiential reconciliation of non-dualism and Trinitarianism; the ideal of "diversity harmonized in love, multiplicity transcended in communion"[49]; acosmism and the vocation of the *jñānī*; the nature of faith; "the bliss of the Spirit." In the course of his explorations Abhishiktananda observes that

> the integration of the advaitic experience into his own faith is for the Christian a necessary task. . . . If Christianity should prove to be incapable of assimilating Hindu spiritual experience from within, Christians would thereby at once lose the right to claim that it is the universal way of salvation.[50]

[46] SAX xiii.

[47] SAC xiii.

[48] SAX xiv.

[49] SAC 134.

[50] SAC 48-49.

It is precisely this "integration of the advaitic experience" into his own Christian faith, thereby breaking a trail for other Christians, that comprises the purpose and substance of *Saccidananda.*

Towards the Renewal of the Indian Church (1970)

This book is a slightly revised memorandum written for a small group of Christians preparing for the All-India Seminar of the Roman Catholic Church in 1969. Its subject is the integration of the "cultural, religious and spiritual heritage" of India into the life of the Church. Although offered as no more than a series of exploratory notes it is one of Abhishiktananda's most coherent and extended considerations of a subject which was one of the main preoccupations of his life in India. It is not our present purpose to consider Abhishiktananda's proposals in any detail, nor to gauge what impact this document actually had on the Church in India, but only to take note of its general thrust.

The book opens with one of Abhishiktananda's most salient themes in his writings about the Church:

> The Church is essentially a spiritual reality and Christian religion is, first of all, a living experience in the Spirit. Its source is nothing other than the inner experience of Jesus. . . . The Church is the social and human milieu in which that experience of Jesus is transmitted though all ages and to all men by the Word and the Sacraments. She is not an end in herself. She is a sign, herself a sacrament . . . just as in man the essential is the spirit, so in the Church, too, the essential is that inner reality in the heart of every man where his spirit is in direct communion with the Holy Spirit.[51]

It follows, then, that the interior life of the spirit is the most important thing in the life of both the Christian individual and of the Church itself. Indeed, "*unless such a conviction is widely disseminated, nothing worthwhile will be achieved in the Church.*"[52] He reminds readers that ecclesiastical authorities have all too often been more concerned with the external aspects of the institution rather than with the work of the Spirit. This has produced "dangerous deviations," "unhealthy and superstitious use of the sacraments" and "a shameless collusion with worldly powers, either political or economical." It has also promoted "an improper rivalry" with other religions. Abhishiktananda also notes that

> We cannot indeed hide the fact in a candid examination of conscience, that too many activities in the Church directed theoretically to spread the Kingdom, are simply the self-satisfying projections in a "mythico-religious" sphere of man's unsuppressible need for self-expression.[53]

Elsewhere Abhishiktananda had written, referring to both the Universal Church and the Church in India, that "The moment in history in which we are living calls us to a stern purification

[51] RC 1-2.

[52] RC 7 (italics mine).

[53] RC 5.

of all our means," a task of which he sometimes despaired.[54] For many Indians, Christians were whites who "ate meat, wore leather, and went into holy places with their shoes on."[55] However, Abhishiktananda always hoped and prayed that the Church could be redeemed by those "deep contemplative souls" who, open to the Spirit, attune the Church to that same Spirit, thus ensuring that even the most humble of worldly-inspired works in the vineyard will not be entirely devoid of spiritual fruits.

Abhishiktananda notes that the Church faces two formidable challenges in the contemporary world: on the one side by those forces in the modern Western world which consider Christianity to be, at best, no more than "a kind of fiduciary currency, lacking security, worth just the credulity of the ignorant man";[56] on the other hand there is the challenge which the civilizations of the East present out of their own spiritual experience. The confrontation with secular atheism and with Eastern spirituality together pose "the most formidable challenge the Church has ever met in the course of her history."[57] Exacerbating the difficulty of meeting these challenges is the unhappy fact that so much Christian theology is abstract, mechanical, divorced from lived experience, over-burdened with historicism. With these salutary and sometimes vinegary reflections to the forefront, Abhishiktananda turns to the question at hand: how is the Church in India to assimilate the spiritual nutrients offered by the Hindu tradition, and how, in turn, is the Church to find "the best openings through which to instill the grace of the Holy Spirit entrusted to her and consequently, the most central and far-reaching channels through which to enable divine grace to fructify a hundredfold."[58] Rather than rehearsing the details of Abhishiktananda's book, suffice it here to give a consolidated summary of those things which he urges the Church to affirm and pursue:

- the primacy of spiritual values and the centrality of contemplation to spiritual life;
- the promotion of inter-religious dialogue, based on a "a common sharing of that "awareness" within," by persons "dedicated to a life of prayer and contemplation," and in places "sanctified by the silence and meditation of holy men";[59]
- the assimilation into Christian practice of various insights and techniques derived from such traditional Indian disciplines as yoga (the control of mind and body so as to achieve that inner silence in which we answer "the call to interiority"), *nāma-japa* (invocation of the holy Name), and various austerities;
- the nurturing of the thirst, in a Christian context, for *brahmavidyā* (knowledge of the Supreme Reality) by the development of the traditional "qualifications": the ability to discriminate between things permanent and impermanent; renunciation of attachment to the fruits of action, both in this world and the hereafter; the six virtues, including the quietening of the mind, and faith in the Scriptures and the guru; the yearning for *moksa* (deliverance);
- the re-animation of the "cosmic covenant" within Christianity;
- the adjustment of various aspects of daily life to accord with the Indian milieu, including

[54] L 14.6.66, 180.

[55] S. du Boulay, *The Cave of the Heart: The Life of Swami Abhishiktananda* (Maryknoll, NY: Orbis, 2005), 60.

[56] RC 10.

[57] RC 10.

[58] RC 26.

[59] RC 21.

fasting, abstinence from flesh-eating, and the regular observance of periods of silence;
- the development of an Indian liturgy *in Sanskrit* (anything else would be "an affair of the studio, an abstract thing, a work of mere scholars"[60]);
- the integration of Hindu Scriptures and Hindu festivals into Christian worship;
- a much deeper study, particularly by the religious, of Hindu Scriptures, mythology, symbolism, iconography, the Sanskrit language etc; the establishment of various courses and centers to this end; such formal studies to be accompanied by regular exposure to the religious life of India by extended stays in Hindu maths, ashrams and the like;
- the development of "a genuine Christian *sannyāsa*";
- the spread of Christian ashrams where Christian communities can live "on traditional Hindu lines" and in which "an authentic Indo-Christian spirituality, liturgy and theology will evolve."[61]

The Mountain of the Lord: Pilgrimage to Gangotri (1966)

In June, 1964, Abhishiktananda and his friend Raimon Panikkar (who appears in the narrative as "Sanat Kumar") walked the ancient Himalayan pilgrim route from Haridwar to Gangotri, climbing to Gomukh where the Ganges finds one of its sources in the melting glaciers. Here, close to the abode of Lord Siva, the two Christian pilgrims celebrated the Eucharist. After farewelling his companion in Uttarkashi, Abhishiktananda returned to Gangotri to spend three weeks in total silence. These experiences are recounted in *The Mountain of the Lord*, first published in 1966 but gaining much wider circulation when it appeared in 1974 as a companion piece to "A Sage of the East," the two together comprising *Guru and Disciple.* Abhishiktananda described it as "an unmistakably Christian meditation on the theme of a Hindu pilgrimage."[62]

This short work is one of Abhishiktananda's most attractive, giving a glimpse of the existential intensity, if one may so put it, with which he lived in the two worlds of Christianity and Hinduism. The account of the outer journey, their fellow pilgrims and the landscape through which they moved finds the author at his most poetical, though the narrative also touches on the penitential hardships of the journey. Early in the piece:

> Behold the great peaks of the Himalaya, the summit of the world, Earth's supreme effort to reach up to Heaven! Thrusting upwards to the greatest possible height, they soar towards the sky, as if to lay hold of the "waters above the firmament," of which *Genesis* speaks—to lay hold of them, and cause them to fall back to earth . . . the meeting point of the world above—that inaccessible world from which none the less we come and to which we go—with the world below in which for the time being we lead our earthly lives.[63]

For Abhishiktananda, surrounded by the sights and sounds of the Hindu faithful, experiencing the grandeur of the mountains was very much a matter of "seeing God everywhere"—not just an aesthetic pleasure but "to those who can discern everywhere the traces of God's handiwork, it [the landscape] gives a call to spiritual joy and thanksgiving."[64]

60 RC 46.

61 RC 74.

62 GD ix.

63 ML 6.

64 ML 14.

The Mountain of the Lord is not only a hymn to the sublime Himalayan peaks, symbolizing transcendence, but also to the solitaries, recluses, renunciates, "acosmics" to be found in the caves and forests on their slopes. By extension it could also be seen as an affirmation of the vocation of the solitary renunciate, whether a Christian monk in the Syrian desert, the Hindu *muni*, the Tibetan *naldjorpa* in the snowy fastness, the Taoist recluse, the shaman on a vision quest, the *staretz* of the Russian forests. Such figures are also symbolized by the mountains with their life-giving waters. "The high mountains point upwards towards heaven, stark naked, *dig-ambara*, clad in space. Such is also the monk—naked, solitary, motionless."[65] The symbolism is, of course, irresistible and one we find expressed by many contemplatives. Thomas Merton, for instance:

> The great, gashed, half-naked mountain is another of God's saints. There is no other like him. He is alone in his own character; nothing else in the world ever did or ever will imitate God in quite the same way. That is his sanctity.[66]

Later Abhishiktananda returns to his theme, calling the solitary witnesses to the Absolute "the pivots of this world, holding it steady by their own stillness within the Unmovable."[67] More than ever before, he writes, both the world at large and the Church in particular need these "immovable pillars" because "the world is more than ever carried away in the stream of events"; today

> the more urgent is the need for some at least to allow themselves to be brought by . . . the Spirit into the mystery of the Unmanifested, and [to] remain there, remote, isolated, naked and silent, both outwardly and inwardly, before God and mankind.[68]

By so doing, the monk "bears witness to the truth that time proceeds from and returns to Eternity."[69]

After musing on the various rites of the *sādhus* and the devotions of the pilgrims, Abhishiktananda reflects that,

> It was surely fitting that a Christian also should come and worship in these high places, that he should come there to "fulfill" all signs, myths and images, and to enable the vast sacrament of the cosmos to pass from the sign to its reality in Christ, in the Eucharist.[70]

On the Feast of the Sacred Heart, soon after sunrise, the two companions climbed to a sheltered spot and bathed in the icy waters of the glacier, thus re-enacting the primordial cosmic rite of the return to the primeval womb, the source of Being, and at the same time recalling the rite

65 ML 48.

66 T. Merton, *New Seeds of Contemplation* (New York: New Directions, 1961), 31.

67 ML, 45.

68 ML 45.

69 Ml 50.

70 ML 21.

of baptism which "so powerfully symbolizes the mystery of our rebirth."[71] Then, with a little wine and a chappati of unleavened flour, the air perfumed with burning incense, with the roar of the holy river "like a mighty organ accompaniment," they celebrated the holy mystery.

> Immediately overhead we had the great heavenly luminary in whose bright light the surrounding snows were a dazzling white—the same sun which sees all that happens on the face of the earth, which enlightened the eyes of our first parents, and at which Jesus gazed as he hung upon the cross—the sun which is the ever present witness of all that is, was, or will be.[72]

And so it was that through this "final and perfect oblation," the countless hymns and prayers of the pilgrims of the ages, their chants and devotions, their austerities and deprivations, the silence and penances of the ascetics, were all "gathered up and fulfilled in the sacrifice of the Lamb."[73]

In the end *The Mountain of the Lord* is itself a kind of prayer, reverberating with the chants of the pilgrims and the sounds of bird and stream, set amidst the majestic Himalayan peaks, and culminating in the celebration of the sacrament. It calls to mind a passage from Frithjof Schuon in which he beautifully depicts man at prayer in the sanctuary of Nature herself:

> The saint has himself become prayer, the meeting place of earth and Heaven; and thus he contains the universe and the universe prays with him. He is everywhere where nature prays and he prays with and in her: in the peaks which touch the void and eternity, in a flower which scatters itself or in the abandoned song of a bird.[74]

The Further Shore (1975)

The Further Shore comprises two separate works, *The Upanishads*, written in 1971 but never finally revised, and *Sannyāsa*, a series of essays written in 1973, first seeing the light of day in serialized form in *The Divine Life*, the monthly organ of the Sivananda Ashram in Rishikesh. Together these writings are the ripest fruit of Abhishiktananda's engagement with Indian spirituality, and can properly be regarded as his "spiritual testament." In this final work, completed only a few months before his passing, Abhishiktananda offers us his most seasoned reflections on many of the subjects which had preoccupied him since he first set foot on Indian soil, nearly a quarter of a century before. *The Further Shore* is the summit of his written work just as those few incandescent weeks between the *diksa* of his disciple and his own "great adventure" in the bazaar of Rishikesh was to be the culmination of his existential journey in search of "the secret of Arunachala." As is suggested by the unidentified writer of the Foreword (almost certainly Marc Chaduc), *Sannyāsa* is written "in letters of fire," and reveals the inner fervor which consumed Abhishiktananda to his very depths and summoned him irresistibly

[71] ML 58.

[72] ML 58.

[73] ML 60.

[74] F. Schuon, *Spiritual Perspectives*, 212-213.

to an ever more acosmic life, totally absorbed in the inward vision."[75] Furthermore, it is altogether appropriate that these writings on renunciation should be published side-by-side with Abhishiktananda's last written meditation on the mystery of *Brahman*, the central theme of the *Upanishads*, these Scriptures themselves affirming that *brahmavidyā* and *sannyāsa* are inseparable. As the *Mahānārāyana Upanishad* has it,

> That mystery of glory and immortality,
> Hidden in the depth of the heart and in highest heaven,
> Which only those can find
> Who have renounced all.[76]

These two subjects were very close to Abhishiktananda's heart: *sannyāsa* most fully expressed the ideal towards which he had been striving throughout the years in India while the *Upanishads* opened the gateway to the advaitic experience.

> His spiritual path essentially consisted in the complete appropriation of the Advaitic experience of the Upanishadic rishis, without however losing hold of his own rootedness in the Christian tradition. He made the *Upanishads* his own, and whenever he happened to comment on them, it was always with a reverent enthusiasm and in order to bring out the radiance of their marvelous intuition.[77]

Sannyāsa presents a limpid exposition of the meaning of this "sign beyond signs," particularly in the Indian tradition but also in its universality, for as Abhishiktananda so rightly claims, "The call to complete renunciation cuts across all *dharmas* and disregards all frontiers . . . it is anterior to every religious formulation."[78] He examines the way the ideal has been practiced over the centuries and considers some of the pressures and degenerations which have come with modernity. Abhishiktananda also ponders the ways in which *sannyāsa* might be assimilated into the Christian tradition to reanimate those spiritual impulses which were so evident in the flight of the Christian solitaries to the deserts of Egypt and Syria and to the forests of Russia. In one of the most arresting passages in *Sannyāsa*, Abhishiktananda explains how the ideal is actually, though paradoxically, embodied in the sacrament of the Eucharist which itself can be a "sign beyond signs."[79]

The Upanishads: An Introduction rehearses themes which Abhishiktananda had explored many times previously—but here he writes with an unsurpassed clarity and power, distilling the insights of both his many years of study of these texts (the *Brihadāranyaka* and *Chandogya Upanishads* being the ones which "most faithfully express Upanishadic thought in its radical purity"[80]), and of his own sometimes vertiginous experiences of *advaita*. The author contextualizes these Scriptures, explicates their controlling themes and offers the readers various

[75] Foreword, FS vii.

[76] Quoted in FS ix.

[77] Foreword FS ix.

[78] FS 27.

[79] FS 50-52. The passage in question implicitly explains why Abhishiktananda himself remained so committed to the celebration of this sacrament.

[80] FS 69.

keys with which to unlock their secrets. This work also presents some wise reflections on a range of questions pertaining to the nature of religion and the so-called problems of religious pluralism. Here, for instance, is one of his last attempts to define "faith":

> Contrary to what is too often supposed, faith does not primarily consist in the mind's acceptance of certain propositions, termed "data of revelation." Faith is essentially that interior sense by which the mind penetrates obscurely into those depths of one's own being which it realizes are beyond its power to explore solely by means of thought and sense-perception.[81]

All in all, *The Further Shore,* written indeed in "letters of fire," must be one of the most stirring expressions of the universal ideal of renunciation, and of the wisdom which is its fruit. To return directly to the *Upanishads* themselves, as Abhishiktananda so frequently does in these pages: *sannyāsa* is the way to

> That mystery of glory and immortality
> Hidden in the depth of the heart, beyond the firmament,
> Which cannot be won either by ritual acts,
> Or by begetting offspring,
> Or by giving one's wealth:
> But which only they can enter
> Who have renounced all.[82]

B. Other Books

An Indian Benedictine Ashram (with Jules Monchanin) (1951)

The first edition of this booklet, written by Monchanin and Abhishiktananda, was published on October 10, 1951, the day on which the chapel at Shantivanam was blessed. Its purpose was to acquaint readers with "the aim and *raison d'être* of the humble hermitage opened discreetly on the Kavery banks on the feast of S. Benedict, the previous year."[83] Only five hundred copies were initially printed. It was expanded for the French edition, *Ermites du Saccidananda* (1956), and a revised edition of the English text appeared as *A Benedictine Ashram,* without the pleonasm of the original title. It portrays its authors' vision of a Christian ashram, and gives a lucid account of the theology underlying it. Much of the book centers on monasticism as the bridge which could link the world of Indian spirituality and the Church. Although the first chapter was written by Monchanin, it fairly represents their shared views at the time. As such it is an invaluable source on both Monchanin and Abhishiktananda, and is a landmark document in the history of the Christian ashram movement. It provoked both excitement and disturbance in ecclesiastical circles in India and France.

81 FS 59-60.

82 Quoted in FS 51.

83 BA 1.

Hindu Christian Meeting Point (1969)

No book written by Abhishiktananda is without its pearls and there is much of interest in *Hindu-Christian Meeting Point*, such as the meditations on the *Upanishads*, and the explication of certain Scriptural passages, particularly Johannine, in a Upanishadic light. Much of what Abhishiktananda has to say about both Christian and Hindu traditions is instructive. But, taken as a whole the book is not one of his more commanding works. There are several readily apparent reasons for this. Firstly, the book suffers from a certain "identity crisis": is it a report of various intra-religious retreats and seminars concerned with the encounter of these two traditions, striving to give a fair account of what transpired, or is it Abhishiktananda's own responses to these encounters? Secondly, perhaps partly as result of the ambiguity raised by this question, there is an unresolved tension in the book between the fulfillment theology then very much in vogue in the Indian Church, and an unequivocal affirmation of the wisdom literature of India and the spiritual experience to which it testifies. Thirdly, various inter-related questions arising out of the general theme are more decisively dealt with in other works by Abhishiktananda—and here one is thinking primarily of *Saccidananda* and *The Further Shore.* As to the practical questions raised by the meeting of Hindus and Christians, both as individuals and as collectivities, these are addressed more coherently in *Towards a Renewal of the Indian Church.* Whilst *Hindu-Christian Meeting Point* gives us some insights into Abhishiktananda's own spiritual experience, it is also the least personal of his published works—and this, too, at least in part, derives from the fact that one of its purposes is to report fairly on the deliberations of the Cuttat Circle as a whole.

The Eyes of Light (1983)

The Eyes of Light is a posthumous compilation of several essays, some previously unpublished, gathered together by Abhishiktananda's friend Fr Joseph Lemarié, and appearing in the first French edition in 1979. The opening essay, "The Experience of God in the Religions of the Far East," is a new translation of an article which had appeared in *Cistercian Studies* in 1974. In it are to be found many of Abhishiktananda's familiar themes about the differing but convergent spiritual/religious traditions of East and West, including more allusions to Buddhism than we find in most of his other writings on the same subject. Other essays concern the contemplative prayer of Silence and Presence, derived from the wisdom of the *Upanishads* and constituting "India's contribution to Christian prayer," the theology of Presence (which was now overtaking the theology of fulfillment in the Indian Church), the formation of priests in the Indian Church, and spiritual childhood. The longest essay, "India and the Carmelite Order" (from *Carmel*, 1965) is another lengthy meditation on the message of the *Upanishads*, the place of contemplative monastic orders in the Church at large, and the role that the Carmelite Order might yet play in Indian Christianity. The book includes excerpts from Abhishiktananda's correspondence to Madame I. Charnelet, Mother Françoise-Thérèse, his family, Fr Lemarié and to Father Miguel, a professed monk of the Abbey Sainte-Marie de Paris. Some fragments from his journal are also presented.

One of the most singular essays, brief though it is, is "Gandhi, Witness of the Truth," reproduced from *Annales de sainte Thérèse de Lisieux* (January 1970).[84] Abhishiktananda's

[84] The title of this essay, as it appears in *Eyes of Light*, misspells the Mahatma's name as "Ghandi," a mistake repeated several times in the text. I have corrected this in the excerpts quoted.

reflections recall those made by the great German theologian, philosopher and comparative religionist, Rudolf Otto. Otto claimed that people in the West mis-read Gandhi if we understand him primarily as a politician, a statesman, a doer of great deeds on the public stage; the key to Gandhi's character and his vocation is that he was a renunciate: his political activities and achievements grew out of his immediate situation; had Gandhi been in different circumstances, he would still have been a *sādhu.*[85] Abhishiktananda hails Gandhi as a prophet and as one of those "in whom the mystery of the invisible Presence has manifested itself in the midst of their brethren with a particularly intense brilliancy."[86] This Presence, to which Gandhi often gave the name "Truth," was "a living and felt reality" in which his life was rooted and which fed all of his activities. The campaign for the liberation of his people from the foreign yoke was paralleled by the inner struggle against the ever-present enemies of the soul—"falsehood and selfishness, hatred and violence, greed."[87] Like Otto, Abhishiktananda finds something quintessentially Indian in Gandhi, without which his appeal would be quite inexplicable:

> To be sure Gandhi had his peculiarities which amused or annoyed his followers. No doubt some of his options can be debated; no doubt free India, on the whole, still remains quite far from the lofty ideal that Gandhi would have liked to inculcate in her soul. Nevertheless it was precisely the idealism of Gandhi, this sense of the absolute, of the Truth, of Love, that he derived from his contemplation of the inner mystery, his sense, in a word, of the sovereign presence of God, which shook and drew his people, which made it attach itself to the Mahatma as to a charismatic leader, as to an emissary of God, and to follow him blindly in defiance of all obstacles. This people recognized itself in him.[88]

Abhishiktananda also comments on Gandhi's attitude to religious pluralism and defends him against the absurd reproach that some Christians (both Indian and European) leveled against him, his failure to enter the Church.

> Some dared even accuse him of insincerity. Had he not read the Bible? Had he not loudly proclaimed that the figure and the message of Christ had exercised a great influence on him? His failure to take this step may have been precisely due to the fact that Gandhi was too attached to truth, to this very truth that Jesus himself preached, to arrive at recognizing in the Church the authentic and unique messenger of this truth. . . . Perhaps it can be attributed also, and above all, to this sense of the absolute of God which is at the base of the whole religious attitude of India. God is beyond all expression, all form, all history. Saints and prophets all manifest him, each in his own way. Each one is the mystery of God become visible among men. The current of the river returns to its source, the manifestation to the manifested, the form to the mystery that goes beyond all form, time to eternity. Attentive to God everywhere, the sage discovers him everywhere. All signs lead

[85] R. Otto, "Gandhi, Saint and Statesman" (1933) in *Autobiographical and Social Essays*, ed. G.D. Alles (Berlin: Mouton de Gruyter, 1996), 195-196.

[86] EL 120.

[87] EL 121.

[88] EL 123.

to him. And he sees no reason to give privileged preference to one or the other of these signs.[89]

Furthermore, it might be added, Gandhi had no reason to abandon the "signs" of the Absolute with which the indigenous traditions of both Hinduism and Jainism had nourished his soul and which found expression in his devotion to that form of the Absolute, Rama, whose very name sprang to his lips at the moment of his death.

C. Unpublished Works and Miscellanea

Amour et Sagesse (1942) (unpublished)

Written for his mother in 1942, this unpublished manuscript is an important way station on Abhishiktananda's spiritual journey. It is a deep pondering on the theme of the Trinity which Abhishiktananda regarded as the "noblest mystery" of Christianity, "so little savored" even by fervent believers.[90] It also introduces some of the mystical themes which were to sound throughout the whole *oeuvre*, and makes some reference to Indian literature, including Tagore's *Gītāñjali*.

Guhantara: au sein du fond (1953) (unpublished)

Monchanin called this work "a spiritual essay born out of silence" while Abhishiktananda himself described it as "the direct expression of my first overwhelming experiences" (at Arunachala).[91] In the words of his biographer, "it was the first detailed articulation of the confrontation between Christianity and *advaita*."[92] It fell foul of the ecclesiastic censor in Paris, one Fr J. Guennou, who found it full of "heresies" and "redolent of relativism, modernism, quietism, modalism and especially pantheism."[93] His report on the book was totally damning and, as James Stuart observes, "so negative as to be ludicrous"—so much so that on receiving it, after the initial shock Abhishiktananda and Monchanin could only burst into laughter.[94] *Guhantara* (which means "the dweller within the cave") was widely circulated in manuscript form amongst some of the French clergy and amongst Abhishiktananda's friends and acquaintances in India. Parts of it were published in other books and as fragments. It adumbrates some of the major themes which were to run through Abhishiktananda's works over the rest of his life.

Swami Parama Arubi Anandam: Fr J. Monchanin 1895-1957 (1959)

This book was edited and largely written by Abhishiktananda—but he is nowhere mentioned by name. It comprises three parts: "glimpses of his [Monchanin's] life and ideals," written by the editor; "a garland of memories" in which we find tributes from both European and Indian friends (including Bishop Mendonça, Bede Griffiths, Raimon Panikkar, Henri de Lubac and

89 EL 123-124.

90 L 7.

91 Monchanin quoted in Vattakuzhy, 77; L 8.3.68, 199.

92 du Boulay, 119.

93 D 86.

94 L 75.

Harold Rose); thirdly, extracts from Monchanin's writings and letters. It is a heartfelt tribute to a man with whom Abhishiktananda had shared many deep experiences, and testifies to Monchanin's many fine qualities.

In Spirit and Truth: An Essay on Prayer and Life (1989)

This essay, concerned largely with the Christian path, derived from some notes written for the Carmel of Lisieux in 1961, and was first published in French as an appendix to *Eveil à soi—éveil à Dieu* (Paris: Centurion, 1971). After its translation into English by Mary Rogers it was further modified by Abhishiktananda in 1972.

D. Diary and Letters

In his Introduction to *Ascent to the Depth of the Heart: The Spiritual Diary (1948-73) of Swami Abhishiktananda (Dom Henri Le Saux)*, the editor makes the following observations:

> We cannot insist too much on the fact that this Diary, which only follows his Indian journey, embodies for Swamiji his personal monologue: he examines himself, sometimes absolutely ruthlessly, clarifies his ideas, and also challenges them. These pages reflect the central preoccupation of his whole life, on which all others converge: the Mystery of the Absolute from the perspective of *advaita*. . .

He also draws a telling distinction (made by the diarist himself):

> The difference between the Diary and his published writings is not only a matter of form and finish. It is also one of perspective. In his books he is aware of his role as a Christian mystic who writes chiefly for Christians (and westerners) in order to open their minds to Hindu wisdom. In his Diary he is more and more the Hindu monk who is faced with the Christian mystery and is desperately trying to reconcile it with Vedanta. . . . This Diary is, so to speak, the laboratory of the alchemist; the forerunner of something unknown.[95]

It might be said that in these "private murmurings of a solitary," these "pages written in the raw flesh of his being—the outpourings of his thought, the expressions of his doubts and seeking, the stammerings or the poetical flights of his ecstasies"[96]—we see Abhishiktananda strip himself naked. The *Diary*, then, is essential reading for anyone trying to retrace Abhishiktananda's existential journey. The editor concedes that the publication of such a diary might be "highly indiscreet, a kind of profanation of what . . . ought to remain hidden." But he finds some sanction in the fact that Abhishiktananda reproduced parts of his journal in his own books and especially prepared others for publication, and also anticipated the possibility of an edited publication. He also believes that Abhishiktananda's journal offers exemplary experiences for those moving across religious frontiers and "symbolizes a life lived in depth in the midst of a world that

[95] R. Panikkar, Introduction, xiv.

[96] D, Editor, xv, xiii.

has fallen apart."[97] He also urges readers to read it in the context of Abhishiktananda's more considered and nuanced published works and in the light of his experience at large.[98]

Abhishiktananda accumulated a set of notebooks, comprising over two thousand pages which, over the years, suffered a good deal of damage from the elements. The notebooks are written in a script by no means easy to read, some of it quite indecipherable. They are littered with terms and phrases from English, Greek, Sanskrit, Latin, Tamil and Hindi, and exhibit a "violent" disregard for grammar. The daunting task of bringing the Diary into a form that might be published was taken up by the Abhishiktananda Society which drew on the work of several people—Madame Baumer-Despeigne who typed out many of the entries, Raimon Panikkar as editor, David Fleming and James Stuart as translators. Abhishiktananda gave his disciple, Marc Chaduc, his diary entries from November 1966 onwards, to do with as he liked. Chaduc transcribed portions of the diary and then threw away the original. As Glenn Friesen has noted, there is no reason to suppose that Chaduc's copying was anything but faithful, but the fact remains that significant portions of the diary are now lost forever.

*   *   *

No less prodigious a labor was entailed in gathering together as much as possible of Abhishiktananda's vast correspondence. We have already observed that he was addicted to reading—no less to letter-writing! (In both respects he is somewhat reminiscent of his fellow-monk, Thomas Merton.) In 1974 some of Abhishiktananda's friends and associates conceived the idea of a memorial volume, under the editorship of Sister Sara Grant, which would include some excerpts from his letters. As the editor came to read through the letters drawn from fifteen separate collections, she was struck by the thought that the letters, with some judicious arrangement, might form the basis of "a vivid mosaic of Swamiji's life in India, told largely in his own words." Because of her other commitments, Sister Sara handed the task over to her colleague, Fr James Stuart. It was not until 1989 that *Swami Abhishiktananda: His life told through his letters* saw the light of day as a publication of ISPCK. But Fr Stuart's labors in the intervening years had garnered a rich harvest. The book is now indispensable for anyone interested in Abhishiktananda's life in India. The letters themselves also reveal facets of Abhishiktananda's personality, his relationships and his daily doings which are either altogether absent or obscured in his other works. Fr Stuart has also done us a fine service in constructing the fullest Bibliography of Abhishiktananda.

*   *   *

All of Abhishiktananda's books contain many treasures and delights. We best appreciate each one not in isolation but when it is situated in the whole existential journey to which each book testifies at a particular moment. Each reader will respond to these works differently. For my own part I would single out four works as especially precious: *The Secret of Arunachala*—a love song to the spirit of India, a rhapsody written in a state of holy intoxication, and a profound

[97] D, Editor, xvi-xvii.

[98] For a provocative review of *Ascent to the Depth of the Heart*, in the form of an imaginary conversation between the reviewer and Swamji, see Sara Grant, "Time-Bomb or Tomb-Stone?: Reflections on the Private Journal of Swami Abhishiktananda," *Vidyajyoti*, 52, 1988, 83-97.

homage to Ramana and Arunachala; *Mountain of the Lord*, a brief but poignant account of a pilgrimage, a glimpse into the density of Abhishiktananda's spiritual life, and a canticle to the Himalayan peaks; *The Further Shore*, the final distillation of Abhishiktananda's hard-earned spiritual insight and including some of the most exalted mystical passages of recent times; and *Ascent to the Depth of the Heart*, a spiritual journal of raw intensity in which a profoundly noble but troubled soul is laid bare.

Sources & Abbreviations (dates are of editions consulted)

BA	*A Benedictine Ashram* (written with Jules Monchanin), Douglas: Times Press, 1964.
D (Diary)	*Ascent to the Depth of the Heart: The Spiritual Diary (1948-1973) of Swami Abhishiktananda (Dom Henri Le Saux)*, ed. Raimon Panikkar, tr. David Fleming and James Stuart, Delhi: ISPCK, 1998.
EL	*The Eyes of Light*, ed. A. Gozier and J. Lemarié, Denville, NJ: Dimension, 1983.
FS	*The Further Shore*, Delhi: ISPCK, 1975.
GD	*Guru and Disciple*, tr. Heather Sandeman, London: SPCK, 1974.
HC	*Hindu-Christian Meeting Point*, tr. Sara Grant, Delhi: ISPCK, 1976.
L (Letters)	*Swami Abhishiktananda: His Life Told through His Letters*, by James Stuart, Delhi: ISPCK, 2000.
ML	*Mountain of the Lord: Pilgrimage to Gangotri*, Delhi: ISPCK, 1990.
Pr	*Prayer*, London: SPCK, 1974.
RC	*Towards the Renewal of the Indian Church*, Bangalore: Dharamaran College, 1970.
SA	*The Secret of Arunachala: A Christian Hermit on Shiva's Holy Mountain*, Delhi: ISPCK, 1997.
SC	*Saccidananda: A Christian Approach to Advaitic Experience*, Delhi: ISPCK, 1984.

The Exiled Immortal: Reconsidering Harold Stewart

Alex Minchinton

> For today the artist has, whether he likes it or not, inherited the combined functions of hermit, pilgrim, prophet, priest, shaman, sorcerer, soothsayer, alchemist and bonze. How could such a man be free? How can he really "find himself" if he plays the role that society has predetermined for him? The freedom of the artist is to be sought precisely in the choice of his work and not in the choice of the role as "artist" which society asks him to play, for reasons that will always remain very mysterious.
>
> *Thomas Merton*[1]

> I never really felt "at home" until I settled here in Kyoto, where I can at last relate to the scenery, religion and culture, even though a gaijin must inevitably remain an outsider to Japanese. That worries me least of all, since to create anything I must be detached from society and need silence and solitude. Other people frighten away the Muse by their mere presence.
>
> *Harold Stewart*[2]

After a controversial career as a poet Harold Stewart left Australia in 1966, never again to return. He was to spend the next 29 years of his life in Kyoto, the ancient capital of Japan, immersed not only in the study and practice of Jōdō Shinshū, "True Pure Land" Buddhism, but in writing his two major works, *By the Old Walls of Kyoto* and his unpublished 5,000 line verse epic, the *Autumn Landscape Roll: A Divine Panorama.* Until very recent times, only a handful of people knew of Stewart's life in Japan but, with the publication of two detailed biographies, we have been able to catch a glimpse into hitherto unknown world of his later years.[3] Still, a full consideration of this remarkable man's unique poetry and inner trajectory has yet to emerge, partly because he was by nature so elusive, partly because he remains defined by the events of his early life, rather than the attainments of his later years. While many attempts have been made at characterizing Stewart, few, if any, have placed his life journey within a spiritual framework, or bothered to ask whether Stewart's life and works did indeed constitute a valiant attempt at realizing his vocation in the face of the many obstacles that confronted him. In this essay, we reconsider Harold Stewart in the light of these concerns. To forestall any objections of an idealized portrait, we assert from the outset that it is precisely Stewart's all-too-human

[1] *The Literary Essays of Thomas Merton*, ed. Patrick Hart (New York: New Directions, 1981).

[2] Stewart, in a letter to Milton Moon 4 Nov., 1984, in Milton Moon, *The Zen Master, The Potter & The Poet* (Stepney: Axiom Publishing, 2006), p. 195. Harold's friend and one of Australia's most distinguished potters, Moon spent time in Kyoto studying under the renowned Zen master, the late Kobori Nanrei, Osho. The final section of this book is dedicated to the author's correspondence with Harold Stewart.

[3] Michael Ackland, *Damaged Men: The Precarious Lives of James McAuley and Harold Stewart* (London: Allen & Unwin, 2001) and Peter Kelly, *Buddha in a Bookshop* (Fitzroy: Ulysses Press, 2007).

flaws—a somewhat inflated ego, messy relationships, hypochondriac tendencies—which make his life achievements of greater interest.[4] In this sense, Stewart's journey to fulfillment resonates that much more powerfully; and in this "decadent age" (*Jap. mappō-ji*)[5] which is marked by diminished spiritual capacities as well as innumerable internal and external obstacles to be overcome, any victories of the spirit must surely be cause for celebration and reflection.

Early Musings

Born in 1916 in the western suburbs of Sydney, as a child Harold Fredrick Stewart displayed considerable musical talent, winning a three-year scholarship to the Sydney Conservatorium High School.[6] But it would be his poetry or, rather, his co-creation "Ern Malley" which would capture the popular spotlight. Stewart demonstrated his poetic bent early on winning poetry prizes throughout high school and, after a brief foray at Sydney university which he described as "mind numbing," Stewart dropped out and instead focused his energies on writing poetry and feeding his newfound fascination for Eastern art, literature and religion. In 1944, Stewart and cohort James McAuley (a gifted poet in his own right), reacting strongly against the excesses of modernist poetry, constructed 17 (16 published) deliberately flawed poems from a random ensemble of texts and passed them off under the auspices of a deceased, unknown poet named Ern Malley. The main target of their efforts was the young upstart, Max Harris, who was the co-editor of the radical cultural journal *Angry Penguins*. What was to follow would be the biggest literary hoax in Australian history, one both would come to regret.

We will not recount all the details of this saga.[7] Needless to say, much to the bemusement of Stewart, Ern Malley was to take on a life of his own, influencing some of Australia's most well-known artists such as Sidney Nolan and Australian Archibald Award winner, Garry Shead, to name just two.[8] In recent years, Ern Malley has been the subject of numerous studies, "artworks" and several doctorates; meanwhile, Stewart's life and works remain largely ignored. In spite of Stewart and McAuley's attempts to expose what they believed to be the pretentiousness and shallowness of the modernist enterprise, the works of the fictional Ern Malley were, and still are, considered to be of high literary value. Shortly before his death, Stewart would joke that "one day it will be irrefutably proved that James McAuley and Harold Stewart were really figments of the imagination of the real-life Ern Malley and in fact never existed!"[9] How sage these words have proven to be.

There are several causes for the disregard of Stewart and his works. On the one hand,

[4] In a Letter to friend Kurt Forrer (1967), Stewart affirms that: "Previously . . . I felt I possessed the necessary spiritual qualifications to achieve Buddhahood in this lifetime. Of course, this was all pretentious ego-inflated nonsense: I am no Maharshi, and I know it: even India can only produce one like him every few centuries" (cited in *Damaged Men*, p. 237). Stewart's interest in the great subcontinent commenced at an early age under the influence of his father, who lived in India for 30 years before relocating to Australia. He also read the writings of the great Indian sage Ramana Maharshi when only a young man, which for the times was quite rare (*Damaged Men*, p. 9).

[5] The Pure Land tradition makes the distinction between *mappō-ji* which corresponds to "the Decadent Age of the Dharma" and *hometsu-ji* "the Age of extinct Dharma."

[6] *Damaged Men*, pp. 10-11.

7 For a detailed account of the events leading up to and surrounding the Ern Malley hoax see Michael Heyward, *The Ern Malley Affair* (St Lucia: University of Queensland Press, 1993).

[8] After 60 years, the Ern Malley affair continues to generate great interest—at the time of writing, the Heide Museum of Modern Art was running an exhibition dedicated to Ern Malley entitled "The Hoax and Beyond."

[9] Stewart in a letter to Milton Moon (20 February 1995) quoted in *Damaged Men*, p. 4.

Stewart focused his attention wholeheartedly on Eastern traditions and all of his later works were published with an international, not Australian, audience in mind. Secondly, there remains a prejudice towards Stewart, since he had scant regard for the *status quo*: he mocked the modernist movement, rejected the literary and intellectual establishment, and scorned the physical and intellectual landscape of Australia. He adopted the wartime enemy as his homeland, took on an unknown foreign religion and, to top it all off, Stewart was gay.[10] To the conservative outlook of the time, he became the "other"—the unknowable, the traitor, the unforgivable villain.

The Bookshop: The Discovery of the Traditionalists

The decisive shift in Stewart's intellectual trajectory came in the early 1950s. After relocating to Melbourne, which Stewart found more agreeable in terms of both physical and intellectual climate, he entered a new phase in his life. Initially, Stewart survived by writing literary articles for journals and magazines, until a more stable income was assured from writing lecture notes for the Council of Adult Education. Fortuitously, Stewart was offered a part-time sales position at the bookshop of his friend, Norman Robb—an offer too good to refuse. This role suited Stewart well, enabling him to apply his considerable expertise in directing customers to suitable reading material, whilst providing a stable income and time to further his writing. In the 1950s, Australia was only just beginning to engage with Asian art, philosophy and culture and, with Stewart's help, the book collection quickly swelled to include a diverse range including such "exotic" items as Chinese and Japanese prints, Moghul or Rajput post cards, as well as hitherto unheard of writers, some of whom came to be known as the "Traditionalists."[11] Having encountered the writings of the art scholar, linguist and metaphysician-extraordinaire, Ananda Coomaraswamy, and the French metaphysician, René Guénon, in the early 1940s, Stewart was one of the first Australians to seriously engage with these "Traditionalist" authors and they were to lay a theoretical foundation which would help shape his later life and works. Coomaraswamy, with his encyclopedic knowledge of the traditional theories and practice of art, and his phenomenal scholarly and linguistic erudition, proved a source of instant delight for Stewart, whose knowledge of Asia art and philosophy was already formidable. Complementing Coomaraswamy were the uncompromising writings of Guénon, offering an extensive re-affirmation of the metaphysical underpinnings of the world's great religious traditions and, furthermore, providing a devastating critique of the erroneous philosophical and "intellectual" foundations of the modern era.

Catering to the increasing interest in Asian philosophy, art and culture, Stewart often directed patrons to the works of Coomaraswamy and Guénon which he had recently imported[12] and, before long, the awareness grew to the extent that Stewart decided to convene regular meetings to discuss the works of these authors. By 1952, meetings were held every Friday and often centered on translations of the French journal *Études traditionnelles*[13] but also included

[10] Stewart would later share a tumultuous long-term relationship with the Japanese artist, Ueshima Masaaki.

[11] *Buddha in a Bookshop*, p. 45.

[12] Ibid, p. 43.

[13] *Études traditionnelles* (1936-1992) was a French journal founded by René Guénon that succeeded *Le Voile d'Isis* (journal founded in 1889) and a publication dedicated to expounding the metaphysical doctrine of the East and West.

topics of individual interest. These meetings continued for the next eleven years until Stewart spent an extended period in Japan. Besides consolidating Stewart's intellectual outlook, these meetings proved to be salutary in several regards. Firstly, Stewart found a forum to sharpen his immense autodidactic knowledge and share ideas with a diverse range of well-educated intellectuals, poets and self-taught seekers. Secondly, for those venturing outside Christianity, the spiritual landscape was particularly disheartening. With Tibetan Buddhism and other religious traditions yet to appear, and universities far from instituting any serious engagement with religious studies, Stewart could at least quench some of his intellectual and spiritual thirst through these gatherings. It was not until 1957 and the emergence of several key texts by the Swiss-German metaphysician, Frithjof Schuon, that the focus of group discussions turned from theory to actively seeking participation in a religious tradition. This secondary phase in the book club group coincided with a fresh influx of members, including Rodney Timmins and Adrian Snodgrass[14] both of whom would later join Stewart on their journey East.

Stewart's theoretical preparation now consisted of a thorough grounding (over almost two decades) in the traditionalist authors Coomaraswamy, Guénon and, most recently, Schuon. At the same time, his poetic endeavors continued and his knowledge of East Asian art, literature, culture and religion was staggering, not to mention his broader reading, the extent of which was reflected in his room which consisted of a "huge library of books which lined the walls on all sides."[15] By 1957, Stewart's introduction to Jōdō Shinshū was drawing nearer. Schuon's writing sparked fresh efforts in establishing a basis of religious theory *and* praxis. Schuon wrote several essays which emphasized the spiritual practice of Pure Land Buddhism as particularly suited to Western needs. Stewart, along with Snodgrass and Timmins, doubled their efforts in establishing an authentic connection with this tradition. Stewart contacted the Buddhist writer, Marco Pallis, seeking advice in finding an introduction in Japan. Up until this point, Stewart had seriously entertained Zen as an intellectual and spiritual avenue, so much so that he succeeded in winning a scholarship to Japan where he intended to study under Professor D.T. Suzuki at Ōtani University in Kyoto. His intention was to combine these studies with

> a work in progress which is to embrace the great periods of Chinese art, literature, philosophy and religion, especially the three great formative influences of Confucianism, Taoism and Zen Buddhism: thus summing up all that was best in the Chinese way of life. Chinese painting provides the setting, and the poem is being written in rhymed couplets in the form of a series of philosophical dialogues between famous poets, painters, sages and religious leaders.[16]

[14] Adrian Snodgrass, a trained architect, would later become an authority on Buddhist art and symbolism, producing landmark works in the field, including: *The Symbolism of the Stupa*, *Architecture, Time and Eternity*, the massive two volume *Matrix and Diamond World Mandalas in Shingon Buddhism* and, most recently, *Interpretation in Architecture: Design as a Way of Thinking*. Snodgrass also personally financed Stewart's travel to Japan on two occasions.

[15] *Buddha in a Bookshop*, p. 41. Stewart's personal library at the time of his death consisted of some 2,500 books, mostly high-quality hardcover publications. Despite the efforts of several people to garner interest from libraries and other institutions, none were forthcoming and the majority of the collection has been purchased and is now in the hands of book dealers.

[16] "Stewart's papers" cited in *Damaged Men*, p. 165. This theme would later emerge as the basis of his great verse epic *Autumn Landscape Roll —A Divine Panorama*.

Stewart turned down the offer, mainly because of the responsibilities attached to the scholarship, which he felt would detract from his writing and burden him with too many non-essential commitments. The culmination of these events and the subsequent effective closure of China meant Stewart's spiritual trajectory was now moving in the direction of Japan, not China.

Stewart continued writing and, after a detailed study of Japanese Haiku, he completed the manuscript for *A Net of Fireflies: Japanese Haiku and Haiku Paintings* (1960).[17] He visited Japan briefly in 1961, still very much interested in Zen and other forms of Buddhism but, on his return voyage, the Divine Name associated with the Pure Land tradition "quite spontaneously . . . began repeating itself in my mind."[18] This calling led to his return trip in 1963 where he enjoined Snodgrass and Timmins to seek official admittance into the Jōdō Shinshū tradition. The trip produced mixed results; Snodgrass, Timmins and Stewart all attended a one-month preparation at the Higashi-Hongan-ji Temple in Tokyo before ordination was to take place. This meeting had been arranged through the efforts of the Buddhist writer, Marco Pallis, and Professor of Japanese at Cambridge University, Dr Carmen Blacker.[19] Professor Blacker offered recommendations for the trio to Bandō Shōjun, the chief priest of the Bando Hoonji Temple, who would later become Professor of Buddhism at Ōtani University in Kyoto. Bandō Shōjun was uniquely qualified to assist these men in their spiritual transition. Not only did he speak English but he was well versed in the writings of the Traditionalists, he corresponded with the likes of the highly-influential Catholic writer Thomas Merton and personally visited Frithjof Schuon in 1966 and 1970.[20] Of the three, it was only Rodney Timmins who would emerge ordained, the first Australian to do so. The reasons behind Stewart's last-minute withdrawal from ordination remain a mystery and he continued as a lay practitioner for the rest of his life. Stewart spent the remaining months with his Japanese partner and supported himself by teaching English, but the whole enterprise had left him at a crossroads:

> The total result of which was a state of mental confusion and doubt as to which was the right way for me. Honen's nama-japa or Shinran's Pure Faith. I left Japan again in uncertainty and frustration and returned to Australia for two years. During this time the Name still continued to work spontaneously, often very much against my will, gradually producing a clarification of mind, until I felt compelled to make yet a third trip to Japan. This time came absolutely certainty: that Shinran's position was the ultimate one for this day and age, and the end-point of development of Buddhism along this line.[21]

17 Somewhat suggestively, Stewart begins his collection of Haiku translations with the poem titled "The Recluse."

18 Cited by Ackland, *Damaged Men*, p. 198.

19 Subsequently, Stewart maintained a long correspondence and friendship with Professor Blacker. Blacker's own works on Japan, which include the famous *The Catalpa Bow: A Study in Shamanistic Practices in Japan* (1975), are regarded among the finest ever written in the field.

20 In his East-West dialogue, Bandō Shōjun follows a long line of Jōdō Shinshū exponents who wrote English works that sought to reach out to a wider Westerner audience. Rev. Zuiken Saizo Inagaki (1885-1981) produced some twenty English publications and his son, Dr. Zuio Hisao Inagaki (1929-) has followed suit. In 1949, the remarkable Kenryo Kanamatsu (1915-1986) published the Shin classic *Naturalness* and even translated the entire works of Plato into Japanese. This long engagement of Shin practitioners with the West has hitherto been completely ignored. In more recent times, the Jōdō Shinshū Hongwanji-ha translation series has published a large volume of high-quality texts.

21 Shinran (1173-1263) gave the Jōdō tradition a completely new emphasis; instead of a spiritual practice cen-

The Decisive Break: *Ex Oriente Lux*

Until this point we have focused on Stewart's general biography. Now we arrive at a decisive phase, since his story is a tale of two halves: Stewart's Australian years constitute his theoretical grounding, with many years spent studying Asian art, literature and culture, to which he added several decades of intense deliberation on the works of the traditionalist authors. Meanwhile his poetry continued to expand and the seeds for a grand narrative were already deeply embedded in his fertile poetic mind. Having already commenced his own Haiku translations,[22] set somewhat peculiarly to the recondite English iambic meter made popular since the time of Chaucer, he was now ready to embark on more epic adventures, personally, poetically and spiritually.

Stewart moved to Kyoto in 1966, residing in a small one-bedroom apartment situated in an old inn, the *Shirakuso*, on the outskirts of the city. While very modest, his room nevertheless was adorned by a collection of stunning statues of Amida Buddha and he even came into possession of three extremely rare mandalas representing the Three Pure Land Sutras,[23] complete with pure gold background and coloring rendered with powdered semi-precious gems, no doubt a source of great inspiration as they hung above his writing desk. During his early years in Japan, Stewart lived frugally until he later enjoyed the patronage of the Swiss doctor, Heinz Karrer, as well as income from literary scholarships and grants. Stewart also kept up a huge correspondence with friends and acquaintances from all over the world, his masterfully-constructed letters acting as a therapeutic outlet for his thoughts and self-deprecating humor, much to the delight of many who received his letters. Although usually living a reclusive lifestyle, Stewart would nevertheless receive guests from around the world and the ensuing visits would be characterized by intense tours of the many temples, shrines, markets and notable landmarks where Stewart would impress his guests with his immense knowledge of local history, geography, art, music, antiques and festivals. In many ways, these activities—letter writing, exploring the many sites of Kyoto, as well as his own inner practice, were all integrated into his writing.

Almost immediately after arriving in Kyoto, Stewart set to work on his first major poetic

tered on simply achieving "birth in the Pure Land" (i.e. the attainment of Nirvana) after death, he taught that the true meaning of the nembutsu teachings were meant to sanctify *this* life *here* and *now*. Shinran explains: "The person who lives true shinjin, however, abides in the stage of the truly settled, for he has already been grasped, never to be abandoned. There is no need to wait in anticipation for the moment of death, no need to rely on Amida's coming. At the time shinjin becomes settled, birth too becomes settled; there is no need for the deathbed rites that prepare one for Amida's coming" (Letter 1). *Shinjin* (信心) literally means "true, real and sincere heart and mind" (*makoto no kokoro*). See *Letters of Shinran—A Translation of Mattōshō*, ed. Yoshifumi Ueda (Kyoto: Hongwanji International Centre, 1978). For Shinran, the nembutsu is the manifestation of *shinjin*. For a detailed consideration of the Buddhist developments in *buddhasmriti/ nembutsu*, see *The Mirror of Memory: Reflection on Mindfulness and Remembrance in Indian and Tibetan Buddhism*, ed. Gyatso (Albany: SUNY, 1992).

22 Steward published his first translation *A Net of Fireflies: Japanese Haiku and Haiku Paintings* in 1960 followed in 1969 by *A Chime of Windbells: A Year of Japanese Haiku in English Verse*. Both were published in Tokyo and beautifully presented. For a critical appraisal of Stewart's haiku see Greg McLaren, "Some Presence Inevitably Shows Through: Harold Stewart's Haiku Versions" [online]. *Australian Literary Studies*, Vol. 22, No. 4, Oct 2006:460-470.

23 The value of these scrolls was such that Stewart's friend and eminent scholar, Dr. Hisao Inagaki (with whom he also collaborated on several English translations), made a detailed study of them, later setting up the "Pure Land Mandala Study Group." Although seldom acknowledged, Marco Pallis' interest in Pure Land traditions was greater than supposed, so much so that he even requested and received *kikyoskiki* (the Shin "confirmation" rite) soon before his death, and he had also previously been a member of Dr. Inagaki's Shin study group in London. An extensive collection of the correspondence between Stewart and Pallis is preserved at the Australian National Library.

enterprise, one which would occupy him for more than a decade. While any detailed examination of his literary output remains well outside the scope of our current concerns, it is worth briefly considering his first great work *By The Old Wall of Kyoto: A Year's Cycle of Landscape Poems With Prose Commentaries* especially as it contains allusions to his own spiritual journey from an otherwise very reserved man. *Old Walls* is, according to the blurb:

> Twelve seasonal poems . . . which capture the atmosphere of the ancient capital, combine to form a short epic in homage to Kyoto's rich heritage of art, nature and religion. From the renowned Stone garden of Ryōan-ji to the Silver Pavilion under snow, the author leads us through the sights and seasons of Kyoto, at the same time as he traces his own spiritual pilgrimage. . . . The poems are complemented by detailed prose commentaries, which illuminate difficult references and provide fascinating historical and cultural background. Deeply learned, these commentaries, which can be read as independent essays, contribute immeasurably to the impact of the poetry. The book is illustrated with twenty-four charming wood-block prints . . . reproduced from *Yōfugachō*, an album of four celebrated artists of the late nineteenth century. . . . This ambitious project is not only a personal tribute to Japan . . . but by its spiritual integrity has also succeeded in bringing the Western reader closer to an understanding of Buddhism.[24]

This statement must be qualified since, throughout Stewart's poetic spiritual journey, we are still left to ponder how much of it is *his* journey and how much is imagined. While we have no reason to doubt that Stewart received glimpses bestowed by the grace of Amida, the deft attention of the poet is always at hand, especially when we remember the many years he had to attend to the minutest of details. Let us briefly consider one such example, mindful that Stewart insisted that his poetry should be read aloud by a reader working sympathetically with the meter. In the eleventh chapter titled "Waiting For Sunrise At The Silver Pavilion Under Snow" the poet wakes up to find that:

> Silence Awoke me, shiveringly aware
> Of even deeper cold, the whiter glare
> That dawn reflected upward from outside.
> Throwing my quilted cover off, I rose,
> And having slid my paper window wide,
> Looked out in wonder: Kyoto city lay
> Transformed by gentle snowfall overnight
> Into a wood-block print in black and white.
> The wintry sea of roofs below that froze
> In still upheaval, bound within it bay
> Of serried mountains, was no longer grey
> But softened into waves of snow, which piles
> In lapping rows of ripples over tiles.
> The white miraculous hush that heavy snows,

[24] Harold Stewart, *By The Old Walls of Kyoto: A Year's Cycle of Landscape Poems with Prose Commentaries* (New York & Tokyo: Weatherhill, 1981).

Muffling the earth with flake on flake, impose
Was only deepened by the bulbuls shrieking
To pierce the cold with mordent cries that trailed
Shrilly behind their flight, as they went streaking
Westward across the twilit sky to where,
Mellow as ivory, the full moon paled,
Declining through the early lilac air,
While dawn along the farthest range's brink
Already tinged the arctic haze with pink

. . . With flakes of grey, which turned intensely white
Before the wooded range's darker height,
But vanished near the snow-enlightened ground.
I saw this impure land, which men have marred
With their industrial crimes of waste and mess
That creep and claw till nature's face is scarred
And ravaged by aggressive ugliness,
Redeemed by heaven, whose fresh descent of grace
Has purified each foul polluted place.
A black cat slunk across a vacant yard
Where rubbish had been dumped and weed let grow,
Transmuted by the alchemic art of snow.

Later, the poet recalls the overwhelming sense of the beauty permeating from the Pure Land before this fleeting glimpse withdraws:

Whence does it come from, this sacred world of white
That has transfigured nature overnight?
Has Amida's Pure Land appeared on earth,
Now sanctified by snow with silent rite,
So that its dark defilement gains rebirth?
No, in that moment when the self, whose vile
Enmity, greed, and foolishness defile
The innate mirror with their mud, has died,
This poisoned world is wholly purified:
Winter's facsimile in snow and ice
Reflects on earth the Western Paradise.
The mind receives this gift of lucid grace
Whose instant crystallizes time in space.
But whither does it go, this rare delight
Of Vision, vanishing by noon from sight,
When our deluded life of everyday
Will falsify the world again to grey?

The accompanying essay begins

> On his fiftieth birthday, the author awoke at dawn to be presented with the most wonderful surprise of his life: the sight of snow for the first time.

Later he writes

> The frozen stillness of the garden reveals to the poetic eye a Vision of the translucency of the physical world, through which the Metaphysical world can be seen to be shining. The poet hopes that, through the crystalline imagery of this scene, he will enable the reader also to envision this season of the spirit. [25]

To a Westerner unfamiliar with the nuances of Japanese culture, little could draw one's attention away from the poet's evocative imagery. Yet, Stewart does leave a clue that may cause one to reconsider his statement. Stewart would have no doubt been well aware of the famous last words of Nobunaga Oda, "Life is merely fifty years looking at things under heaven, everything is nothing but dream and illusion." In the context of the poem, the symbolism adds yet another layer to his poetic creation: it is when Stewart turns fifty that he receives "this gift of lucid grace Whose instant crystallizes time in space," from which "everything under heaven" "Reflects on earth the Western paradise." The death at the end of the fifty years is the death and overcoming of ignorance which then removes the "dream and illusion" revealing "this rare delight." There is nothing arbitrary in Stewart's works, and the fact that he chose to associate his realization with an age which has great cultural significance is, I believe, less of an attempt at self-aggrandizement or deception and more a case of symbolic integration. Stewart's Kyoto is simultaneously the past and the present, an accurate description *and* a reimagining of the old capital in all its glory:

> I have felt obliged to describe in minute detail those things uniquely Japanese which are of everyday familiarity to residents but whose strangeness to those who are not may need to be clarified if they are to be brought vividly before the eye and ear of imagination. For the uninitiated, this should open poetic windows on to a remote and fascinating world. . .[26]

Leaving aside Stewart's apparent spiritual move from "self power" to "Other power," Stewart's work raises a most important issue for the neophyte: how do I identify myself with this world? The title "The Old Walls of Kyoto" is a brilliant metaphor, since Stewart is encouraging us to recognize that the "Old Walls" are at once a symbol of everything of beauty, truth and harmony which the Old capital re-presents, and also a symbol of the decay and erosion, not only of the old capital, but of the present day which is in the decadent age of *mappō-ji*.[27] While Stewart initially despairs and laments such a loss, as his wisdom matures throughout his poetic journey (and indeed his life), he sees that the past and the present, the old and new, the beautiful and

[25] *By The Old Walls of Kyoto*, pp. 397-398.

[26] *By The Old Walls of Kyoto*, p. 15.

[27] The Pure Land schools emphasize the fact that we reside in the *mappō-ji*, "the Decadent Age of the Dharma." This is not intended to lead to pessimism but simply reaffirms the appropriateness of Amida Buddha's Name and Vow for these times, which can be seen as one of the last great "cyclic compensations," hence illustrating the compassionate activity of Amida Buddha working for the benefit of all beings.

the ugly, are dichotomies which exist in our mind but not in reality, since Samsara *is* Nirvana!

After completing *Old Walls*, Stewart moved on to his most ambitious project, the as yet unpublished *Autumn Landscape Roll: A Divine Panorama* which would occupy him for the rest of his life.[28] Briefly, this work is an imaginary metaphysical journey through the many Buddhism realms, including not only the many hells but also vividly describing the majestic Pure Lands. This massive poem is divided into 32 cantos and framed around Wu Tao-tzü, the most celebrated Chinese artist of the T'ang dynasty who incredibly steps into his landscape roll to journey in search of wisdom. This work expands to include non-Buddhist elements, fulfilling and building upon Stewart's earlier goal of completing a work encompassing the great Confucian, Taoist and Zen traditions. At the time, Stewart had not yet discovered the Jōdō Shinshū path which was to shape and giving meaning to his later life but, here in this work, it now becomes the inspiration for the poetic world he inhabits.

Reimagining Harold Stewart

In the English manner of speaking, which is also to say, thinking, "to wander" is understood in two senses, firstly; "to wander" is to go from place to place aimlessly, to drift, rove and, essentially, it conjures a sense of freedom or openness to discover or, literally, to be open to all possibilities. Secondly, and perhaps more commonly, is the sense of wandering as being lost, digressing, straying from a path, veering into "no man's land." Stewart opened himself up to many of these possibilities: through his walks, he stumbled on the many temples, parks, gardens, markets and natural splendors which would be the inspiration for his poetic output. Through his wanderings, he would find Jōdō Shinshū, a spiritual mentor and scholarly company. Through his wandering and associations, he would find himself in possession of three extremely rare and beautiful Pure Land scrolls through which he must have wandered as he admired them from his writing desk. Harold Stewart wandered through life, not as a bitter, disaffected exile but as a man following the way which would allow him to bring into being a poetic output, a venture which projected, or revealed, the unfolding of a vision that may have started under his "own power" but was fulfilled by *tariki*, the "Other power."

Coomaraswamy would have seen in Stewart's total commitment to his poetic vocation nothing that does not fully accord with either the Hindu or Platonic doctrine of work of which he was such an outstanding advocate. No doubt, Guénon would have approved of his deep engagement with Eastern traditions; his numerous penetrating essays on symbolism[29] and his full commitment to seek the "Light from the East." And finally, Schuon would have approved of a life culminating in prayer and poetry. Stewart's encounter with Schuon's writings in the 1950s had highlighted the importance of prayer in these days of *mappō-ji*; undoubtedly Stewart would have endorsed Schuon's remark that "He who lives in prayer has not lived in vain."[30]

The accounts of Stewart in his final years speak of his mellowed disposition, warmth, humour and wisdom.[31] We can only assume that true *shinjin* had begun to quell the fire of the

[28] An online version can be seen at: http://www.nembutsu.info/alr/

[29] An outstanding example of Stewart's deft prose writing is evident in his second commentary in *Old Walls*; "On the Metaphysics of the Stone Garden of Ryōan-ji" provides a detailed study of one of Japan's finest Zen Gardens. Stewart offers six levels of interpretation which include: a Physical, Existential, Ethical, Cosmological, Mythical, and Metaphysical Interpretation.

[30] Frithjof Schuon, *Prayer Fashions Man*, ed. James Cutsinger (Bloomington: World Wisdom, 2005) p. 182.

[31] Several citations are given in both Ackland, *Damaged Men* and Kelly, *Buddha in a Bookshop*. Peter Kelly and

ego and, with this, the ability to "truly hear" (*monpo*) the call of the infinite was actualized. In a self-reflective passage from one of his commentaries, Stewart writes

> Yet how can we purify ourselves spiritually by own individual or social efforts? This is manifestly impossible, as anyone knows who has tried, since it is the ego that, by its own self-will and effort, undertakes the task. And so all its endeavor, no matter how altruistic and well-intentioned, must inevitably end in failure.... Only the Awakening of Faith, that radical change of heart caused by ... Amida Buddha from his suprahuman store can now purify us spiritually and, so, mentally and morally. Individual unselfishness or social morality, economic and political panaceas, cannot accomplish this alone. Only the death of the ego in utter selflessness ... can transfigure us and our world with wonder, like the silent benediction of snow.[32]

Weeks before his death Dr. Hisao Inagaki told Stewart that he was now an "auspicious dragon" a telling indication of how far he had come from his troubled beginnings. Admittedly, here we have only been able to convey a sketch of Harold Stewart—poet, scholar and Jōdō Shinshū adept—who walked a unique path in times where spiritual attainment is hard won. After many years spent dedicated to his poetry, often under the shadow of long-term ill health (which at one point looked like preventing him from completing his poetic endeavors), Stewart put the finishing touches on his *magnum opus*, *Autumn Landscape Roll*,just weeks before his death in August 1995. In light of this, and the praises offered by his closest spiritual mentors, it is not too much of an exaggeration to state that, in his own way, he had succeeded. Shinran reminds us that:

> We who aspire for Amida's fulfilled land,
> Though we differ in outward condition and conduct,
> Should truly receive the Name of the Primal Vow
> And never forget it, whether waking or sleeping (*Koso Wasan*, Verse 96)

In light of the Jōdō Shinshū tradition there is nothing in Harold Stewart's life that does not properly conform to an authentic, if not heroic, attempt at spiritual salvation. His unique path was shaped by poetic drives which were later tempered by the corrective of the Jōdō Shinshū tradition and, most notably, the workings of the Name and Vow of Amida Buddha. It has been disingenuous of overly-zealous critics to suggest that Stewart passed away as a lonely and disaffected man, especially when one considers the substance of his inner life, the difficulties (including those of his own character) which he resolved, his tremendous autodidactic knowledge, and his fierce commitment to his poetry despite his precarious financial and personal situation. Stewart did not live the life of an austere monk; instead, like many lay Jōdō Shinshū practitioners, he did the best he could in times when many forces conspired to hold him back. While we may never truly know what lay at the deepest recesses of Harold Stewart's being, his life and works demand a timely reassessment of the man who thought himself, rightly or wrongly, "The Exiled Immortal."

Rev. John Paraskevopoulus (who met Stewart in 1994 in the year prior to his death) have echoed these sentiments.

32 *By The Old Walls of Kyoto*, p. 391.

A Visit to the Jagadguru

William Stoddart

Historically speaking, there can be little doubt that the greatest exponent ever of pure and unconditional metaphysics made his appearance in the world of Hinduism. This was Shankara, who lived in India in the 9th century A.D. He is often referred to as Shri Shankaracharya. In India, *Shrī*, the literal Sanscrit meaning of which is "Lord," is widely used as an honorific, and *achārya* means "teacher." The metaphysical doctrine of Shankara is known as *advaita* or "non-dualism"—a double negative, so to speak, which has its parallels in the Neoplatonic expression "the One without a second" and in the Islamic expression "He who has no associate" (*lā sharīka la-Hu*).

Shankara's function was to formulate the truth, to give expression to ultimate reality. There is an authentic line of spiritual descent from the original Shankaracharya down to the present day. It is refracted into five traditional functions or offices, all of them regular and valid. All five of the holders of these offices bear the title of *Shankarāchārya*, and these Shankaracharyas have their official seats respectively at Badrinath (in the north), Puri (in the east), Dwarkā (in the west), Kanchipuram (in the south), and Sringeri (also in the south). Each Shankaracharya also has the title of *Jagadguru* or "universal teacher" (*jagad* literally signifying "world").

There are many paths that lead to God. In India, as elsewhere, the one that is most widespread is that of "devotion" (*bhakti*). However, for their respective regions of India, these spiritual descendents of the original Shankaracharya traditionally and symbolically represent the uncolored light of knowledge or gnosis (*jñāna*).

During a visit to India in March-April of 1963, I accompanied two of his Indian devotees on a visit to the Shankaracharya of Kanchipuram. Kanchipuram (in Sanscrit, "Golden City") is in Madras State (*Tamilnad*), and in the Tamil language it is known as Conjeeveram.

Each Shankaracharya has, so to speak, a circuit: that is to say, he travels publicly and ceremonially, accompanied by his suite. In the case of the Jagadguru of Kanchipuram, the suite includes elephants, camels, cows, and musicians. For the collectivity in general, he exercises his function in a manner that the Buddhists might describe as an "activity of presence": he is a blessing, not merely for what he teaches, but above all for what he (or his office) *is*. In this respect at least, his role is analogous to, and has the importance of, that of a temporal monarch. (Miraculously, this role still has validity even in modern and democratic monarchies which have long since forgotten their traditional and sacred past.)

At the moment concerned, the Jagadguru was known to be at Tanjore, and we set forth from Madras on the afternoon of 3 April 1963. The journey was of approximately two hundred miles, and it took about seven or eight hours to complete it. On the way we passed through the towns of Pondicherry, Cuddalore, Chidambaram and Kumbakonam, and arrived at Tanjore fairly late at night. It was a beautiful drive, both during the daylight hours and after dark, when we traversed the Tamilnad countryside by full moon. (I had already visited the towns of Chidambaram and Tanjore on my way from the southern tip of India to Madras.)

In Pondicherry, we stopped for a moment at the "ashram" of the late Aurobindo, the modernist-evolutionist pseudo-mystic, where one of our party had some minor errand to perform. I did not get out of the car. A few signs of the erstwhile French presence in Pondicherry were still visible, such as the imposing Catholic church "Notre Dame des Anges," a statue of Saint Joan of Arc, and, less sublimely, the name of the main square: Place Charles de Gaulle!

In the delightful small town of Kumbakonam, we stopped for a while, and took photographs of the magnificent temple with its large square enclosure, impressive towers (*gopurams*), and "tank" (*teppakulam*). Here we seemed to be at the very heart of Hindu India. On reaching Tanjore, we took a room at the Rajah Guest House.

Next morning, having risen early, we went out to purchase some fruit which we could later offer to the Jagadguru. After seeking vainly for a long time, we finally obtained this from a Muslim fruit-seller named 'Abd al-Quddūs ("the slave of the All-Holy"), who had a shop near the railway station. Then we made our way to the place where the Jagadguru and his entourage were camped—a spot just south-west of the Brihadeshwara Temple.

The Jagadguru's full designation is: His Holiness the Jagadguru Shrī Chandrasekharendra Sarasvati, the 68th Shankarāchārya Svāmigal of Kāñchī Kāmakoti Pītha. He was born in 1894, and assumed his function in 1907. He died in 1994 at the age of 99 years. His successor, Shri Jayendra Sarasvati, had been appointed many years before his death, and it is now he who, as the 69th Shankarāchārya Svāmigal, fills the role of head of the Kāmakoti Math (Mathādhipati). A successor to the last-named, known as the junior *svamigal,* was also appointed during the lifetime of the 68th Shankarāchārya, and thus at the time of my visit in 1963, three "generations" of Shankarāchāryas were present in Kanchi.

On the occasion of his death, an appreciation of the 68th Shankarāchārya was published in *Time Magazine* (24 January, 1994). Mention was made of his friendship with Mahatma Gandhi, and of his deep knowledge of Christianity. Like another great Hindu spiritual figure of the 20th century, Swami Ramdas, he also had a profound respect for Islam, and the Indian Prime Minister mourned him as "one who symbolized peace and harmony in a turbulent world."

Preliminary arrangements for an audience had previously been made, and we now informed members of the Jagadguru's entourage of our arrival. Usually, at this stage, a period of waiting is involved, sometimes extending to several days. Devotees regard the waiting-period as a sort of "retreat" and give it over to spiritual preparation and prayer.

To our great surprise, however, as soon as the Jagadguru had been informed of our arrival, he let it be known that he would receive us at once. My companions hastened to prepare themselves in matters of dress. The proper dress is a *dhoti,* with bare chest and bare feet. The two devotees were dressed thus and, as *Vaishnava* brahmins, also applied the mark of Vishnu to their foreheads. (The Jagadguru, descendent of the original Shankaracharya, is a *Shaiva.*) I was wearing European dress, but I removed my shirt, shoes and socks, and thus appeared, suitably bare-chested, to merge acceptably with my two companions. Our preparations took less than five minutes.

On entering the compound, we found the Jagadguru sitting cross-legged on a mat, and with a staff in his hand, just as he most often appears in photographs. We prostrated ourselves before him in the prescribed manner. We offered him the fruit that we had brought with us, and he motioned us to sit down on a mat near him. The only others present in the compound were his *aide-de-camp* and a servant.

All remained silent for some moments. Then His Holiness put some questions regarding the European visitor: where he came from, what his profession was, etc. The Jagadguru spoke mainly in Kanarese, the language of Mysore, from which the Jagadguru—and did also, as it happened, the two devotees—originated. The two friends kindly interpreted for my benefit. The Jagadguru also spoke a little in Tamil, and occasionally used English expressions. He knows English well, but normally does not speak it.

The Jagadguru then referred to Frithjof Schuon, concerning whom he was well aware, since the latter had dedicated his book *Language of the Self* to him. This had been mediated by Mr. Macleod Matheson, one of the translators of the book, who visited the Jagadguru in February 1959, presented him with the English manuscript, and received the Jagadguru's acceptance of the dedication. The book was published in India later that year. His Holiness referred to the chapter in the book dealing with the sacred pipe of the North American Indians, and also to the book *Black Elk Speaks*, and said that the rites of the Red Man resembled those of Hinduism. He then spoke of the Algerian Sheikh Ahmad al-'Alawī and of Martin Lings's impressive monograph on him, *A Sufi Saint of the Twentieth Century*, which had been published in 1961.

Having mentioned the Jagadguru's interest in Schuon's book, and in the rites of the Plains Indians, it is appropriate to recall that Schuon, in his book *The Feathered Sun*, refers to a meeting that he had, during his first visit to North America in 1959, with a holy man of the Cheyenne tribe. Schuon showed the venerable elder a picture of the Jagadguru, and spoke to him of the spirituality of Hinduism. The Cheyenne priest took the picture in one hand, and raised the other towards the sky—the Red Indian gesture of prayer. He prayed a long time while gazing at the picture, and finally put his hand on it and then, in the Red Indian manner, rubbed his face and breast with his hand so as to impregnate himself with the Jagadguru's blessing. Finally, he reverently kissed the picture.

Our discussion with the Jagaguru then turned to the dissemination in Europe and North America, thanks to the Guénon-Schuon books, of the ideas of metaphysics, intellectuality, orthodoxy, and tradition. Reference was made to the three forms of Christianity: Eastern Orthodoxy, Roman Catholicism, and Protestantism, and to the possibilities within them, in twentieth-century conditions, for following a spiritual path based on faith and prayer. His Holiness expressed interest in both the collective and individual prayer of these denominations, and enquired in detail about the Christian sacraments. He classified the Hindu rites as *dikshas* and *samskaras*, and made it clear from what he said that the former correspond to the sacraments of Baptism and Confirmation (which have an initiatic character), while the latter correspond to the sacraments of Eucharist, Penance, and Extreme Unction (which mediate sanctifying grace), and of Matrimony and Ordination (which confer a grace of state).

Towards the end of the audience the Jagadguru blessed the basket of fruit which we had given him, and from it gave each of us a piece of fruit, to eat later. He also blessed a photograph of himself, and presented it to me. His Holiness then gave us his blessing, which indicated that the audience was at an end. We made our obeisances, and took our leave, never turning our backs on him as we departed the compound. The whole audience lasted the best part of an hour. We returned to our guesthouse, where we ate the fruit that we had been given.

For a little while, we drove around Tanjore, and I saw again some of the sights that I had seen six days previously while on my way, by train, bus and bullock-cart, from the southern tip of India to Madras. Soon we started on our return journey, and drove to Tiruvannamalai, where we spent the night in the ashram of the late Shrī Rāmana Mahārshi, the great *jñānin* who had died in 1950. We had our evening meal (South Indian vegetarian style) in the ashram, and briefly met Mrs. MacIver, a Parsi lady, who was the widow of an early English acquaintance of René Guénon. We also met a *sadhu* ("devotee") from the ashram, at Kahangad near Mangalore, of Swami Ramdas, the great votary of the Name of *Ram*.

In the ashram of the Shrī Rāmana Mahārshi, we continued to visit some of the places that had been hallowed by his presence, and then went out for a delightful evening stroll. The next morning, we climbed half-way up the sacred hill of Arunachala, where we visited the samadhi (place of meditation) of the Mahārshi. From the hillside we had a splendid overview of the large temple of Tiruvannamalai and, on descending again into the village, paid a visit to it. We gave the priest in the temple a small stipend, and he offered worship on our behalf. After that, we continued on our journey, passing through the small Tamil town of Madhurantakam where, in 1884, an Englishman named Lionel Place had a vision of Shrī Rama (the seventh incarnation of Vishnu). We arrived back in Madras later in the day.

BOOK REVIEWS

Frithjof Schuon: Messenger of the Perennial Philosophy by Michael Oren Fitzgerald
Bloomington, IN: World Wisdom, 2010

An issue of *Studies in Comparative Religion* dedicated to the theme "Crossing Religious Frontiers" could hardly find a more apposite subject than the life and work of Frithjof Schuon. Indeed, two of Schuon's essays feature in this very issue. His work first appeared in the Anglophone world with the publication in 1953 of *The Transcendent Unity of Religions*, a book which articulated the metaphysical basis of the inner or essential unity of the world's great religious traditions. This remarkable work was followed, over the next half-century, by more than thirty books in which Schuon provided a peerless exegesis of immutable metaphysical and cosmological principles, and an explication of their applications and ramifications in the boundless world of Tradition. These works, written in crystalline prose, stand as a beacon for those lost in the spiritual wastelands of modernity. Many years ago, in introducing one of Schuon's books, Seyyed Hossein Nasr wrote: "His authoritative tone, clarity of expression, and an 'alchemy' which transmutes human language to enable it to present the profoundest truths, make of it a unique expression of the *sophia perennis*".[1] Quite so. Now we have to hand a biography of this frontier-crosser *extraordinaire.*

For many readers of this journal, Schuon—metaphysician, poet, artist, spiritual master—requires no introduction. Amidst the clamor and confusion of modernity those few still willing to heed the lessons of Tradition have long since recognized Schuon as the most commanding exponent of that timeless wisdom which lies at the heart of all integral mythological, sapiential, and religious traditions. But both the life and work of Frithjof Schuon have remained more or less unknown to the public at large. There are many reasons for this. Schuon's writings are, in the main, addressed to that small minority of jnanic disposition, capable of discerning the inner convergence of apparently divergent and manifold religious forms. Schuon's primary task has been to expound the *philosophia perennis*—"the totality of the primordial and universal truths—and the metaphysical axioms—whose formulation does not belong to any particular system"[2]. Likewise, he has been the foremost exponent of the *religio perennis*—that is, "the essence of every form of worship, every form of prayer, and every system of morality".[3]

His *oeuvre* is necessarily somewhat difficult of access, not only because metaphysics demands intellectual rigor and contemplative intelligence, but because modernity is characterized by a pervasive ignorance of metaphysical principles. Then, too, there is the fact that Schuon deliberately shrouded his own life from public view, living a somewhat reclusive existence and abjuring public acclaim. Nonetheless, over the last three decades a number of studies have appeared, some dealing with the more recondite aspects of Schuon's metaphysical expositions, as well as many essays and articles addressing other facets of his work. Mention might be made of several landmarks: Nasr's percipient Introduction to *The Essential Frithjof Schuon* (1986), a substantial compilation of many of Schuon's essays, organized around various themes; James Cutsinger's *Advice to the Serious Seeker* (1996), subtitled *Meditations on the Teaching of Frithjof*

[1] Preface to *Islam and the Perennial Philosophy* (London: World of Islam Publishing Festival, 1976), p. viii.

[2] Frithjof Schuon, "The Perennial Philosophy", in *The Unanimous Tradition*, ed. Ranjit Fernando (Colombo: The Sri Lanka Institute of Traditional Studies, 1991), p. 21.

[3] Ibid., p. 21.

Schuon, a manual for wayfarers treading the spiritual path signposted by Schuon's writings; the memorial issue of *Sophia* which appeared soon after Schuon's passing in 1998; and the French anthology of articles, *Frithjof Schuon: Les Dossiers H* (2002). These were followed in 2004 by Jean-Baptiste Aymard and Patrick Laude's excellent study, *Frithjof Schuon: Life and Teachings*, which includes both metaphysical and biographical material. Now, more than a decade after Schuon's death, Michael Fitzgerald has furnished us with the first intimate, full-scale biography of the sage.

Fitzgerald is particularly well-equipped for the task at hand. He was a disciple, adviser, friend, and executor of Schuon's estate, and is thus able to draw not only on his own long personal association with the metaphysician but on a wealth of unpublished material—letters, diaries, notes, manuscripts, poems, drawings—which has hitherto only come within the purview of a very small circle. He has also enjoyed direct access to some of Schuon's closest friends, associates, and disciples whose recollections texture his account.

We cannot here recount Schuon's biography except in its most general contours: his childhood in Basle in an ambience redolent of the medieval, the Romantic, and the Oriental; the early apprenticeship in Paris in textile design; the immersion in the Scriptures and commentaries of the East, especially the *Advaita Vedanta* which provided the foundations for Schuon's metaphysical works; the travels to North Africa, where he entered Islam and was initiated into Sufism by Shaykh Ahmad al-'Alawi; his vocation as Sufi master; the association with René Guénon; military service and incarceration during World War 2; marriage to Catherine Feer and the long residence in Lausanne where Schuon produced many of his books; visionary experiences of the Virgin and the Marial graces which subsequently flowed through his life; the therapeutic sojourns with the American Plains Indians who had a special place in his heart from childhood years; the eventual move to America in the early 1980s and the growth of the *Maryamiyyah tariqah* over which he presided. All this, and much more, is seamlessly recounted in Fitzgerald's narrative, frequently embellished with Schuon's own words. In the process we come to sense something of those qualities which moved another luminary of our time, Swami Ramdas, to recall: "[Schuon's] face was bright with inner illumination. He possessed a regal bearing . . . but he was at heart so humble, simple, and loving. The love in his heart was manifest on his face . . . . [He was] a very prince among saints" (p. 79).

Throughout Schuon's life and work we can discern several themes which run like brightly colored threads through a variegated tapestry. To mention a few: the prodigious intellectual gifts and astonishing spiritual plasticity, evident from an early age in the youthful attraction to Plato, the *Vedanta*, and the *Gita*; the spontaneous and intuitive understanding of the symbols and messages of sacred art; the uncanny, more or less miraculous ability to penetrate religious forms of all kinds—texts, myths, doctrines, rituals, symbols—to uncover their deepest and most universal significance; the love of Virgin Nature and the singular role of the American Plains Indians in Schuon's personal life, writings, and paintings; the privileged position of the Virgin, of Celestial Femininity and of Beauty throughout the *oeuvre*; the implacable defense of Tradition and the unflinching arraignment of modernity in many of its ugliest and most sinister guises (particularly the aberrations of modern philosophy and the Promethean claims of a totalitarian scientism); the centrality of prayer, particularly Invocation, in the spiritual economy extolled in Schuon's works and exemplified by his life. Without intruding with superfluous commentary, and often allowing Schuon to speak in his own words, Fitzgerald deftly draws our attention to these leitmotifs. The book also includes Schuon's essay, "*Sophia Perennis*", the text of an interview first published in 1996, excerpts from previously unpublished writings about the spiritual life, a glossary of foreign terms, and a highly useful Bibliography and Index. The biography is quite free of pretentious academic jargon and the repellent "theorizing" which infects much so-called "scholarship" nowadays, but the material is scrupulously documented in detailed but unobtrusively placed endnotes.

Unlike many modern biographers Fitzgerald does not swamp us with tediously accumulating details—he does not belong to what has been called the "laundry list school" of biography wherein the reader is numbed into submission by ever-proliferating minutiae of the most mundane kind. Nor, to change the image, does Fitzgerald imagine that the mere aggregation of stones produces a building. What is on offer here is a carefully crafted and nuanced portrait which gives us the essentials of a life in both its outer and inner dimensions without ever descending into the impudent psychologizing which, so often, is the very calling card of the modern biographer. Fitzgerald skillfully renders the salient features of Schuon's life, his family background and upbringing, his personality and character, his daily habits and disciplines, his travels and friendships, his relations with an extraordinary range of spiritual masters and representatives of the world's religious traditions. Much of this is quite fascinating. For my own part I was particularly moved by the account of Schuon's childhood and youth, and by Fitzgerald's evocative treatment of Schuon's relations with the Plains Indians, especially his friendship with Chief Thomas Yellowtail and his little known but quite pivotal role in the preservation of the Lakota heritage. The biography recounts Schuon's indirect but potent relationship with the Lakota visionary Black Elk, mediated by Joseph Epes Brown whom Schuon had sent to seek out the aging holy man—and so it was that Brown was able to compile that treasury of ancestral wisdom and traditional Lakota rituals, *The Sacred Pipe.* In *The Feathered Sun,* a luminous collection of Schuon's writings and paintings on Indian themes, he observed that "a stoical and combative heroism with a priestly bearing conferred on the Indian of the Plains and Forest a sort of majesty at once aquiline and solar";[4] how apt these words are in relation to Schuon himself!

It is not surprising that Fitzgerald should handle the place of the Indians in Schuon's life and work with such sensitivity and surety, not only because of his own long association with Yellowtail and other Indian figures, but because he is himself one of the most authoritative and penetrating of contemporary writers on their spiritual legacy. (Fitzgerald's first major work was *Yellowtail: Crow Medicine Man and Sun Dance Chief,* published in 1991; a stream of books has followed in its wake, including *Indian Spirit* and *The Spirit of Indian Women,* both co-authored with Judith Fitzgerald.)

Frithjof Schuon: Messenger of the Perennial Philosophy is studded with many captivating anecdotes and flashing insights into its subject. Not the least interesting aspect of the book concerns Schuon's encounters with some of the most impressive spiritual figures of our time—Shaykh Ahmad al-'Alawi, Staretz Sophrony, Shojun Bando, Swami Ramdas, and the Jagadguru of Kanchipuram, to mention a representative sample. Then, too, there are accounts of Schuon's relations with his brother Erich, who as a Trappist monk became Father Gall, with his schooldays friend Titus Burckhardt who became an immensely erudite writer on metaphysics and cosmology, and with others who played various roles in the recovery of the Wisdom of the Ages in these latter days—René Guénon, Marco Pallis, Leo Schaya, Whitall Perry, Martin Lings and others. Schuon's wife Catherine provides engaging glimpses of his disposition, daily

[4] Frithjof Schuon, *The Feathered Sun: Plains Indians in Art and Philosophy* (Bloomington, IN: World Wisdom Books, 1990), pp. 39-40.

routines, work habits, and spiritual practice. However, anecdotal and illustrative material is never allowed to derail the book's governing purpose which is to throw into sharp relief Schuon's peculiar vocation as "messenger of the perennial philosophy", to accent the astounding gifts and the unwavering commitment he brought to this life-long task, to acclaim the majestic corpus of work (not only the metaphysical explications but also the paintings and poems), and to show how Schuon actualized in his own person the spirituality which he extolled in his work. In Schuon's own words, "The *Sophia perennis* is to know total Truth and, in consequence, to will the Good and to love Beauty".[5] Elsewhere: "Knowledge saves only on condition that it engages all that we are; only when it constitutes a path which works and transforms and wounds our nature as the plough wounds the soil".[6] For Schuon the *sophia perennis* could never be a matter of mere abstractions, abstruse speculations, and what Shankara called "subtle argument"—though to be sure Schuon, like the Indian sage, was a master dialectician; it was, rather, a matter of *living* and *lived* verities, of spiritual realities both understood and realized. To put it another way, in both the life and work of Schuon we find a fusion of the intellectual and spiritual, of doctrine and method, of principle and way. As he himself so pithily put it, "If we want truth to live in us we must live in it".[7]

The book is generously illustrated with photographs and with Schuon's own drawings and paintings; along with the biographer's commentary these provide vital insights into Schuon's spiritual personality, if one may so put it. Many of the photographs, not previously exposed to public view, allow us to savor something of the ambience of the various milieux in which Schuon lived. We find, for instance, arresting photos of Schuon as a child and youth, as a young man in Paris and North Africa, in the precinct of the pyramids of Egypt, in his military uniform in 1939, with Plains Indians in the American West, as well as some charming images which reveal the more gentle side of his temperament. The book is also a veritable treasure-house of rare photos of Schuon's family, friends, and associates—parents, siblings, and wife Catherine, Guénon, Burckhardt, Marco Pallis, Leo Schaya, Thomas and Suzie Yellowtail, Hans Küry, and Lucy von Dechend among them.

Also interspersed throughout the biographical narrative are excerpts from the immense and glittering collection of poems which flowed from Schuon's pen in his later years, offering an immediate, concrete, lyrical, and succinct expression of the metaphysical and spiritual insights which had inspired his formal expositions over half a century and more. This kaleidoscope of visual and poetic material, as well as the abundant quotations from Schuon's metaphysical and autobiographical writings, enrich the biography and make the book a thing of beauty. It is produced with the meticulous attention to detail and commitment to quality which characterizes the productions of World Wisdom. Readers will also be pleased to learn that Fitzgerald's biography will soon be complemented by a film which has been in preparation for some time, and which includes interviews with Schuon himself.

Much of the contemporary mania for biographies is really thinly-disguised voyeurism, fuelled by an insatiable appetite for gossip, for trivia, for the sensational, and the salacious. Here is a book of a different kind, one drawing out the exemplary significance of a heroic and saintly life—a life dedicated to the pursuit of Truth, to the preservation of the revealed and

[5] Frithjof Schuon, *Roots of the Human Condition* (Bloomington, IN: World Wisdom Books, 1990), p. 93.

[6] Frithjof Schuon, *Spiritual Perspectives and Human Facts* (Bloomington, IN: World Wisdom, 2007), p. 146.

[7] Frithjof Schuon, *Echoes of Perennial Wisdom* (Bloomington, IN: World Wisdom Books, 1992), p. 31.

traditional forms in which that Truth has been enshrined, and to the spiritual life which is the very realization and living-out of that Truth. And so it is that this biography necessarily calls us back to a sense of the sacred and the way of prayer which is a constant refrain in Schuon's life. Like Gandhi, Schuon might well have said, "My life is my message"—though in the latter case we have an imposing body of writings and paintings which will endure quite independently.

As Fitzgerald remarks in his Preface, the lives of the great sages lend themselves to diverse interpretations and inflections; no single account can ever be exhaustive or finally definitive. True, but one must say that Fitzgerald's biography, the fruit of many years of research and reflection, is unlikely to be surpassed. It is a precious document which will, assuredly, prove to be of abiding interest and significance to all those who seek that Light which is of neither East nor West, a Light dazzlingly refracted through the life and work of Frithjof Schuon.

Harry Oldmeadow

Parmenides and the Way of Truth
by Richard Geldard
Rhinebeck, NY: Monkfish Book Publishing Company, 2007

Richard Geldard's *Parmenides and the Way of Truth* reexamines the early Greek philosopher Parmenides of Elea, a vitally important figure for the western tradition. The founder of logic in the West, called "our father" by Plato himself, Parmenides lies at the very root of western culture. But his fragmentary poetry is notoriously difficult to understand—full of obscure language, riddles, even outright trickery and deception. Geldard's goal in this ambitious study is to "reassess Parmenides" so that we can learn "just how and why" contemporary philosophy "has argued itself into paralysis and gnostic dissatisfaction" (x). This recovery of Parmenides will serve, he hopes, as a way out of our postmodern philosophical impasse.

Parmenides' poem is monumentally important for western mystical, philosophical, and scientific tradition. Written in the epic meter of hexameter verse, the poem has three main parts. In the introduction, Parmenides uses incantatory, shamanic poetry to describe—and invoke—an initiatory journey to the underworld. Specifically, he presents himself as an initiate who has traveled to the world of the dead to learn from an unnamed goddess. The second part of the poem, from which Geldard's book takes its title, is commonly called the "Way of Truth." Here the goddess, through a very rigorous and formal logic, introduces Parmenides—and us—to the oneness behind and inside of everything that exists. She proves that reality is birth-less, deathless, motionless, eternal, and absolutely one. More than a few modern academics have tried to strip the Way of Truth of its clear mysticism. They follow Aristotle, who intellectualized the esoteric wisdom of ancient Greece to further his own hyper-rational philosophical agenda. But students of the world's sacred traditions will immediately recognize the goddess's words for what they are: an ancient demonstration of the timeless truth of oneness. In the third part of the poem, the goddess tells Parmenides—quite openly—that she is about to deceive him. She then goes on to give an intricate and detailed account of our apparent world of change, motion, and multiplicity. Her deception, or the "Way of Seeming," as it is called, is now all but lost. But the fragments of the Way of Seeming that survive, coupled with the ancient reports of its contents, are enough to show us that it was a stunningly sophisticated account of the natural world. Parmenides, in this final part of his poem, introduced—for the first time in the West—the idea of the Earth as a sphere. He explained that the globe had cold poles, temperate tropics, and a hot equatorial belt. He pointed out that the moon's light was not its own, but a reflection of the sun's. He delivered, in sum, a scientific understanding of the physical universe decades, perhaps centuries ahead of its time. Mystic that he was, he declared it an illusion, but an illusion to be cared for with great seriousness.

Geldard, to his credit, rejects the modern academic fiction of Parmenides as a mere theoretician. Instead, he sees—and explicitly embraces—the experiential core of Parmenides' poetry. The journey to the goddess described by Parmenides is, Geldard writes, the record of "an actual experience" (41). The message of oneness at the heart of Parmenides' poem comes through "grace" and is not "a work of the reason," but instead "a surprising gift" and "an experience without precedent" (81). In his attempt to convey the love and intimacy involved in such an initiatory experience, Geldard even invokes the relationship between the initiate and the divine feminine in the Eleusinian mysteries (41-42). As for the goddess herself, he writes that she is "not an icon or an idol, nor is she merely a symbol of intuitive understanding. She is a reality. . ." (81). This emphasis on lived experience is all too rare in modern treatments of early Greek philosophy. But it is the absolute prerequisite, the necessary starting point, for any real understanding of what philosophy was in the ancient world: a way of life and a sacred tradition. This aspect of Geldard's book distinguishes it from many other works, and for this he is to be commended.

But a starting point is only a starting point, and sadly, Geldard's reading of Parmenides wanders far from this auspicious beginning. Most troublingly, he seems determined to sever Parmenides and his poem from their sacred origins. Parmenides is re-imagined as part of a "siege" of "the ancient mythological world view" (vii). His poem is treated as an intellectual exercise, an "exploration into the nature of unity" (x). This perspective offers Geldard "intriguing" opportunities for "speculative" interpretations (x). He is aided in his work of interpretation by sources as diverse as the Pythagoreans, Plato, Plotinus, Schelling, Emerson and Voegelin. But there is no indication of how Geldard arrived at his translation of Parmenides. He gives no sign of any direct familiarity with the Greek language spoken and used by Parmenides himself; and it's difficult to avoid the impression that Geldard is more interested in building something out of Parmenides' words than in entering into them intuitively so he can grasp what they really say.

This is more than just a lost opportunity for scholarship, because Geldard's book has a truly urgent task. It is not aimed at academics, but at everyone who lives in the chaos of the modern western world—a world that has forgotten its spiritual purpose. Geldard rightly urges all of us to see the danger in having lost touch with the Divine, an "immense, perhaps even fatal" loss (115). It is imperative that we "remember once again the sacred reality of our lost heritage" (116). We must make that heritage real in our own experience, as he so correctly says: "Our destiny lies in the experience of life, in conscious action" (116). But unfortunately, Geldard's clear humanistic bias drives him to imagine a "sacred reality" unencumbered by "the burdens of religious layering" (81). Sacred names like "Jesus" and "Buddha" are reduced to "terms-as-symbols" that—according to his very questionable interpretation of Parmenides—"do not meet the criteria for Being" (123). The Divine is experienced physically, emotionally and intellectually; but spiritually only "in rarer circumstances" (123). This secularist version of the sacred will, I suspect, leave many readers cold. And to offer it in Parmenides' name is historically inaccurate at best—contradicted by the last half century's revolution in the study of Presocratic philosophy, which Geldard very strangely ignores. The work of classical scholars like Martin West, Walter Burkert, Laura Gemelli Marciano and Peter Kingsley has revealed a rich, living mysticism at the heart of early Greek philosophy.[1] Kingsley's work, in particular, makes it completely clear how wrong Geldard is in claiming that Parmenides was "more a naturalist than a mystic" (31, where he misquotes Plutarch and Giorgio di Santillana in support of this view). Parmenides was a mystic, indeed, and one who belonged to a very real and powerful religious lineage: the indigenous mystical tradition of the West. That tradition spanned centuries. It was of decisive importance for Hermetic, Gnostic and alchemical tradition, and eventually for Sufi tradition as well.

[1] See Walter Burkert, "Das Proömium des Parmenides und die Katabasis des Pythagoras," (*Phronesis* 14: pp. 1-30) and *Lore and Science in Ancient Pythagoreanism* (1972); M. Laura Gemelli Marciano, "Images and Experience: At the Roots of Parmenides' *Aletheia*," (*Ancient Philosophy* 28/1: pp. 21-48); Peter Kingsley, *Ancient Philosophy, Mystery, and Magic: Empedocles and Pythagorean Tradition* (1995), *In the Dark Places of Wisdom* (1999) and *Reality* (2003); and Martin West, *Early Greek Philosophy and the Orient* (1972).

Geldard's dismissal of this tradition creates a jarring incongruity between his presentation of Parmenides and Parmenides' presentation of himself—which Geldard even points out: "Parmenides himself makes no claim to have arrived at his knowledge by himself, or through his own efforts . . . it is revelation" (81). But of course Parmenides was well aware of his role as a messenger, and of his function as a bearer of divine revelation, because he understood his place in sacred tradition. Geldard vacillates awkwardly between acknowledging Parmenides' links to that tradition and ignoring them in the service of his own philosophical enterprise, which is aptly summed up as an attempt "to re-vision Being without the 'sacred transport' of Parmenides" (120). And while Geldard's plain distaste for "orthodoxy" (116) is completely understandable, to conflate dogmatic orthodoxy and sacred tradition—as he seems to do—is a mistake as counterproductive as it is unnecessary. Real mystical tradition is anything but dogmatic and rigid. It is always fluid—and always timeless—because it is alive. This was the reality of the tradition that Parmenides served—a tradition that he and others like him worked with to sow the seeds of our civilization.

Geldard has seen something real. We in the West must reconnect to our sacred roots—or face extinction. His book has a deep value just through sharing this message with us. But ironically, his own refusal to see those sacred origins as a real tradition is a symptom of the "immense, perhaps even fatal" loss he writes about; and his many interpretive errors stem from cutting Parmenides' poem off from its source. This strange predicament is one we all share, because it happens to be the predicament our whole western civilization is faced with—of desperately searching for, but failing to honor, its own sacred source and purpose. Unfortunately, it also is what prevents Geldard from accomplishing what he might have in his book.

Nicolas Leon Ruiz

The Way and the Mountain
by Marco Pallis
Bloomington, IN: World Wisdom, 2008

> The difference between . . . the traditional and anti-traditional outlooks, lies in the fact that the first-named derives the lesser reality of the changing and moving world from a principle or "sufficient cause" residing in the universal realm, which is by its nature the seat of the changeless and the uncompounded, while the second of the two mentalities attempts to place all reality in the realm of change. The difference of these two ways of looking at things is of fundamental importance, as affecting not only general ideas but even the minutest details of daily life: for whereas the traditional outlook fosters a habit of always looking to the cause rather than to the effect in all orders . . . the anti-traditional attitude encourages precisely the contrary tendency, namely the paying of more attention to applications than to principles, to effects than to causes, to symptoms rather than to disease—and still less to health—to the absence of open warfare than to the things that make peace. This mental habit, which is all the more dangerous in that it is largely unconscious, lies at the root of most of our troubles, and so long as it is prevalent among us we shall be condemned to remain the dreamers we are, instead of the men of awareness that we might be. (p. 39)

The name Marco Pallis will be familiar to readers who remember the early days of this journal, to which he was a regular contributor between 1968 and 1972. Pallis was born in England of Greek parents in 1895. He was a classically trained musician, an accomplished mountaineer, and among the Perennialist writers, a peerless spokesman for the Tibetan tradition. Pallis first came into contact with Tibetan Buddhism during a mountaineering exhibition in the Himalayas in 1933, and both the Tibetan people and their religion made such an impression on him that he resolved to return to the region to study under traditional authorities. In 1936 he visited both Sikkim and Ladak. It was during this visit that he became a practicing Buddhist, absorbing the Tibetan tradition in monasteries in both regions. The fact that Pallis was able to immerse himself in the tradition in an environment that was still virtually unaffected by modernity makes his elucidation of Tibetan Buddhism particularly valuable. But Pallis was not an academic. He was a formidable metaphysician and a spiritual wayfarer who always wrote for the benefit of fellow pilgrims, and herein lies the real value of his work.

Pallis described his encounters with the Tibetan tradition up to 1936 in his first book, *Peaks and Lamas* (1949). In this unique blend of travel literature, mountaineering lore, botanical observations, and doctrinal expositions, Pallis takes us on a spellbinding journey through a traditional civilization. In 1980, several later essays which appeared in this journal were collected together with some new material to form *A Buddhist Spectrum*, a book which Pallis himself said "is not a consecutive treatise on Buddhism yet deals with a number of Buddhist themes of prime importance in such a fashion as to make up a whole." *A Buddhist Spectrum* represents "a gentle but clear-eyed wisdom that was the fruit of long years of study, spiritual practice, and first-hand experience" (Harry Oldmeadow, Foreword, p. x).

The work with which we are presently concerned was the fruit of an extended visit to the East which Pallis undertook after World War II. It was during his studies under Tibetan lamas at Shigaste that he was initiated into one of the lineages, most probably the Gelugpas, and given the Tibetan name Thubten Tendzin. Pallis was reticent about his own spiritual practice, his concern always being with universal principles and their practical applications.

Pallis' extended sojourn matured his understanding of the Tibetan tradition, and *The Way and the Mountain*, first published in 1960, reflects a remarkable sympathy with both Tibetan Buddhism and the *sophia perennis* from whence it issues. The epigraph with which we began this review neatly illustrates the *leitmotif* of *The Way and the Mountain*—Tradition. However, this book is more than just an exposition of Tibetan Buddhism. The book might be roughly divided into two sections. The first four chapters address practical issues of the spiritual life from a Perennialist perspective. The second part is concerned with various aspects of the Tibetan tradition. Pallis approach is not systematic or exhaustive; he explains that "the nine essays forming the present collection . . . [were] . . . composed at intervals and in answer to particular requests." But nor is the composition arbitrary or *ad hoc*. The chapters containing practical advice provide guidance for anyone setting out on the spiritual journey in our confusing and abnormal times, for Pallis is adamantine in his opposition to the sentimental notions of modern, profane man. The chapters concerning the Tibetan tradition brightly illuminate the particular spiritual genius of the *Vajrayana* branch of the Buddhist heritage. Indeed, Pallis skillfully communicates the essence of the Tibetan tradition for the aspiring Buddhist wayfarer.

In the first chapter, "The Way and the Mountain," Pallis launches a wide-ranging discourse on the idea of the spiritual Way. He visits traditions as disparate as Taoism and Christianity, and seamlessly integrates their symbolism of spiritual wayfaring into a coherent argument. Take for instance the comparison of Odysseus steering clear of Scylla and Charybdis to the Buddhist doctrine of aiming for the "middle way." He also explores the spiritual symbolism inherent in mountaineering and in any excursion into Virgin Nature, these activities recalling the primordial state, that of all mankind before the "fall." So,

> it is to this symbolism of the "primordial state" that should logically be attached all those movements that take the form of a cultivation of the simple life or of a flight from the artificiality and distraction of the city, and which might well include, among necessary aids to realization, both wayfaring and mountaineering as we know them. (p. 19)

Pallis' elucidation of spiritual benefits of Nature is also significant for the contemporary environmental debate:

> in the love and companionship of wild Nature and of solitude one must recognize a distant echo of the original harmony in which Man, instead of acting like a tyrant and exploiter, was on the contrary the acknowledged protector and ruler of his fellow-creatures and their spokesman with the celestial Powers ... he himself played the part of the axis for them, and this in view of his own firm adherence to the axial position... "fallen" man, on the other hand, lacks this sureness of judgment... he is only too apt, in his enthusiasm, to turn it into an idol, that is to say to abstract it from the whole by losing sight of its relativity and treating it as a self-contained reality. (p. 19)

At one stroke Pallis situates the "environmental crisis" in its proper context, and disqualifies the profane view that its solution can be found in the more skilful management the earth's "resources."

Chapters 2, 3, and 4 are well described by their titles, "The Active Life," "On Crossing Religious Frontiers," and "On Soliciting and Imparting Spiritual Council," respectively. All are lucid expressions of timeless principles which have been expounded by various witnesses of the *sophia perennis*. Indeed, Pallis acknowledges the contribution of Frithjof Schuon and René Guénon to his own understanding.

The second part of the book sharpens its focus on Tibetan Buddhism and contains essays as various as an exploration of the nature of compassion in Tibetan Spirituality: a tour through contemporary Sikkim to examine the state of the *Dharma* there; an insightful piece about the real significance of the office of the Dalai Lama; a penetrating examination of the "presiding idea" of the Tibetan tradition; and an Afterword which is effectively an exhortation to Buddhists to practice diligently. This last mentioned chapter, entitled "The Tibetan Tradition—Its Presiding Idea," is an exposition of the *Vajrayana* doctrine of the *Bodhisattva*:

> The status of the Bodhisattva has been defined (though, strictly speaking, the very word "definition," implying as it does the idea of limitation, is here inapplicable) as that of one who realizes Wisdom as Knowledge of the Void, and Method as Universal Compassion; the first-named representing the purely transcendent aspect of his realization, while the second implies an unblurred recognition of the Face of Divinity even through the veil of separability as constituted by the worlds—in other words, a not merely theoretical but an effective awareness that the transcendent aspect of Truth is not other than the immanent and vice versa. (p. 199)

Pallis here also unpacks the real meaning of the formula "*Nirvana* is *Samsara*." In this context, an oft quoted vow of the Bodhisattva "to remain in *Samsara* until every being is enlightened down to the last blade of grass," can also lead to a dualistic error. This formula, though correct at its own level, is particularly vulnerable to misinterpretation if taken too literally:

> The Bodhisattva's vow must never be taken to imply that the saving of mankind, or even of all creation, should become *an end in itself* for the apprentice in spirituality. Nothing short of the naked Truth, shorn of all contingencies and restrictions, merits to be called desirable . . . having attained it, he does, in fact, become qualified to save the world, but should he at any stage yield to the supremely diabolical temptation (the one offered by Satan to Christ upon the high mountain) of making the world's salvation into his overriding aim, then he must pay the price of his altruistic idolatry and remain irremediably chained to the world and its otherness (pp. 218-19).

This chapter, the longest in the book, is a comprehensive treatment of its subject from the perspective of a man who had himself traversed a long way down the path. Pallis deftly avoids the many pitfalls into which an essay on such a difficult and at times paradoxical doctrine might fall. This essay, in my view, is the masterwork of the entire Pallis *oeuvre*. I return to it time and again to find yet more insights.

Perhaps Chapter 7, "Do Clothes Make the Man?" is something of an anomaly in this company. It is a perfectly competent essay about the significance of human attire and its attendant symbolism. However, it does not carry the same weight as the other essays about the spiritual life, nor is it specifically Buddhist in content. One possible explanation is that Pallis was fiercely opposed to the industrialization of traditional art and crafts. In his "Appreciation," Paul Goble recounts that Marco, who was ever generous, once supplied a friend the financial wherewithal to set-up a traditional weaving workshop in India. The essay may well be somehow connected to these events.

The new edition of this book published by World Wisdom adds three new Appendices as well as a new Foreword by Harry Oldmeadow, an Introduction by Joseph Fitzgerald, and Paul Goble's Appreciation which round out the picture of Marco Pallis the man. The Appendices include an essay on the interplay of "Own-power" and "Other-power" in different branches of Buddhism, a lecture which Pallis gave to a conference of Catholic headmistresses in 1968 called "On Discovering the Interior Life," and a tribute to the 68th Jagadguru of Kanchi Kamakoti Pitha on the occasion of his 76th birthday. These are valuable additions to the work.

World Wisdom is to be commended for maintaining its usual high standards of presentation in the current volume which also contains excellent reproductions of many photographs, some of which are published here for the first time.

Pallis said that "action on the relative plane has no other justification than its dependence on a superior principle, which it helps the being to realize, thus earning its only possible reward" (p. 42). His work is firmly anchored in the transcendent principles which alone justify any action on the relative plane. In this book, Pallis demonstrates how one can conform aspects of one's life to transcendent principles, for it is precisely this which constitutes the Active Life, which, moreover, is the "normal" life of most men in a traditional society. I can only agree with Harry Oldmeadow that "the essays to be found within these covers should be of interest not only to those on the Buddhist path but to all spiritual wayfarers" (p. x).

Paul Weeks

Acknowledgments

We are grateful to the following journals and publishers for permission to reproduce articles and excerpts. (Articles not listed below are here published for the first time.)

Abhishiktananda. "The Depth Dimension of Religious Dialogue." *Vidyajyoti*, May 1981.

Titus Burckhardt. "Ito's Cave." In *The Essential Titus Burckhardt*, ed. William Stoddart. Bloomington: World Wisdom, 2003.

Ananda Coomaraswamy. "Sri Ramakrishna and Religious Tolerance." In *Coomaraswamy Vol. 2: Metaphysics*, ed. R. Lipsey. Princeton: Princeton University Press, 1977.

Stephen Cross. "St Augustine, Coomaraswamy, and the Perennial Philosophy." *Avaloka*, 6, 1992.

René Guénon. "Not Fusion but Mutual Understanding." In *East and West* (originally published as *Orient et Occident*, 1924). Ghent, NY: Sophia Perennis, 1995.

Harry Oldmeadow. "The Writings of Swami Abhishiktananda." Modified excerpt from *A Christian Pilgrim in India: The Spiritual Journey of Swami Abhishiktananda.* Bloomington: World Wisdom, 2008.

Marco Pallis. "Crossing Religious Frontiers." In *The Way and the Mountain.* Bloomington: World Wisdom, 2008.

Roland Pietsch. "Religious Pluralism and the Transcendent Unity of Religions." *Al-Taqrib: A Quarterly Journal of Islamic Unity* 2:3, Winter 2008.

Frithjof Schuon. "*Religio Perennis*" and "The Universality and Timeliness of Monasticism." In *Light on the Ancient Worlds.* Bloomington: World Wisdom, 2006. New translations by Mark Perry.

William Stoddart. "Visit to the Jagadguru." In *Remembering in a World of Forgetting.* Bloomington: World Wisdom, 2008.

Sri Chandrasekharendra Saraswati Swamigal, The Jagadguru of Kanchi. "On Religion." In *Introduction to Hindu Dharma*, ed. Michael Oren Fitzgerald. Bloomington: World Wisdom, 2008.

Charles Upton. "The Transcendent Unity of Religions as Spiritual Practice." In *The System of Antichrist: Truth and Falsehood in Postmodernism and the New Age.* Hillsdale, NY: Sophia Perennis, 2001.

Thomas Yellowtail & Michael Fitzgerald. "Make Your Choice." In *Yellowtail: Crow Medicine Man and Sun Dance Chief.* Norman: University of Oklahoma Press, 1991.

Notes on Contributors

Abhishiktananda was the name assumed by the French Benedictine monk, Henri Le Saux (1910-1973), who spent the last 25 years of his life in India where he immersed himself in the doctrines and practices of Advaita Vedanta. His many books include *The Secret of Arunachala* and *The Further Shore.*

Rodney Blackhirst teaches Religious Studies at La Trobe University Bendigo and is the author of *Primordial Alchemy and Modern Religion.*

Titus Burckhardt (1908-1984) was one of the most authoritative exponents of the perennial school. A compendium of some of his most important writings, *The Essential Titus Burckhardt*, was published by World Wisdom in 2003.

Ananda Coomaraswamy (1877-1947) was the first well-known author of the modern era to expound the importance of traditional arts, culture, and thought as more than simply relics of a bygone past. Some of his seminal writings can be found in *The Essential Ananda K. Coomaraswamy* (World Wisdom, 2004).

Stephen Cross is the author of *The Elements of Hinduism* and a Fellow of the Temenos Academy.

James Cutsinger is Professor of Theology and Religious Thought at the University of South Carolina, and has published many books and articles concerning the perennial philosophy, the work of Frithjof Schuon, and the spirituality of Eastern Christianity.

Michael Oren Fitzgerald is the author of many books on the spiritual heritage of the American Indians, and was a close friend of Chief Thomas Yellowtail whose autobiography he recorded in *Yellowtail: Crow Medicine Man and Sun Dance Chief.*

René Guénon (1886-1951) was a French metaphysician who, in the modern era, first explicated the immutable metaphysical and cosmological principles which inform all integral traditions. His master work is *The Reign of Quantity and the Signs of the Times*, first published in 1945.

Peter Kingsley is an internationally renowned expert on the philosophical and mystical roots of the Western tradition, especially in Parmenides and Empedocles. His books include *Reality* and *In the Dark Places of Wisdom.* His website address is: www.peterkingsley.org.

Patrick Laude teaches at the Doha campus of Georgetown University and is the author of *Singing the Way* and co-author, with Jean-Baptiste Aymard, of *Frithjof Schuon: Life and Teachings.*

Barry McDonald is a widely-published poet. His most recently published collection is *The Eagle's Flight.*

Alex Minchinton is a student in the Religious Studies Program at La Trobe University Bendigo. His interests include Pure Land Buddhism and spiritual poetry.

Marco Pallis (1895-1989) was a writer, musician, and mountaineer who immersed himself in the doctrines and practices of Tibetan Buddhism. His works include *The Way and the Mountain* (1960) and *A Buddhist Spectrum* (1980).

Roland Pietsch is a Professor of Philosophy and Religious Studies who has taught at several universities in Germany, the Ukraine, Uzbekistan, and Iran.

Nicolas Leon Ruiz earned his PhD in philosophy from the State University of New York, Stony Brook, specializing in ancient philosophy.

Frithjof Schuon (1907-1998) was the pre-eminent exponent of the *religio perennis* in the twentieth century, and the author of works covering all of the world's major religious and sapiential traditions. Many of the principles underpinning his work were first articulated in *The Transcendent Unity of Religions* (1953).

Timothy Scott is the editor of *Eye of the Heart: A Journal of Traditional Wisdom* and author of *The Symbolism of the Ark* (forthcoming).

Aminah Smith is a student in the Religious Studies Program at La Trobe University Bendigo. Her interests include Sufism and the spiritual traditions of indigenous peoples.

William Stoddart is a Perennialist author, editor, and translator, and an expert on the work of Frithjof Schuon and Titus Burckhardt. Some of his writings were compiled in *Remembering in a World of Forgetting.*

Mark Stone is an artist and a student in the Religious Studies Program at La Trobe University Bendigo. His interests include mysticism and traditional theories of art.

Sri Chandrasekharendra Saraswati Swamigal (1894-1994) was the 68th Jagadguru of Kanchi in the lineage of Shankara, and one of India's most honored spiritual teachers.

Charles Upton is a poet, author, and activist whose books include *The System of Antichrist* and *The Shadow of the Rose* (co-authored with his wife, Jennifer Doane Upton).

Paul Weeks is a doctoral student at La Trobe University Bendigo where he is researching Western adaptations of Tibetan Buddhism.

Thomas Yellowtail (1903-1993) was a Sun Dance Chief of the Crow Indians and a pivotal figure in the preservation of the spiritual heritage of the American Indians.

Note on the Editor

Harry Oldmeadow is Coordinator of Religious Studies in the Department of Arts, La Trobe University, Bendigo, Australia. He studied history, politics, and literature at the Australian National University, obtaining a First Class Honors degree in history. In 1971 a Commonwealth Overseas Research Scholarship led to further studies at Oxford University. In 1980 Oldmeadow completed a Masters dissertation on the "perennialist" or "traditionalist" school of comparative religious thought. This study was awarded the University of Sydney Medal for excellence in research and was later published under the title, *Traditionalism: Religion in the Light of the Perennial Philosophy* (2000). Oldmeadow's principal intellectual interests include the perennialist school of thinkers, on whom he has written extensively during the last two decades, and the mystical and esoteric dimensions of the major religious traditions, especially Christianity, Hinduism, and Buddhism. He also has an abiding interest in the primal traditions of the Plains Indians of North America and the Aborigines of Australia.

His latest works include *Journeys East: 20th Century Western Encounters with Eastern Religious Traditions* (2004), *The Betrayal of Tradition: Essays on the Spiritual Crisis of Modernity* (2005), *Light from the East: Eastern Wisdom for the Modern West* (2007), *A Christian Pilgrim in India: The Spiritual Journey of Abhishiktananda (Henri Le Saux)* (2008), and *Frithjof Schuon and the Perennial Philosophy* (2010) all published by World Wisdom, and *Mediations: Essays on Religious Pluralism and the Perennial Philosophy* (2008). He has published extensively in such journals as *Sophia*, *Sacred Web*, *Vincit Omnia Veritas*, *Eye of the Heart*, and *Studies in Comparative Religion*. He currently resides with his wife on a small property outside Bendigo.